RESEARCH TECHNIQUES FOR
CLINICAL SOCIAL WORKERS

Research Techniques for Clinical Social Workers

Second Edition

M. Elizabeth Vonk
Tony Tripodi
Irwin Epstein

COLUMBIA UNIVERSITY PRESS  New York

Columbia University Press
Publishers Since 1893

New York   Chichester, West Sussex
Copyright 2007 © Columbia University Press
All rights reserved

Library of Congress Cataloging-in-Publication Data
Vonk, M. Elizabeth
Research techniques for clinical social workers /
M. Elizabeth Vonk, Tony Tripodi, Irwin Epstein. — 2nd ed..
p.   cm.
Includes bibliographical references and index.
ISBN 0–231–13388–X (cloth : alk. paper) — ISBN 0–231–13389–8 (pbk. : alk. paper) —
ISBN 0–231–50854–9 (pbk. : alk. paper)
1. Social service—Research. I. Tripodi, Tony. II. Epstein, Irwin. III. Title.
HV11.T747 2006
361.3072—dc22
2006017789

Casebound editions of Columbia University Press books are printed on
permanent and durable acid-free paper.

Printed in the United States of America

c 10 9 8 7 6 5 4 3 2 1
p 10 9 8 7 6 5 4 3 2 1

To Rand, Camille, and Elise
Betsy Vonk

To Jimmy, Chrissy, Maria, Tina, and Toni Ann
Tony Tripodi

To Edward and Fran
Irwin Epstein

Contents

RESEARCH TECHNIQUES FOR
CLINICAL SOCIAL WORKERS

Introduction

The purpose of this book is to provide an introduction to the use of research concepts and techniques for collecting, analyzing, and interpreting information relevant to clinical social work practice. By this last term we refer to the efforts of social workers to help individuals, families, and groups of clients to resolve their psychosocial problems. These efforts may involve changing the clients, changing others in the clients' environment, or both. They take place in a range of organizational settings and are rooted in a variety of theoretical perspectives.

The book is written for social work students and practitioners who are not research trained. It presents selected research concepts and techniques that can be applied by clinical social workers irrespective of their theoretical orientations or practice settings. Accordingly, examples will be provided throughout the book that incorporate various practice theories and programmatic locations. Neither the research concepts and techniques nor the practice theories and settings are exhaustive. They simply represent a beginning attempt to incorporate research into clinical social work practice.

Our basic assumption in writing this book is that the use of research concepts and techniques can facilitate the rational use of information by social workers engaged in direct practice with individuals, families, or groups. Our emphasis, however, is on the collection and use of information concerning individual clients and "significant others" in their lives. Consequently, we primarily employ concepts that treat the individual as the basic unit of analysis. And while we do not utilize concepts that focus on the family or group per se, such as family power structure or group cohesiveness, we do indicate how clients involved in family therapy or group treatment can be clinically assessed as individuals. Moreover, we suggest ways in which individual data can be aggregated or combined to make inferences about families and groups.

PRACTICE AND RESEARCH

Although research courses are required in any social work curriculum, clinically oriented social work students often tend to view these courses as irrelevant to practice. Sometimes they are. As a result, many practicing social workers who have merely "done their time" in required research courses fail to see how research can aid them in their work. When they do recognize its potential utility, often they do not know how to integrate research into practice.

Despite their lack of applied research training and competence, practicing social workers are under increasing pressure from funding sources, client groups, and agency administrators for more objective information describing their efforts and their effectiveness. Among the many forces moving social work practice toward objective evaluation is the delivery of health and mental health services through managed care systems. Managed care controls and distributes health care by a variety of mechanisms, including utilization review processes that require providers such as social workers to present evidence of the necessity and potential effectiveness of proposed interventions. Moreover, for quality assurance reviews, providers are asked to show that clients have achieved specified outcomes through their interventions.

In addition, most practitioners undoubtedly are aware of the increasing interest in evidence-based-practice (EBP) within social work and other helping professions, including medicine and psychology. EBP involves a process of systematically searching and evaluating current research related to a particular clinical problem in order to inform and guide practice with the best evidence available. Interest in EBP, related to both the empirical practice movement and the demand for accountability, is reflective of a desire on the part of many social work researchers to develop a systematic, research-validated knowledge base for practice.

Still other developments in social work practice and research have affected the need for clinical social work practitioners to develop or sharpen research skills. As the population of the United States becomes increasingly diverse, social workers are challenged to meet the needs of clients of many and varied ethnicities. While some practice and research guidelines have emerged for cross-cultural practice, empirical support of treatment effectiveness has only rarely been studied among ethnic minorities. Practitioners who offer assessments and interventions to ethnic minority clients must rely on a variety of research techniques to obtain feedback from clients regarding both cultural relevance and effectiveness of services.

Fueled in part by increased diversity and the need for cultural competence in practice, another research trend in social work has been the increased use of qualitative research methods. Qualitative methodology is flexible, subjective, and results in a descriptive narrative of a particular phenomenon. Techniques and concepts of this methodology have been useful to practitioners in a variety of areas, including assessing service needs within communities, monitoring interventions, and evaluating consumers' perceptions about an agency or the service it provides.

Social work research and practice have also been deeply affected by the growth of information technology (IT). From electronic record keeping to computer-based administration and scoring of evaluation instruments, social workers are increasingly in need of computer skills and Internet capability. With such skills and capability, social workers can make use of IT to integrate research and practice in many ways, including computer-based assessments, management of clients' evaluation data, analysis of assessment and evaluation data, access to research literature related to treatment effectiveness, and participation in "virtual" communities of practitioners among whom knowledge may be shared.

Finally, the NASW Code of Ethics not only outlines guidelines for ethical conduct when engaged in research, it also requires practitioners to stay current with and base practice on relevant practice-related knowledge. Further, the code requires social workers to monitor and evaluate their practice interventions. In sum, the code makes it clear that research skills are mandatory for ethical social work practice. Social workers must possess research knowledge and skills that enable them to utilize existing research to inform practice as well as to engage in research in order to evaluate practice and build practice knowledge.

Our intention with this book is to make research more accessible for practitioners. Without assuming a high level of research sophistication on the part of the reader, the book will describe ways in which clinical social workers and their supervisors can make use of existing research for the improvement of practice, utilize research techniques to evaluate practice, and potentially contribute to the base of knowledge that will inform future practice.

To achieve this end, our approach involves conceptualizing and dividing practice into parts in which major tasks are performed; delineating practice objectives within each practice division; identifying research concepts and techniques that can be employed to achieve these objectives; describing the principles and procedures involved in using these concepts and techniques; identifying relevant ethical considerations; providing illustrations of their use in diverse practice situations; and, finally, demonstrating how the information they generate can inform practice decisions.

ORGANIZATION

Our conception of clinical social work practice and the book itself are divided into three sections: diagnostic assessment; intervention selection, implementation, and monitoring; and evaluation. These divisions reflect critical areas or decision making in clinical practice and are consistent with many existing models of social work practice. For example, they closely parallel the "problem-solving model" articulated in Compton, Galaway, and Cournoyer's book, *Social Work Processes*. Our conceptualization is also consistent with the practice skill areas identified in *Direct Social Work Practice* by Hepworth, Rooney, and Larson. Both texts are widely used introductions to social work practice.

More broadly, a review of current social work theories concerning individuals, families, and groups suggests that these conceptual divisions describe major components in a wide variety of theoretical approaches such as ego psychology, behavior modification, case advocacy, task-centered social work, psychosocial practice in small groups, and group problem-solving approaches. It should be emphasized, however, that we are not arguing that all aspects of clinical social work can be reduced to this three-part conceptualization. Nor are we saying that all clinical practice is reducible to research techniques. Nonetheless, our three-part division makes useful distinctions between different aspects of practice in each of the foregoing theories. It is also heuristic in that it makes it easier to envision possible applications of research concepts and techniques to direct practice.

Diagnostic assessment involves decisions about the nature and extent of a client's problem as well as the choice of targets of intervention. Intervention selection, implementation, and monitoring refers to that phase of practice in which interventions are chosen and carried out. This involves judgments about the extent to which the client is actually receiving the prescribed intervention in a manner consistent with professional standards, the practicing social worker's initial planning, and the contractual understanding between client and social worker. Evaluation refers to the decision about the effectiveness and efficiency with which the clinical objectives are attained and whether interventions should be modified or terminated.

Within the three major sections of the book, chapters will present suggested uses of selected research concepts and techniques for assessment, intervention, and evaluation. Although a technique may be introduced in the context of one of these functions, its use may not be confined to that function. Thus, for example, standardized interviewing techniques are introduced in the section devoted to client assessment. Clearly, however, these techniques can be applied to monitoring and evaluation as well. Each chapter provides principles for implementing a given technique and hypothetical examples of how the technique can be applied to actual practice situations. This is followed by an applied research exercise for the reader. A selected bibliography concludes each chapter.

Rather than being exhaustive in our survey of research methods, we have selected those that we believe can be learned easily and readily applied by social work students and practitioners. By our application of these methods to a broad range of practice examples, our intent is to show that the incorporation of research into clinical social work practice need not be bound to any particular theoretical approach or agency setting.

This book is intended for use as an introductory research text for graduate social work students. It also can be used as a supplementary text for direct practice courses along with basic practice texts such as the aforementioned books by Compton, Galaway, and Cournoyer; and by Hepworth, Rooney, and Larson. Finally, the book is intended for practicing social workers who value the increased integration of research into their social work practice.

SELECTED BIBLIOGRAPHY

Anastas, J. W. 2004. Quality in qualitative evaluation: Issues and possible answers. *Research on Social Work Practice, 14*(1), 57–65.

Antle, B. J., and Regehr, C. 2003. Beyond individual rights and freedoms: Metaethics in social work research. *Social Work, 48*(1), 315–324.

Cohen, J. A. 2003. Managed care and the evolving role of the clinical social worker in mental health. *Social Work, 48*(1), 34–43.

Compton, B. R., Galaway, B., and Cournoyer, B. R. 2005. *Social Work Processes.* 7th ed. Pacific Grove, CA: Brooks/Cole.

Dziegielewski, S. F., and Holliman, D. 2001. Managed care and social work: Practice implications in an era of change. *Journal of Sociology and Social Welfare,* 28(2), 15–138.

Hepworth, D. H., Rooney, R., and Larson, J. 2002. *Direct social work practice: Theory and skills.* 6th ed. Pacific Grove, CA: Brooks/Cole.

Kirk, S. A., Reid, W. J., and Petrucci, C. 2002. Computer-assisted social work practice: The promise of technology. In S. A. Kirk and W. J. Reid (eds.), *Science and social work: A critical appraisal,* pp. 114–150. New York: Columbia University Press.

Lum, D. 2003. Culturally competent practice: A framework for understanding diverse groups and justice issues. Pacific Grove, CA: Brooks/Cole.

NASW. 1999. *Code of Ethics.* Silver Spring, MD: National Association of Social Workers.

Potocky-Tripodi, M., and Rodgers-Farmer, A. Y. (eds.) 1998. *Social work research with minority and oppressed populations: Methodological issues and innovations.* Binghamton, NY: Haworth.

Roberts, A. R., and Yeager, K. R. (eds.) 2004. *Evidence-based practice manual.* New York: Oxford University Press.

Turner, F. J. 1996. *Social work treatment: Interlocking theoretical approaches.* 4th ed. New York: Simon and Schuster.

Diagnostic assessment is the first phase of clinical social work practice. It involves a number of interrelated tasks and decision points for the social worker. In this section we describe these tasks, discuss the ways in which research can and should inform them, and identify relevant diversity issues and ethical concerns. The following five chapters describe, in greater detail, the use of specific research concepts and techniques in client assessment.

TASKS

As we indicated above, diagnostic assessment requires that the clinical social worker accomplish a number of tasks and make a number of decisions. These tasks are as follows:

1. First, the social worker must obtain information from the prospective client to determine the nature and extent of the presenting problem. With signed consent from the client, the social worker may also want to obtain information from the referral source, if there is one, and significant others in the client's life. In most practice settings the social worker will need to have information

sufficient for both a biopsychosocial assessment as well as the appropriate five-axis diagnosis from the most current *Diagnostic and Statistical Manual* (DSM) (APA, 2000). Clients' initial presenting problems vary greatly, from concrete needs such as help in finding employment to more ambiguous and diffuse difficulties such as experiencing feelings of anxiety or depression. The latter form of presenting problem requires more active involvement on the part of the social worker in order to specify those problems that require or allow social work intervention.

Whatever form the presenting problem takes, the task is to make a thorough initial assessment of the prospective client's social, psychological, economic, and health needs as well as the client's requests or needs for service. In cases in which clients do not present themselves voluntarily for treatment, such as those encountered in prisons or involuntary mental hospital admissions, social workers must still secure enough information from clients to make reasonable and humane assessments of need.

2. The second major task for the clinical social worker is to determine whether the prospective client meets the eligibility requirements imposed on clients by the social agency and its funding sources. Equally important is to determine whether the services provided by the agency are appropriate to the client's problem. The former, determining eligibility, may require information about income, health insurance or Medicaid coverage, place of residence, age, marital status, or other demographics. The latter, determining whether the services offered are most appropriate, requires not only a knowledge of the potential client's need but information as well about the full range of services offered by the agency, those services available from other agencies in the client's environment, and information about those values, beliefs, attitudes, and abilities that might affect the potential client's utilization of the available services. Fulfilling these information requirements may involve contact with a variety of sources in the client's environment such as other social agencies, schools, or places of employment. Whatever the source, the information gathered must be reliable enough to serve as a basis for decision making.

3. Once it has been determined that the prospective client can benefit from what the social worker and the agency have to offer, further specification must take place in the assessment process. This process involves refining and coherently organizing information about the client's problems and needs in order to determine appropriate targets of social work intervention. Social workers should make use of relevant research literature, practice theory, and practice wisdom in order to increase their understanding of the client's problem, including its etiology, parameters, complications, and prognosis. Based on the

information gathered in assessment and on the conceptualization of the problem, the social worker and client can develop an initial understanding of the focus of intervention.

In most cases clients have presenting problems that consist of many inter-related difficulties that may require intervention. For example a child who has been physically abused may be having trouble in school, living in inadequate housing, and in need of medical or psychiatric attention. The child's parents may be unemployed, have a psychiatric disorder, and lack adequate child management skills. In such cases, priorities must be set for targets of intervention. Even the most skillful social worker cannot intervene on all fronts at the same time. Moreover, clients cannot productively engage in a social work process if they are trying to solve all their problems at once. Consequently, the social worker and client must prioritize the difficulties, deciding which of them is most pressing and requires most immediate attention. In some cases, such as with physical abuse, the priority is quite clear; medical needs and the need to protect the child from future abuse require immediate intervention. Establishing priorities for intervention is more flexible for other presenting problems that do not pose an immediate threat of harm to the client or to others.

4. After problems have been identified and prioritized, a final task remains in the assessment phase. This involves "operationalization" of the target of intervention. In other words, social workers must clearly specify both the problem and the goals or what they are trying to achieve through intervention. This should be done in precise enough language so that it would be possible to determine whether the intended outcomes have been achieved by the time intervention is over. The specification of problems and treatment goals is not only a necessary component of the diagnostic assessment phase of clinical practice; it is required for evaluation as well. In addition, operationalization of the target of intervention, discussed in more depth in chapter 4, combined with specification of the means for achieving the outcomes, discussed in part 2, are the basis of a complete treatment plan.

So, for example, a school social worker may work with a group of children whose disruptive behaviors are keeping them in trouble in school and interfering with their learning. The social worker will specify the characteristics of the children's educational performance and disruptive behaviors as well as the desired changes in each of the children in terms of a reduction of disruptive behavior and an increase in educational achievement. By carefully specifying both the problem and the goals, the target of intervention is clear and it now becomes possible both to select appropriate intervention methods and to evaluate the outcomes of the intervention.

ASSESSMENT DECISIONS

Clinical social workers make many crucial decisions during the process of diagnostic assessment. As much as possible these decisions should be guided by complete and factual information. Often, however, crisis situations and agency or managed care pressures deny social workers the luxury of enough time to do a full biopsychosocial study. Here, previous experience with similar cases, intuition, knowledge of relevant research studies and consultation with colleagues or supervisors can supplement social workers' ability to correctly diagnose and effectively intervene.

Even when social workers are able to gather extensive information prior to intervention, skilled clinicians recognize that they are basing the treatment decisions on a "working hypothesis" about the client's problem, its causes, and its solution. This tentative hypothesis is validated, refined or totally rejected in the course of treatment as new information about the client's situation emerges. For this reason, the process of diagnostic assessment continues throughout the actual implementation of treatment.

Whether diagnostic and treatment decisions are made before or during the treatment process, certain questions must be answered about the client and his or her problems if effective intervention is to take place. Some of these questions are as follows:

1. Who is the client? What are his or her social and psychological attributes?
2. How and why did the client come into contact with the agency?
3. What are the client's problems and can they be ameliorated through social work intervention?
4. Is the client motivated to participate in a social work process?
5. What are the treatment objectives?

SOME ASSUMPTIONS AND REQUIREMENTS

Although five steps have been presented in describing the tasks involved in diagnostic assessment and five decisions have been listed above, it should be clear that five is not presented as a magic number and ours is not a magic formula. Many different models exist that describe the first phase of treatment. We have presented a straightforward model that hopefully captures the essentials of many of them.

Moreover, while we have described these tasks in a neat, logical order, practice does not always conform to our linear model. For example, information necessary for more than one task may be gathered during one interview. Further, the task of operationalization may require additional information gathering in order to sufficiently specify the problem and goals. And, as we indicated earlier, even after treatment begins, the social worker continues to gather information that informs and helps to refine assessment. The process that actually takes place is more like a circle or a spiral than the straight line implied by our model. The most important issue here, however, is arriving at an appropriate set of intervention goals and objectives that are agreeable to the client and are likely to lead to effective intervention strategies. The route the social worker takes in getting there is much less important.

The growing diversity of social work clientele creates challenges for social workers in the assessment phase. As can be seen in the table below, each of the tasks and decisions requires skills for culturally competent assessment. Culturally competent assessment is the ability to utilize awareness of and knowledge about clients' culture in order to establish rapport and collect meaningful information that will lead to effective interventions. First, social workers must be aware of cultural issues that may present barriers to obtaining reliable and valid information. Two such barriers are spoken language and nonverbal communication differences. In order to overcome these barriers social workers must either be proficient in the client's language or employ interpreters or consultants. Even when language is not a barrier, social workers must take care to fully understand the cultural context of nonverbal communications, such as the use of eye contact or accepted level of social distance, to avoid misunderstandings. In addition, any instruments used to gather information must be reliable and valid among the group of people to which the client belongs as a member. The information gathered must then be interpreted with awareness of clients' world view and cultural norms. Further, when determining eligibility, social workers must examine whether the services offered are respectful of clients' needs within their cultural contexts. Finally, the prioritization and specification of problems and goals for intervention must be compatible with the client's cultural values and beliefs.

Diversity Issues in Assessment and Treatment Formulation Phase

Task	Issue
Information gathering	Culturally competent assessment methods
Determination of eligibility	Ability to meet needs in culturally competent manner
Determining/Prioritizing targets	Selecting culturally compatible targets for change
Specifying target of intervention	Selecting culturally compatible goals and objectives

The tasks and decisions of assessment outlined here also require consideration of potential ethical issues, such as those in the following table. Whenever client information is gathered, social workers must safeguard the confidentiality of that information. If the information is to be shared with others, it should only be done with explicit consent of the client. In addition, determination of eligibility must include an honest appraisal by social workers as to their ability to meet clients' needs. When it is determined that the social worker or agency cannot do so, the social worker has an ethical responsibility to help the client find appropriate care through referral. Further, the social work values of self-determination and autonomy are paramount when determining and prioritizing targets of change. Finally, specification of the target of intervention—and all parts of assessment for that matter—should be guided by informed practice. As social workers, we have a responsibility to base practice decisions on what is known to be effective.

Ethical Issues in Assessment and Treatment Formulation Phase

Task	Issue
Information gathering	Confidentiality; consent to share information
Determining Eligibility	Ability to meet identified needs; duty to refer
Determining/Prioritizing targets	Self-determination; autonomy
Specifying target of intervention	Informed practice (evidence-based assessment)

Finally, our model assumes that clinical social workers will be motivated and skilled enough to guide their selection of intervention strategies based on available knowledge from practice research. In addition, they will be sufficiently "eclectic" to then utilize the most effective and efficient interventions to achieve treatment goals. This assumption may be unrealistic. Some social workers, for example, are bound by limits in competence or training, by their own treatment preferences, or by therapeutic or ideological dogmatism. Social agencies may offer some kinds of treatment and proscribe others. Therefore, rather than a description of what is, our model represents an ideal that may be approximated in the course of social work history, but never really reached. Nonetheless, it is based on a value of rationality and effectiveness the authors blatantly endorse.

RESEARCH CONCEPTS AND TECHNIQUES

Sound diagnostic assessment is dependent upon information that accurately portrays the client's situation. Research concepts and techniques can increase the quality and quantity of information gathered as well as improve the interpretation of this information. Three key research concepts that directly relate to the adequacy and accuracy of information are *reliability, validity,* and *representativeness.* Definitions and key questions related to information gathering follow. Reliability refers to the extent to which the information gathered is internally consistent. In other words, is information from and about the client consistent or contradictory? Validity concerns the accuracy of the information. Is there objective evidence to support the information provided by the client? Representativeness involves the extent to which the information gathered characterizes the clients' life circumstances. Are the client's assertions about his or her situation based on typical or unique events?

These concepts will be discussed in greater detail as they relate to specific research techniques for gathering information necessary for diagnostic assessment and treatment formulation. In chapter 1, for example, we demonstrate the use of standardized research interviewing and questionnaires for gathering reliable, valid, and representative information from clients about their needs and problems. This technique is particularly useful for obtaining a client's self-assessment.

In addition to gathering information through interviewing, the social worker may choose to utilize one or more of the many available diagnostic instruments. Instruments are available to measure a variety of relevant concepts, from levels of depression and anxiety to clients' satisfaction with agency service. In chapter 2 we discuss how social workers can locate these clinical assessment instruments and make judgments about the reliability, validity, representativeness, and utility of the information they generate.

Chapter 3 introduces another information-gathering research technique, systematic observation. This technique is particularly useful in making diagnostic assessment based on the potential client's behavior in natural settings such as at home or at school. Here, again, the key concepts of reliability, validity, and representativeness are employed whether the social worker chooses to develop or to use an existing observation instrument.

Chapter 4 further describes the process of specifying the targets of intervention, including the problems, goals, and objectives. In this process the social worker and client move from what may be a general or vague articulation of a problem to a specific measurable description of the problem and desired outcomes. Specificity allows for a clear understanding of the problem as well as the opportunity to measure progress throughout the intervention. Two techniques that may assist the process of operationalization, goal-attainment scaling and individualized rating scales, are also described. Rating scales may be designed to be completed by the client or completed about the client by others. In either case the reliability and validity of the information from the rating scales must be considered.

SELECTED BIBLIOGRAPHY

American Psychiatric Association (APA). 2000. *Diagnostic and statistical manual.* 4th ed. American Psychiatric Association.

Conrad, A. P. 1988. Ethical considerations in the psychosocial process. *Social Case-Work,* 69(10), 603–610.

Garvin, C. 2002. Developing goals. In A. Roberts and G. Greene (eds.), *Social workers' desk reference,* pp. 309–313. New York: Oxford University Press.

Hepworth, D. H., Rooney, R., and Larson, J. 2002. *Direct social work practice: Theory and skills.* 6th ed. Pacific Grove, CA: Brooks/Cole.

Lum, D. 2003. Culturally competent practice: A framework for understanding diverse groups and justice issues. Pacific Grove, CA: Brooks/Cole.

Manoleas, P. 1994. An outcome approach to assessing the cultural competence of MSW students. *Journal of Multicultural Social Work, 3,* 43–57.

NASW. 1999. *Code of Ethics.* Silver Spring, MD: National Association of Social Workers.

Reamer, F. G. 1999. *Social work values and ethics.* 2d ed. New York: Columbia University Press.

Siegel, C. Davis, Chambers, E., Haugland, G., Bank, R., Aponte, C., and McCombs, H. 2000. Performance measure of cultural competency in mental health organizations. *Administration and Policy in Mental Health,* 28(2), 91–106.

The research interview is perhaps the most powerful and versatile of techniques for gathering information directly from another person. Routinely, it involves a face-to-face exchange between the person seeking information and the person giving it. It may also take place over the telephone. Whether in person or over the phone, successful interviewing requires that interviewers give a good deal of attention to the research instrument as well as to their role in the interview situation. The interviewers' primary goal is to gather relevant data by encouraging, facilitating, and guiding the respondents to provide unbiased and clear answers to necessary questions.

Interviews vary from relatively *unstructured* formats to *semistructured* and *highly structured* ones. A highly structured interview is organized according to themes or topics and presents the respondent with a set of specific questions the interviewer reads aloud. The answer categories are also structured, so that the respondent must choose from a set of predesignated or *forced-choice* response categories. In this type of interview the interview situation is *standardized* as well. Hence there are explicit instructions for the interviewer to follow regarding the location of the interview, its duration, and even things to say when the respondent is having difficulty answering. Consequently, the structured interview is characterized by a high degree of control over both the interviewer and the respondent. In addition, it offers a high degree of consistency from one interview to another. Some interview schedules are so highly structured that they permit respondents to interview themselves. These are called *self-administered questionnaires*. For example, standardized, structured interviews are sometimes used in clinical settings to determine or confirm *DSM-IV-TR* (APA, 2000) diagnoses of mental disorders, while questionnaires may be used to gather specific factual information from clients.

At the other end of the continuum is the unstructured interview. This approach is best suited for studying highly sensitive or unexplored subjects in depth. Rather than offering the respondent forced-choice response categories, the unstructured interview presents open-ended questions that may be answered in any way. The interviewer is also free to rephrase questions and to use whatever supportive or probing comments are necessary to elicit desired information. This technique demands great sensitivity to respondents' feelings, attitudes, and opinions as well as to their nonverbal behaviors. Although the unstructured interview involves little control over the interviewers and respondents, the interview situation cannot go unattended. To be successful, an unstructured interview must take place in surroundings that are physically comfortable and free from distraction or stress. Most clinical interviews are unstructured.

Somewhere between these extremes is the semistructured interview. It usually involves some combination of open-ended and forced-choice questions. Within specified limits, the interviewer may rephrase questions or probe responses. The interviewer's task, however, is to keep the respondent focused on particular issues and questions, thus exercising more control over the direction of the interview than in an unstructured interview.

Whatever the type of interview, successful information retrieval requires that respondents understand the questions, be motivated to answer them honestly, and be knowledgeable about the matters covered in the interview. Moreover, interviewers should conduct themselves in a warm but professional manner and show interest in and knowledge about the topics discussed. Most important, they should be nonjudgmental and accepting of the opinions and information offered by the respondents.

INTERVIEWING AND DIAGNOSTIC ASSESSMENT

Diagnostic assessment requires reliable and valid information about the type and severity of the client's problem, the client's internal and external strengths, the need for clinical social work intervention, the level of client motivation, and the client's social and cultural context. In most clinical settings a formal five-axis *DSM-IV-TR* diagnosis is needed as well. Social workers have traditionally employed "clinical interviewing" to secure this information. This form of interviewing is most similar to what researchers refer to as unstructured interviewing. It is flexible, sensitive, and attuned to verbal as well as nonverbal client behavior.

Clinical interviewing has been used historically by social workers and is an essential component of clinical assessment. It does, however, have limitations. Through its focus on unique aspects of the client's situation, the clinical interview may ignore elements that are common to many clients. This may, in turn, prevent the evaluation of the progress of whole classes of clients through the accumulation of information about them. In addition, it may obscure intervention possibilities that are aimed at more than the individual client. Finally, clinical interviewing is very time-consuming and requires motivation and emotional investment on the part of the interviewer and respondent. Often the managed care environment or crisis situations among clients make in-depth clinical interviewing by itself an unrealistic and inefficient mode of information gathering. Diagnostic clinical assessment can be aided by the additional use of structured and standardized interviewing or questionnaires.

Structured and standardized research interviewing procedures are well codified and documented in the social research literature. While these procedures do not generate information with the richness and depth of clinical interviews, standardized research interviews are more efficient and consistent in the information they produce. They can be employed at intake for diagnostic assessment, during treatment for monitoring purposes, and after treatment has terminated for evaluation. These standardized techniques also may be introduced into clinical interviews as a supplement for gathering less sensitive factual information through questionnaires. It should be kept in mind that the information-gathering purposes of a standardized interview or questionnaire may have to be compromised at times for the sake of clinical demands.

Many agencies have well-developed interview schedules that include semistructured and structured components. They may, in addition, have questionnaires that are part of the established intake and assessment procedures.

PRINCIPLES OF RESEARCH AND DIAGNOSTIC INTERVIEWING

The Purpose of the Interview

When conducting a research interview or a clinical assessment interview, social workers should be clear about the purpose, the kind of information to be gathered, the characteristics of the clients, the role of the interviewer, and the characteristics of the interview setting. For clinical social workers, this means fitting the interview to the context of the social agency in which they are employed. More specifically, social workers will want to know how and why the applicant came to the agency for help, how the applicant defines the problem or need, whether the applicant's problems can potentially be ameliorated by the services that the agency offers, and whether the applicant is eligible for those services. To facilitate trust and openness, the applicant should be told in a few brief introductory comments the purpose of the interview, why the information is desired, and how it will be used. In addition, confidentiality and protection of the privacy of clients' information should be discussed. Finally, questions should be limited to areas that are relevant for diagnostic assessment and intervention decisions.

The Content of the Interview Schedule or Questionnaire

Interview schedules or questionnaires have two basic functions: they serve as guides to the interviewers and pose the questions to respondents. In diagnostic interviewing the content of interview schedules should be consistent with the theoretical viewpoints of the social workers and agencies they represent. Questions posed should provide social workers with the information required to make sound diagnostic and intervention decisions within their theoretical framework. Thus, for example, a clinical social worker operating within a systems framework will require information about a number of different systems in which the client is implicated such as work, family, school, and cultural context. A social worker in an advocacy agency may be concerned primarily with questions about a client's relationship to a particular agency that has failed to provide appropriate services. In a mental health setting the diagnostic interview is more likely to focus on descriptions of signs and symptoms of psychopathology and related biopsychosocial factors. Irrespective of which theoretical framework is employed, it is essential that questions asked are consistent with it.

Having considered the interviewer's need for information, we now turn our attention to the clients. First, since a primary function of diagnostic interviewing is to elicit clients' perceptions of their needs, problems, and potential solutions, the language, timing, level of formality, and syntax of the questions should correspond to that of the clients. In the case of cross-cultural assessment, the practitioner must develop awareness and knowledge of clients' cultural context in order to design effective diagnostic interview questions. More generally, the questions should be clearly worded, unbiased in relation to gender, age, race, and culture, and each focused on a single idea or issue.

The Structure of the Interview

Many research interviews move from the general to the specific. This is called a funnel approach. The interview begins with general, nonthreatening orienting questions and gradually leads to more specific, detailed ones. As we indicated earlier, highly structured interviews may contain instructions to the interviewer for rephrasing questions that are not receiving clear, complete, or relevant responses. This attempt to standardize the interviewer's language increases the chances that information gathered from different respondents will be comparable. A couples' therapist, for example, may attempt to ask partners in a relationship exactly the same questions about their relationship problems in separate interviews. If questions are posed differently to the two respondents, differences in response might be more a consequence of the ways in which the questions were asked than a reflection of conflicting perceptions of the two persons in the relationship. Moreover, if the two persons in the couple are interviewed by different social workers, the workers should be trained through direct instruction and role-playing techniques so that their interviewing behavior is similar. Finally, if any useful generalizations are to be made about the kinds of problems people are bringing to the agency, the questions asked at intake must be standardized from worker to worker and from case to case. This standardization is equally important in monitoring and evaluating client progress.

Sometimes, during the course of an interview, respondents may give vague or irrelevant responses. A technique for encouraging respondents to clarify their responses is probing. Probing is "continued neutral questioning" that has the purpose of either clarifying responses or redirecting the respondents to answer questions more precisely. Many times expectant silence is enough to elicit more of a response from clients, but there are helpful phrases as well. Some examples of common interviewers' probes include "In what ways?" "Could you explain that in more detail?" and "What does that mean to you?" Or a simple relative probe might be used. Here the interviewer repeats the respondent's last few words or a key phrase from a preceding response in a questioning manner. This encourages respondents to expand on their previous response.

Ideally, the interview should not exceed an hour. Interviews beyond an hour are exhausting for the interviewer and respondent alike. In some agencies, such as psychiatric hospitals or residential child-care institutions, multiple interviews might be possible if the necessary information cannot be gathered in one sitting. In other settings a second intake session is impractical, if not impossible, because of agency and managed-care restraints. Regardless of the setting, however, the interview should be as efficient as possible and confined to essential information gathering. Semistructured and structured interviews promote this kind of efficiency.

The interview should conclude with the interviewer briefly summarizing how the information will be used in the assessment and treatment planning process, or for evaluation, and by offering the respondent the opportunity to make any brief additional comments about issues covered or neglected in the interview. It is important that positive rapport be maintained throughout the interview and that respondents feel that their self-disclosures have been appreciated. In addition, the concluding comments made by respondents often serve as a useful bridge for future interviews.

The Interview Schedule

When constructing an interview schedule, the social worker should list the types of information necessary and relevant to the purpose of the interview. After this list has been prepared, topics should be ranked in order of importance. Finally, the list should be carefully edited in order to keep the length of the interview within the allowable time-frame.

Having identified the areas to be covered, the social worker must then decide how structured the interview should be. The semistructured interview specifies the types of information sought and leaves respondents free to answer in their own way. The structured interview, on the other hand, specifies the types of information sought, the specific questions to be asked, and even provides the choice of available responses to these questions. In general, more structured questions are best for gathering factual information that is not emotionally charged. When the range of responses to these questions is well known, closed-ended questions should be provided. Semistructured, open-ended questions are best for eliciting expressions of emotion, personal need, and answers to questions in areas in which the social worker and/or the agency have little previous knowledge of response possibilities.

Interviews need not be completely structured or completely lacking in structure. In fact, some combination of structure and flexibility is often preferable. Moreover, as knowledge and experience are accumulated, interview formats may be revised and become more or less structured over time.

If a semistructured format is employed, the basic types of information to be covered in the interview are specified and sample questions and probes that the interviewer may use might be provided. For example, an area to be explored might be the client's presenting problem. Questions might be formulated about what the client sees as the reason for coming to the agency, why the client chose the agency, and what services are desired.

Although the funnel approach, moving from the general to the specific, is almost always used in structured and semistructured interviews, a format referred to as the *umbrella approach* is sometimes used in semistructured interviews. In this format, instead of moving from general to specific, the interview comprehensively covers all facets of a given dimension exhaustively. The respondent is given a chance to raise any additional thoughts in relation to the dimension before moving to the next one. The umbrella approach helps to define the broad parameters of an issue, but can lead to the collection of information that is never utilized. Alternatively, the funnel approach is especially useful for approaching sensitive topics gradually yet ultimately retrieving detailed information.

In formulating questions for structured and semistructured interviews, four general principles should be followed: 1. questions should be clearly stated, 2. questions should not reflect bias, 3. each question should contain one thought only, and 4. questions should flow in a logical order. The art of asking questions is to ask them simply and concisely in understandable language and in a logical sequence.

Once questions have been written a decision must be made about the degree to which responses will be structured. Should questions be open-ended or closed? While open-ended questions require less advance knowledge about the kinds of responses the questions are likely to elicit, responses to these questions may wander widely from the topics to be covered. Open-ended questions are preferable, however, for in-depth exploration of issues with clients. Closed questions, on the other hand, require advance knowledge about the range of responses and are preferable for collecting straightforward and behaviorally specific data.

The following list indicates some of the various response systems available for what is basically the same question about parents' problems with their children.

a. The open-ended question:
    1. Can you tell me something about any problems you are having with your children? (Respondents answer in any way they choose).

b. Closed questions:
    1. Simple "yes" or "no."
        (01) Do you have problems with your children? Yes____(1) No____(2)
    2. Frequency of occurrence using adverb modifiers.
        (02) How often do you have problems with your children?
        Always____ (1) Almost always____ (2) Occasionally____ (3)
        Rarely____ (4) Never____(5)

3. Frequency of occurrence using numerical categories.

(03) How often do you have problems with your children?

Daily____ (1) Every other day (2) Two to four times a week____(3)

About once a week____(4)

4. Frequency of occurrence using percentages.

How often do you have problems with your children?

0–10% of the time____ 11–50% of the time____ Over 50% of the time____

5. Indication of level of agreement or Likert scales.

Indicate how much you agree with the following statement: I often have problems with my children.

Strongly agree____ Agree____ Disagree____ Strongly disagree____

6. Comparative response scales.

Compared to other problems you now have, how important are the problems you have with your children?

Very important____ Somewhat important____ Unimportant____

The questions above are only a few of the response formats available. Others include rank ordering the respondents' problems, asking respondents to identify their problems from a list of problems, or asking respondents to rate the intensity of a given problem on a numerical scale from 1 to 10. In selecting response systems one should choose those that appear to be most appropriate to the interview and to typical respondents. Complicated systems should not be used when a simple "yes" or "no" would suffice.

For closed-ended questions, several additional rules apply to the construction of response alternatives. First, response alternatives should be *mutually exclusive* to preclude clients' from feeling that they need to choose more than one response. This means that for any given question the respondent's answer should fit in one and only one response category. In other words, the response choices may not overlap. The responses for question number four above provide an example of response choices that may cause confusion because they are not mutually exclusive. The second and third answers, "every other day" and "two to four times per week," overlap, and respondents may feel forced to choose both responses.

Next, response alternatives should be *exhaustive,* including the entire range of possible responses. To ensure this, many interview schedules, include a choice of "Other" among the responses. In addition, the use of noncommittal response categories such as "Undecided" or "Don't know" should be avoided. These options discourage thoughtful deliberation on the part of the respondent in answering difficult or sensitive questions.

Additionally, in constructing an interview schedule or questionnaire, it is preferable to choose one or two types of response systems that are readily understood by most respondents. Excessive variation of the response system leads to confusion and unreliable information gathering.

Similar unreliable results may occur if clear instructions are not provided to the interviewer or client about how to indicate which response is being given for each item. For example, the instructions may ask the interviewer or client to "circle one," "check the box to the left of the response," or "write the number of your response on the blank line." Each set of items that utilize a particular response system should have clear instructions about the information that should be used in making the ratings and the information that should be excluded from consideration. As an example, the instructions may explain that the rater should only consider the client's experiences within the past seven days when answering the items.

As a final point, when constructing an interview schedule or questionnaire it is helpful to keep in mind that the information gathered will most likely be transferred to a computer as data contained in a spreadsheet, database, or statistical software program. In order to transfer the data from the interview schedule to the computer, it is necessary to *code* it first. With closed-ended questions, coding involves assigning numbers to each question and each possible response. This can be accomplished in several ways, but one of the easiest methods is to assign and mark the code on the interview schedule itself prior to its administration. An example of coding can be seen in questions 1 through 3 above.

Coding of responses to open-ended questions is more complicated, but the idea is the same in that responses must be converted into data that can be understood by a computer. In order to perform quantitative analysis of open-ended responses, the information must be categorized and then numbered. Generally, this is accomplished through a process called *content analysis*. Inductive, *qualitiative* methods may also be used to analyze the word-for-word responses gathered from open-ended questions. Computer software programs are available to assist with both content analysis and qualitiative analysis. Generally in clinical assessment, however, the social worker "analyzes" the clients' responses without the aid of computer technology, arriving at a conceptualization of the clients' situation based on the current information, practice research knowledge, and practice wisdom.

The Interview Environment

In addition to specifying the content of the diagnostic interview, the environment in which itvf will be conducted should also be standardized. Standardization of the interview environment increases the efficiency and reduces the potential bias in information retrieval. Thus, interviews should be conducted in similar surroundings from client to client and from social worker to social worker. Where possible, the amount of time given to each interview should be uniform as well as the number of interviews social workers conduct in a day. Other aspects of the interview situation should be made routine whenever possible. These efforts at standardization of the interview environment not only promote efficiency but make possible more valid comparison of the responses of those interviewed, better decisions about resource allocations to different clients, and the accumulation of information about groups of comparable clients.

Rehearsing the Interview

Before an interview schedule is implemented with clients, it should be rehearsed by the social workers who will be using it. This can be done by asking colleagues to take the role of a typical respondent presenting a typical problem. During the role-play, the interviewer should practice conveying the purpose of the interview, get familiar with the questions, try various probing techniques, and so on. In a rehearsal, the interviewer can get feedback from the person playing the respondent about ambiguous questions, distracting gestures and habits, and inaccurate reflective statements. The roles can then be reversed. Finally, videotaping mock interviews, listening to and discussing the playback may be additionally instructive.

Pretesting the Interview

After the interview has been rehearsed and refined, it should be pretested with two or three clients. If possible, and with the clients' permissions, these interviews should be videotaped. After completion, the interview tapes can be played back to determine whether they provide necessary information, whether they are too long, and whether the interview schedule or interviewer are introducing sources of bias. The interviewer may also ask the respondent for feedback about the length of the interview, clarity of questions, uncovered topics, and so forth.

Conducting the Interview

Once the interview schedule is refined and in final form it is ready to be used in social work practice. Nevertheless, there are certain principles of successful interviewing that must continue to be observed by those using the information-gathering device. Successful interviewing is not simply a matter of reading aloud the words on the page. The interviewer must show an active, concerned interest in what the respondent has to say. In seeking accurate information, and in clarifying responses, the interviewer may need to request validating information through documentation or names of others who may verify information. In doing so, however, the interviewer should be direct, accepting, and empathic, using neutral probes to ask for clarification of responses. Here is an example of part of an intake interview in a child abuse agency with a parent suspected of abusing her child.

RESPONDENT: Children need to be punished, otherwise they go bad.

INTERVIEWER: What sorts of punishment do you use when your child is bad?

RESPONDENT: Whatever he deserves.

INTERVIEWER: Can you give me an example of a situation in which he was bad and you gave him punishment?

RESPONDENT: I can't remember. Anyway it's my business and not yours.

INTERVIEWER: I know it's difficult to have a stranger asking you all these personal questions, but for your sake and for your child's it's important that we get all this information. Your child shows signs of severe beatings from the doctor's reports.

RESPONDENT: He falls a lot.

INTERVIEWER: Is there anyone else who we can talk to who can tell us something about that, like a doctor, babysitter, or a teacher?

Interviews are also useful tools for generating information about the interviewer's feelings and attitudes. Thus, the content of the interview, the characteristics of the respondents, and the interview context can generate powerful emotional responses in the interviewer. Does the respondent provoke anger in the interviewer? Does the interviewer empathize so much with the respondent that unsubstantiated favorable assumptions are made about what the respondent is saying? Social workers must develop self-awareness and sensitivity to their own emotional responses during and after the interview in order to fully utilize information gathered through interviewing. This is no simple task when the interviewer is writing the responses to questions, attending to the respondent's nonverbal behavior, and conscious of the time.

Recording the Information

In some situations—for example, in semistructured interviews with mostly open-ended questions—it may be helpful to record the responses on videotape or audiotape if possible. At times the interview situation is emotionally charged, making it impossible or grossly insensitive for the interviewer to be writing while clients are disclosing their most intimate problems, thoughts, or experiences. In situations such as these, when taping is not used, interviewers should write down relevant information immediately after termination of the interview. Structured interviews, on the other hand, with closed-ended questions may employ self administered sections to be completed by the respondent. If respondents are literate, they may be able to give a great deal of straightforward factual, demographic information such as name, address, and employment status by filling out a form while waiting to be interviewed. Finally, regardless of how the information is gathered, it must, at some point, be entered into a computer for storage and future retrieval purposes. This may be accomplished through numerical coding, inductive analysis in the form of case formulation or progress notes, or some combination of the two.

Regardless of how information is recorded, whether on videotapes, case notes, or computerized records, protection of clients' confidentiality is a primary ethical obligation. Paper records should be well organized and in locked storage when not in use by the social worker. Electronic records should be password protected and out of view from passers-by when in use on the computer screen. Similarly, video- or audiotapes should be kept in a secure, locked facility and erased when no longer useful for case planning, intervention, or evaluation.

Successful interviewing takes hard work, self-awareness, and experience. Over time, however, the ability to develop and conduct interviews can be one of the most useful information-gathering aids available to the social worker.

INTERVIEWING IN ACTION

A private nonprofit service agency that endeavors to promote healthy family functioning provides couples' counseling and child management services. There are ten direct service clinical social workers on staff, two of whom have primary responsibility for intake interviewing. The other eight social workers also do intake interviewing, but on a much more limited basis.

This agency, though small, has many referrals for service as well as direct applicants. The clinicians and the agency's administrator would like to manage the intake function more efficiently in order to generate data-based information about the applicants, their problems, their sources of referral, and their progress through treatment. This information is important for the agency in order to understand future needs as well as to provide evidence of need for continued funding from community sources. Until now clients have been asked to complete a very brief questionnaire to provide demographic and contact information before intake. Social workers then have used their own individual intake interview formats leading to considerable variation in the kind of information gathered. There is a particular need to standardize that portion of the intake interview concerned with couples' relationship problems and child management difficulties since these are the agency's primary foci. The task, then, is to develop a standardized interview for assessing applicants' problems in these areas.

The Purpose of the Interview

The primary purpose of the intake interview is to determine the type and severity of the problems experienced by applicants and whether agency services can help alleviate them. The intake interviewers, on the basis of information gathered, must decide whether clients are eligible for agency services or whether they should be referred to a private practitioner, a more specialized agency, or an agency in another geographic area.

Articulation of the Conceptual Framework and Interview Content

Although the social workers in this agency differ in the specific kinds of treatment interventions they routinely employ, they do share a problem-solving orientation emphasizing the current situation with which a client is struggling to cope. Since agency clients are voluntary and participate in agency service on a contractual basis, they need to be adequately motivated for treatment to take place and be effective. The social workers, however, are considering implementation of community-based services for clients who are unable to regularly attend office-based sessions.

To begin, the primary intake workers organize a meeting with the rest of the agency staff in which the categories of information that they all agree are essential for diagnostic, treatment, and referral decision are listed. These categories include applicant identifying information, indications of the range and severity of family problems, descriptions of the conditions that exacerbate these, expressed satisfaction and dissatisfaction with the couple's relationship, level of motivation for treatment, barriers to participation in office-based services, previous involvement in professional counseling, and personal, interpersonal, and environmental resources.

Constructing the Interview Schedule

Because the social workers in this agency vary in their interviewing styles and treatment approach, a flexible, semistructured interview schedule is chosen. Once the major categories or information dimensions are identified, open- and closed-ended questions can be developed. The social workers decide to expand the questionnaire completed by clients prior to intake, to request more information that may be asked in the form of specific, closed-ended questions. In addition to the demographic and contact information currently requested of clients, the agency adds several questions, including those specific to the general types of problems for which clients seek intervention and employment and income information. These questions may look like the following:

For what problem(s) are you seeking help? Please check all that apply.
___ Difficulties with my spouse or partner
___ Difficulties with my child(ren) at home
___ Difficulties with my child(ren) at school
___ Difficulties with aging parent(s)
___ Physical, emotional, or sexual abuse
___ Alcohol or other drug-related problems
___ Medical problems
___ Other—please specify: _____

Employment status and income
Are you currently employed? Yes____ No____
Is your spouse or partner currently employed? Yes____ No____
What is your combined annual income?
____Less than $20,000 per year
____Between $20,000 and $39,999
____Between $40,000 and $59,999
____Between $60,000 and $79,999
____Between $80,000 and $99,999
____Over $100,000

The social workers decide that much of the necessary information still needs to be asked in an open-ended format. In order to increase consistency among interviewers, however, they next specify examples of questions within each important information category. The categories and questions are organized in a logical order, eliminating question overlap or redundancy. Some of the questions might look like the following:

Presenting Problem(s)
- Why did you come to this agency?
- What do you see as your major family or relationship problems?
- When did these problems start?
- Has anything happened recently to make them worse and to lead you to seek outside help?
- What kind of help would you like to receive?

In addition, the social workers decide to develop an introductory statement to inform the applicant of the purpose of the interview, assure the applicant of confidentiality, and indicate how the collected information will be used. Instructions for the interviewers with regard to probing and clarifying interview responses and gathering necessary documentation are also developed. Next, the interview guide is compiled, making sure it is uncluttered and that open-ended questions have sufficient space provided after them for the intake workers to record full and complete responses to them. In addition, a closing statement is composed including information for the client regarding what and when to expect to hear from the agency in the days and weeks to come. Finally, instructions for transferring information from the notes on the interview schedule to the computer are detailed.

Standardization of the Interview Environment

The social workers are also faced with decisions regarding the interview environment. For example, should the couple be interviewed together or separately? How will children be included in the interview process? How long should each interview take? Where should the interviews take place? What style of address, demeanor, and clothing are appropriate to the agency and interview context?

Rehearsing the Interview

After coming to a decision concerning the foregoing questions, the social workers rehearse the interview, alternating in the roles of client and interviewer. Various types of clients, such as adult, child, noncompliant, anxious, hostile, and depressed applicants are role-played. Probes and clarifying questions are practiced. The role-played interviews are videotaped and then discussed among the social workers so that necessary changes can be made in the interview schedules and in individual interviewer behavior. The interview schedule is adjusted accordingly.

Pretesting the Interview Schedule

Next, the social workers try the interview with one or two clients, asking their permission to videotape the interview and explaining why. After the formal interview is completed, respondents are asked to indicate whether they felt that any important questions had been left out and/or whether any questions seemed unnecessary or repetitious. The tape recordings are then reviewed, and further modifications in the schedule are made.

Conducting the interviews

The new interview schedule is now ready for routine implementation with agency clients. Efforts are made by the primary intake workers and other social workers who occasionally do intakes to use the schedule in a standardized manner. Problems that seem to occur in a number of interviews are discussed at staff meetings so that necessary modifications in the interview schedule can be considered.

Recording the Information

When a number of interviews have been completed, interview protocols are reviewed to see whether all interviewers are asking all relevant questions, to check the accuracy of data transfer from interview schedule to computer, and to determine whether necessary supporting information and documentation is being gathered. Final revisions in the interview schedule or instructions to interviewers take place at this point.

EXERCISES

1. Consider the responses provided in the case illustration above for the question "For what problem(s) are you seeking help?" Are the responses mutually exclusive? Are they exhaustive? How would you improve the question and the response set?
2. Identify a major task of or service provided by a social work agency in which you are currently working. For that service, identify the information that needs to be

gathered in order for diagnostic decisions to be made. Devise a questionnaire to elicit that information from prospective clients. Compare your questionnaire with the method currently used in your agency to gather this information. How does your procedure compare with existing agency procedures?

SELECTED BIBILIOGRAPHY

Allen-Meares, P. 1985. Content analysis: It does have a place in social work research. *Journal of Social Service Research, 7,* 51–68.

First, M. B., Spitzer, R. L., Williams, J. B. W., and Gibbon, M. 2000. Structured clinical interview for DSM-IV Axis I Disorders (SCID-I). In American Psychiatric Association (ed.), *Handbook of psychiatric measures,* pp. 49–53. Washington, DC: American Psychiatric Association.

Gingerich, W. J. 2002. Computer applications for social work practice. In A. Roberts and G. Greene (eds.), *Social workers' desk reference,* pp. 23–28. New York: Oxford University Press.

Kadushin, A. 1997. *The social work interview: A guide for human service professionals.* 4th ed. New York: Columbia University Press.

Kagle, J. D. 2002. Record-keeping. In A. Roberts and G. Greene (eds.), *Social workers' desk reference,* pp. 28–33. New York: Oxford University Press.

Klein, W. C., and Bloom, M. 1995. Practice wisdom. *Social Work, 40,* 799–807.

Krippendorff, K. 2004. *Content analysis: An introduction to its methodology.* 2d ed. Thousand Oaks, CA: Sage.

Manoleas, P. 1994. An outcome approach to assessing the cultural competence of MSW students. *Journal of Multicultural Social Work, 3,* 43–57.

Patton, M. Q. 2002. *Qualitative research and evaluation methods.* Thousand Oaks, CA: Sage.

Rubin, A., and Babbie, E. 2001. *Research methods for social work.* 4th ed. Belmont, CA: Wadsworth/Thomson Learning.

Using Available Instruments | **TWO**

Some applied research problems require the development of original research instruments such as interview schedules or questionnaires. Others do not. In the latter cases, existing research instruments can be used directly or modified slightly to suit the unique features of the context to which they will be applied. Consequently, to employ research tools in their practice, clinical social workers need not invent new information-gathering devices every time they wish to collect valid and reliable information. In fact, they should first determine whether suitable instruments or rating scales already exist before launching into the development of original ones.

Existing instruments are quite varied and appear in many forms. There are standardized questionnaires, statistical forms, observation guides, rating scales, and draw-a-picture tests, to name a few. Clinical social workers most frequently use structured interviews, self-report measures, and instruments that measure perceptions of others who are in close contact with clients. While development of structured interviews was discussed previously, it is important to know that standardized structured interviews are available for a variety of purposes, including *DSM* diagnosis. The variety of self-report and other-report measures is seemingly limitless. They vary not only in content, but in length, ease, or difficulty in scoring, and readability. *Rapid assessment instruments* are self-report scales that are short, simple, easy to score, and have proven to be valuable for use in the managed care environment. While some measure a broad range of potential problems, others are more narrowly focused on a specific area of interest, such as eating disorders.

Instruments relevant to clinical social work practice are described in scholarly journals, in agency reports, in books, and on Web sites accessible through the Internet. If they are copyrighted, permission must be secured to use them. In addition, the use of some instruments requires payment of a fee. Some instruments, of course, require considerable training to be used properly, and we do not recommend their use without adequate training. Thus, for example, we are not suggesting that clinical social workers without proper training routinely incorporate projective tests such as the Rorschach or Thematic Apperception Test (TAT) into their diagnostic interviews. However, many other existing instruments can be obtained and applied easily, by clinical social workers, without extensive training.

In this chapter we describe the ways in which instruments may be utilized in clinical settings. In addition, we offer guidelines for locating, selecting, and applying available research instruments to diagnostic assessment.

THE CLINICAL USE OF AVAILABLE INSTRUMENTS

As we suggested earlier, existing research instruments can be used directly, that is, in their original form. They can also be used indirectly and modified, revised, or adapted to the unique requirements of a new practice or research situation. Some of the ways in which existing instruments can be used for diagnostic assessment follow:

1. They can generate information directly relevant to diagnostic assessment. For example, problem checklists may be used in settings or contexts in which client self-assessments of problems are required. Self-report or structured interview instruments may also be used to confirm or indicate *DSM-IV-TR* diagnoses.

2. They can provide information about how a client compares with a normative population that has already been tested with the instrument. For example, a standardized scale to measure reactive attachment disorder can provide information about the presence and severity of the disorder for a child in foster

care who is referred to a clinical social worker for assessment and placement recommendations.

3. They can provide evidence of necessity for social work intervention within managed care systems. For example, a client who requests therapy for anxiety-related signs and symptoms may be allowed to begin or continue treatment based on the social worker's assessment. The results of a rapid assessment instrument, or standardized scale to indicate the severity of anxiety, allows social workers to justify their request for sessions.

4. They can generate discussion that is relevant to diagnostic assessment. For example, a scale to measure parenting behaviors may be completed independently by two parents and then compared to generate discussion between them at the beginning of family therapy. The discussion can be a source of critical information about the similarities and differences in parenting between the two as well as an indicator of how they communicate with each other.

5. They can serve as a starting point for the development of an original measurement instrument. An existing instrument may provide ideas about issues to be covered, question format, or response systems; which when properly modified could be used for generating information relevant to the particular topic of significance to the social worker or agency.

In addition to diagnostic assessment, the use of available instruments is applicable to treatment monitoring and evaluation. In monitoring a client's compliance with a group treatment contract, for example, an existing group observation instrument can be used to monitor the character and frequency of clients' participation in group sessions.

Perhaps the most frequent use of available instruments, however, is in gathering data to measure the extent to which client and social worker objectives have been realized as a result of social work intervention. This evaluative use of available instruments is exemplified in the widespread employment of standardized scales in a variety of mental health settings. These instruments generate detailed information about treatment efficacy.

Although this chapter presents a set of principles for locating, selecting, and utilizing existing research instruments for diagnostic assessment, treatment monitoring and evaluative uses should also be kept in mind. In other words, the following principles are equally applicable to locating, selecting, and utilizing existing research instruments for diagnostic assessment, treatment monitoring, and evaluation.

PRINCIPLES FOR USING AVAILABLE INSTRUMENTS

The Purpose of the Instrument

In considering the use of an existing research instrument, one should first specify its purpose. Is it intended for diagnostic, treatment monitoring, or evaluative purposes? At which stage in the clinical process will the instrument be used?

Another important question involves the type of knowledge, information, or data that best suits the purpose. Should the information take the form of quantitative or qualitative data? Quantitative data puts information into numerical form. Questions about the frequency of drug use, incidents of depression, marital conflicts, and the like, yield quantitative information. In addition, many complex concepts such as depression or relationship satisfaction have been *operationalized,* that is, precisely defined in order to allow for quantitative measurement. Quite frequently, standardized instruments can be located to measure concepts useful in clinical work.

Qualitative data offer information in narrative form. Thus, asking clients to describe their thoughts and feelings concerning matters such as divorce, death, marriage, parenting, or career will generally yield rich narrative or qualitative responses. Open-ended response systems encourage such responses. Information of this sort may be presented in the form of *hypotheses.* Hypotheses are statements about possible cause-effect relationships. Some research instruments, for example, are suited to generating hypotheses about the causes of client problems. Asking clients to describe their life circumstances when they began experiencing sadness or loss might generate causal hypotheses about potential sources of their depression. At the very least, such questions will generate *correlational hypotheses* about which problems seem to occur at the same time. Accordingly, asking applicants whether incidents of partner abuse are likely to take place when they have been drinking may yield correlational hypotheses about the problems associated with applicants' drinking behavior. Structured interviews can be located to guide collection of qualitative data.

One more question is needed related to the purpose of the instrument. From whom does the social worker need information? Information may be provided by clients themselves through self-report questionnaires or structured interviews, but it may also be desirable to seek information from others in clients' lives. For example, when working with a child, the social worker will need information from parents and perhaps teachers or others with whom the child is involved.

Most instruments are designed specifically to collect information either from the client or from particular others.

Locating Available Instruments

The more specific social workers can be about the purpose for which an instrument is to be used, and the kind of information which is required from it, the more efficient the search will be for it. How does one locate relevant, available research instruments? There are several paths.

Research instruments are routinely employed in some forms of therapy or intervention. For example, behavioral assessment instruments are frequently used by behavioral therapists. In addition, social workers who specialize in the treatment of particular disorders often utilize relevant measurement tools. For instance, social workers who frequently treat persons with eating disorders often use a rapid assessment instrument designed to measure anorexia and bulimia. Asking colleagues who use such instruments as a standard part of their practice is one way to locate relevant instruments.

Relevant instruments also may be located in the professional literature devoted to the kinds of problems or forms of intervention in which the social worker is interested. Basic practice journals such as *Social Work Research, Research on Social Work Practice,* and *Behavior Therapy,* among many others, frequently publish articles describing research instruments. Problem-focused journals such as the *Journal of Addictive Diseases, Journal of Multicultural Social Work, Journal of Family Social Work,* and many others, publish descriptions and critiques of such instruments as well. If the instruments are not fully described, or if the author's permission is necessary to use the instrument, the journals generally indicate the author's contact information. Relevant articles in these and other journals may be identified through the use of one or more databases, including *Social Work Abstracts* and *PsychInfo,* available at most academic libraries.

Probably the most efficient way to locate instruments as well as critical reviews of them is by using collections of research instruments. One of the most frequently used collections in social work is Corcoran and Fisher's *Measures for Clinical Practice: A Sourcebook.* Another excellent resource is Roberts' and Yeager's *Evidence-Based Practice Manual: Research and Outcome Measures in Health and Human Services.* While the *Manual* does not provide the actual instruments, it does provide a wealth of information about a variety of instruments and how to locate them. Table 2.1 provides a list of such books that may be useful in social work practice.

Further, research institutes, centers, and departments within social agencies often describe research instruments on their Web sites. These organizations may be located within universities, such as the University of North Carolina's Jordan Institute for Families; or within private and governmental agencies, such as the Child Welfare League of America. In some cases the instruments are freely available; in others the measures may be used with permission or payment of a fee. Further, some Web sites allow clients to complete instruments online and then automatically provide the score and interpretive feedback to the therapist. Table 2.2 provides a list of organizations and their Web addresses from which standardized instruments may be purchased.

Finally, instruments may be located by performing searches on the World Wide Web. This is done most successfully when the exact title of the desired instrument is known. For example, a search of the Internet for the Composite International Diagnostic Interview (CIDI) quickly reveals a site (www.crufad. unsw.edu.au/cidi/discuss.htm) where this structured interview is available for purchase, in paper-and-pencil or self-administered computerized forms. The site also includes a wealth of information about CIDI, the purpose of which is to provide highly reliable *DSM-IV* diagnoses. If searching by the concept to be measured, however, World Wide Web searches are not practical, in that they are most likely overly time-consuming. For example, a search on "depression and measurement" returns over seven thousand possible sites, far too many to look over when attempting to locate an assessment instrument.

Determining the Relevance of Available Instruments

In the context of diagnostic assessment, social workers should seek instruments that provide information pertinent to diagnostic decision making. Further, for treatment monitoring and evaluation purposes, the instrument should measure the relevant concept as directly as possible. In addition, the information generated by the instrument should be consistent with the intervention techniques and treatment goals being utilized. Equally important, the instrument should be appropriate to the clientele of the agency. This includes consideration of clients' age, abilities, level of literacy, range of presenting problems, and culture. For example, self-administered questionnaires are not applicable to those who cannot read or are literate in a different language. No matter how reliable and valid the instrument, it is only relevant if it facilitates diagnostic assessment by the social worker.

Looking for Built-in Bias as a Source of Measurement Error

Closely related to the issue of relevance is the question whether existing instruments contain any built-in biases that might lead to systematic *measurement error*. Biased wording or content of an instrument may alienate or distort assessments of certain groups of respondents. Accordingly, some instruments have been shown to favor some groups of individuals at the expense of others. It has been asserted, for example, that IQ tests are biased in favor of urban, middle-class, white males. Marital conflict assessment tests standardized with middle-class professional-managerial respondents may lead to incorrect judgments of pathology when applied to working-class families. Additionally, instruments that display assumptions based on gender, age, race, or ability may be offensive to clients who do not fit neatly into traditional roles. While there is no ironclad rule for determining whether such bias exists in an instrument, some effort should be made to look over the instrument for obvious bias, to determine the sociocultural characteristics of the groups on which the instrument was developed and tested, and, finally, to read the published critiques of the instrument. Interpretation based on built-in biases can lead to serious errors in diagnostic assessment.

It is important to note, that there are many potential sources of measurement error in addition to biased wording or content of an instrument. Error may also result from such things as the method by which information is gathered or to clerical recording errors. Potential error associated with self-report instruments will be discussed below.

Determining the Reliability of Available Instruments

An instrument is reliable if it produces the same results with repeated trials on the same basic information. For example, a reliable rating scale for measuring the level of physical impairment of a disabled person will produce the same rating when applied repeatedly to the same person, assuming there have been no changes in the actual level of disability.

Researchers commonly assess instrument reliability in several ways, including test-retest, interrater, parallel-instrument, and internal consistency reliability. Test-retest reliability is assessed by taking repeated measurements of the same variable; it is a measure of the stability of the instrument over time. As an example, consider the level of client anxiety prior to psychotherapy. Assuming that the anxiety level has remained relatively constant over a short period of time, a reliable instrument would produce consistent anxiety ratings. Test-retest reliability is reported in the form of a statistic called a correlation coefficient. Correlation coefficients used to measure reliability generally vary in strength from 0.00 to 1.00. A test-retest reliability coefficient of 0.00 represents a complete lack of reliability; 0.50, only moderate reliability; 0.80, high reliability; and 1.00, perfect reliability.

When more than one observer rates a phenomenon, interobserver or interrater reliability refers to the extent to which different observers produce the same rating. For example, if two equally experienced clinical social workers utilize a standardized instrument to assess *DSM-IV* diagnoses among the same group of clients; the extent to which their diagnoses are consistent is referred to as interrater reliability. Measures of interobserver reliability are often expressed as correlation coefficients, as above. They also can be expressed, however, in terms of percentage agreement, with 80 percent agreement or more indicating an adequate level of interobserver reliability.

A third approach to assessing the reliability of research instruments involves correlating the results of "parallel" measures of the same phenomenon. Say, for example, we are interested in utilizing an available measure of school adjustment. The concept of school adjustment would include variables such as academic grades and classroom conduct. To assess the reliability of these variables as parallel measures of school adjustment, we would look at the correlations between grades and conduct. In doing so, a researcher would utilize correlation coefficients, such as Pearson's r or Spearman's rho, that describe relationships in positive or negative terms. These results range from -1.00 to +1.00 and indicate the direction as well as the strength of the relationship between measures. A negative correlation would indicate an inverse relationship between grades and classroom conduct. This finding would suggest that the measures are not consistent and one or both were unreliable measures of school adjustment. A correlation around 0.00 would indicate no relationship between grades and classroom conduct and would again suggest that at least one of the measures was unreliable. A positive correlation would indicate a direct relationship between grades and classroom conduct. However, in order to justify the assumption that each of these measures is a reliable measure of school adjustment, one would expect a positive correlation of +.90 or better. Only such a positive correlation would indicate that the two measures were consistent or parallel measures of school adjustment.

Internal consistency reliability is based on logic similar to the preceding approach. The difference is that internal consistency reliability assesses the consistency of responses to multiple items within a single measure. In this form of reliability testing an attempt is made to judge the homogeneity of the component parts of a single measure. One method of determining internal consistency, called split-half reliability, is done by dividing the items into two groups for comparison. For example, in order to test the split-half reliability of a ten-question instrument developed to measure marital compatibility, the ten questions would be randomly assigned to two groups of five questions each. The cumulative scores on these two groups of items would then be correlated. Another way of testing internal consistency is by determining the coefficient alpha, the average intercorrelation among all the items in the measure. Cronbach's alpha is the statistical test most often employed to determine internal consistency and is easily calculated using statistical software. Instruments used for clinical decision making should demonstrate high internal consistency among the component parts or items of the instrument indicated by a positive correlation of +.80 or better.

When choosing an instrument, it is important to have information about the methods by which the reliability of the data collected with the instrument was tested. Each of the tests of reliability discussed above provides a slightly different piece of information about the instrument. The tests used should fit the practice situation. First, if more than one rater will be used, interrater reliability is important. Next, if more than one measure will be used, parallel instrument reliability should be examined. If a single instrument with many component questions is used, the internal consistency reliability is important. Finally, if the instrument will be used to measure change or stability over time, test-retest reliability is essential.

In sum, when choosing an instrument for use in practice, it is important to determine whether previous uses of the instrument indicate a high level of appropriate reliability with a population similar to the social workers' clients. If they do not, or if no reliability tests are reported, the instrument probably should not be used or the reliability should be tested first. Ideally, even if reports of appropriate reliability do exist, it is a good idea for social workers to do their own testing. This would ensure the fact that there is nothing different about the process or the particular group of clients that would reduce the reliability of the data from the instrument. Recognizing that constraints of time and resources in practice would rarely, if ever, allow for reliability testing, it is best to choose instruments with well-established support of reliability.

Determining the Validity of Available Instruments

An instrument is valid if it measures what it claims to measure. From a purely logical standpoint, validity concerns itself with the extent to which the measurement device is directly relevant to the concept being measured. More simply, it answers an extremely important question. Does the instrument actually measure what it is intended to measure?

There are several types of validity. The least complicated is referred to as face validity. Face validity is simply the opinion of someone who has looked over the instrument that it appears to measure what it says it measures. For example, an instrument intended to measure whether a couple would be suitable as adoptive parents that included questions about how many times a week and where the family grocery shops would have low face validity. These questions appear "on the face of it" to be irrelevant to suitability for parenthood. Closely related to face validity is content validity. Content validity again depends on opinion, but refers to the extent to which the instrument includes all aspects of the concept being measured. While there are no clearly defined procedures for establishing content validity, developers of instruments often ask experts to critique their work before conducting empirical tests of validity. Going back to the instrument to measure suitability for adoptive parenting, content validity would be low if it did not include questions about parents' attitudes toward child-rearing practices.

Criterion validity is an empirical test of validity that examines how well the measure relates to other known indicators or measures of the same concept. The criterion may be concurrent, based on current known indicators; or predictive, based on future indicators. Predictive validity refers to whether the measure predicts other phenomena that are assumed to be associated with the concept being measured. Using the previous example, the instrument would have high predictive validity if those couples who scored high on the suitability index were more likely to successfully complete the home-study process, receive adoptive placements, and become better adoptive parents than those who scored low in suitability. These relationships are expressed in the form of correlation coefficients.

Sometimes it is impossible to wait long enough to test the predictive validity of an instrument. In such instances researchers assess concurrent criterion validity by correlating the instrument with other measures that are presumed to measure the same or similar variable. Considering our prospective adoptive parents again, their scores on the suitability index could be correlated with scores obtained with an observational instrument that assesses the manner in which they relate to children currently in their home. A high positive correlation between the new measure and the criterion measure would indicate support for concurrent validity.

Finally, construct validity refers to the extent to which the instrument being tested relates to other measures of similar concepts in theoretically predictable ways. When a measure has high convergent validity, it is highly correlated with other measures of the same or similar concepts. If the measure has strong discriminant validity, it is not significantly correlated with measures of different concepts. Construct validity is further supported if instruments are sensitive to change, that is, if the measurement changes predictably through the course of an intervention.

Returning once again to the suitability index, the complexity of construct validity can be demonstrated. Theoretically, we would hypothesize that suitability for adoptive parenting would be positively associated with emotional maturity at a moderate level. Therefore, construct validity would be supported if scores on the suitability index were moderately associated with tests designed to measure emotional maturity. Convergent validity would be demonstrated by the positive association, but, if the correlation was very close to +1.0, the discriminant validity would be questioned. In other words, if the association was very strong, we would have to question whether the suitability index was actually measuring emotional maturity. Sensitivity to change would be supported if the measure increased following social work intervention to educate prospective parents about adoption issues, child rearing, and so forth.

Ideally, all research instruments should be validated in all of the above-mentioned ways. Typically, however, content and criterion validity are more commonly reported, particularly in the early stages of instrument development. In instruments that are better developed, reports on construct validity should be available. Correlation coefficients reported in criterion or construct validity are likely to be weaker than those reported in tests of reliability. In the context of validity, then, correlations of +.30 to +.50 would be high enough to warrant the cautious use of the instrument. If an unproven instrument is utilized, social workers should at the very least assess the fit between the concept to be measured and the instrument used to measure it. Are they logically related? Are there significant components of the concept to be measured that are left out of the instrument? Ideally, social workers would choose standardized instruments with known support of reliability and validity.

Determining the Availability of Test Norms

Along with the reliability and validity reports, the user of an available instrument should obtain a description of the population or populations with whom the instrument was tested and standardized. An instrument that was developed and first used in an urban context may be inappropriate for use in a rural community. Tests developed with one class or cultural group may not be valid and reliable with another.

Some tests have been so widely used and broadly standardized that test norms have been established for comparing individual respondents to a larger population in order to make judgments about the individual's relative performance. This is particularly true for certain academic performance and intelligence tests conducted in the schools. These statistical norms are valuable for assessing a child's or a group of children's relative performance as compared with other children of the same age.

When test norms are not available, one should, at a minimum, attempt to find out the social characteristics of those who were subjects in the original development of the instrument. How similar are they to the population with whom they are intended to be used?

Determining the Adequacy of Knowledge Generated by Available Instruments

As we indicated earlier, available instruments can aid diagnostic assessment in numerous ways. Specifically, they can 1. generate information directly relevant to diagnostic assessment, 2. generate information about how a potential client compares with a normative population, 3. provide evidence of necessity for social work intervention within managed care systems, 4. generate discussion with the service applicant, which, in turn, can serve as a basis for diagnostic assessment, and 5. serve as a starting point for the generation of an original research instrument.

Once the purpose, relevance, sources of bias, reliability, validity, and normative bases of an instrument have been assessed, it is possible for clinical social workers to judge the adequacy of the information generated by the instrument relative to their intended purpose. Any instrument that is desired for use as a direct diagnostic tool for a large pool of clients over a period of time should demonstrate relatively high degrees of criterion and construct validity and test-retest reliability. In addition, it should be standardized on a population similar to the client population, particularly if individual applicant scores are to be compared with normative scores. Any dissimilarity between the client and normative populations are likely to be exaggerated with a clinical population, leading to useless, misleading, or even harmful generalization from test results. Strong psychometric support is also needed for instruments used to show necessity for treatment.

Alternatively, if available instruments are to serve as stimuli for discussion or for instrument generation, issues of reliability, validity, and standardization are less important. Instrument relevance and content validity, however, remain as important dimensions for instrument assessment.

Determining the Feasibility of Using Available Instruments

Having assessed the extent to which an instrument is likely to satisfy knowledge requirements, a final consideration is its feasibility, sometimes referred to as ease of use. This refers to the practical factors involved in an instrument's use. Among these factors are the following: financial cost, time required for administration and scoring, respondent requirements, and staff training requirements.

Financial costs include the fees for purchasing and administering an instrument as well as indirect costs associated with staff members' time. In general, copyrighted, standardized test forms are more expensive than nonstandardized instruments, but they yield more reliable results. Some instruments are designed to be administered and scored by computer, in which case the expense of computer hardware and software must be considered. In addition, one must consider the direct and indirect costs of analyzing and interpreting the information generated by the instrument in assessing its feasibility.

A second set of considerations is the time involved in administering, analyzing, and interpreting the information. In most cases information from the administration of diagnostic instruments is needed quickly to inform assessment. Tests that require a lengthy scoring process or involve complicated interpretation are not practical in most practice settings. In addition, more frequent administration of an instrument generally provides more reliable information. Frequent administration also costs more money and time. More than likely, a balance needs to be found between the time and cost factors, on the one hand, and the need for reliability, on the other. Alternative sources of information as well as validating information, such as behavioral measures, should also be considered as a way of keeping costs down.

Some instruments, particularly self-administered questionnaires, require a relatively high degree of literacy and understanding on the part of respondents. Here the fit between the characteristics of those who are likely to be respondents and the requirements of competent instrument completion must be considered. Self-administered questionnaires completed by clients who are illiterate or only partially literate result in a complete but meaningless set of information. This issue comes up as well when respondents are not fluent in the language in which the questionnaire is written or are not familiar with the culture in which the questionnaire is situated. Computer literacy is an added concern when questionnaires are administered by computer.

Finally, the knowledge requirements associated with administering and interpreting the instrument should be considered. Some instruments, such as TAT and Rorschach tests, require a great deal of training and experience in order to be administered and interpreted competently. These instruments should be used by qualified experts only. Many other available instruments, however, are not difficult to understand and to employ. When these instruments serve clinicians' purposes, function within the ethical and value constraints of their profession, and are acceptable and understandable to clients, they can greatly facilitate diagnostic decision making and evaluation of progress.

INSTRUMENTS IN ACTION

The social workers and other clinicians employed by the university's student counseling center spend much of their time working with young adults who are experiencing depression related to a variety of life problems. The clinicians are guided by a variety of practice theories that includes psychodynamic, cognitive-behavioral, and solution-focused. They are interested in using a standardized measure of depression in their screening process in order to identify those students who are experiencing suicidal ideation or are otherwise in greatest need of immediate service.

The Purpose of the Instrument

The purpose of the instrument is to assess signs and symptoms of depression. The social worker is also interested in finding an instrument that is not specific to a particular practice theory, does not require a high level of specialized training or expertise for its administration, is not costly, and is easily administered, scored, and interpreted.

Locating and Assessing an Instrument.

On the recommendation of the counseling center director, the social worker first explores the possibility of utilizing the Beck Depression Inventory (BDI-II). Finding the BDI-II easily on the Web, the social worker learns that it is a psychometrically sound measurement tool for depression and meets most of the practical requirements for the counseling center. The cost for using it, however, is more than the director has allocated. Next, the social worker looks through Corcoran and Fisher's *Measures for Clinical Practice*. In this collection of measurement tools the social worker finds over twenty different instruments with which to measure depression. Reviewing each of them, the social worker chooses the Generalized Contentment Scale (GCS) developed by Walter Hudson. It too is reported to be psychometrically sound and it is, as well, within the allotted budget (Corcoran, 2004).

Determining the Relevance of the Instrument

The GCS is highly relevant to the social workers' purpose. It measures the respondents' level of depression but is not situated within a particular practice theory. In addition, it is excellent for a screening device because it includes clinical cutting scores, one of which indicates clinically significant levels of depression, and the other suicidal ideation.

Looking for Built-in Bias as a Source of Measurement Error

Although no bias is obvious in the wording or content of the GCS, it is clear that two major sources of bias will emerge from total reliance on its use. First, the instrument is based on clients' self report. The use of self-report alone leaves clinicians vulnerable to systematic distortions due to clients' worldviews or to clients' desire to choose the "right" answers. In addition, the answers are only as accurate as the clients' level of willingness to disclose the information requested. Next, the ratings are not behaviorally specific; what may seem to occur "very rarely" to one person may seem like "a good bit of the time" to another.

Recognizing these sources of potential error because of the method by which information is being requested, it is important for the social workers to balance information based on the GCS with information based on their observations of the client. In addition, the social workers may wish to gather more behaviorally specific information about the signs of depression such as weight loss/gain, changes in sleep patterns, and so forth. The process of gathering similar information from several sources and by varying methods is called *triangulation*. Validation of the clients' perceptions is important for sound diagnostic decision making.

Determining the Reliability of the Instrument

The report on the Generalized Contentment Scale in *Measures for Clinical Practice* indicates strong support for internal consistency. In addition, strong support is reported for its test-retest reliability.

Determining the Validity of the Instrument

The instrument appears to have a high level of face and content validity. Thus the statements are directly related to symptoms commonly seen in depressed clients. This form of validity is based, however, on the judgment of the social worker rather than on any statistical tests.

As far as statistical measures of validity are concerned, there is ample evidence of concurrent validity, that is, the scores on the GCS are highly correlated with other respected measures of depression, including the BDI. In addition, construct validity is supported in that the instrument demonstrates sensitivity to change when administered repeatedly through the course of interventions. This is particularly important as the social workers wish to use the scale not only for assessment but for evaluation as well.

Determining the Availability of Test Norms

Although the GCS does not have established norms, it does have clinical cutting scores that indicate clinically significant levels of depression and suicidal ideation. The cutting scores can provide the social workers with information pertinent to screening clients for service. In addition, the test was developed with a very large sample that included a variety of people among whom were college students.

Determining the Adequacy of Knowledge Generated by the Instrument

Although the instrument is neither an exhaustive nor a definitive diagnostic instrument, the knowledge it produces can facilitate diagnostic decision making in a number of ways. First, it can provide direct information about how severely depressed the clients sees themselves. Second, it can quickly identify those clients who are experiencing suicidal ideation, at least among those who are willing to disclose that information. Third, though no test norms are available, the instrument can be used to compare subpopulations of students applying to the clinic for counseling. Thus male students can be compared to females, undergraduates to graduate students, and so on. Such comparisons can provide important implications for planning, policy development, and staff training programs. Finally, the GCS can be reliably administered repeatedly, allowing the social workers to use the instrument to measure change in clients' levels of depression throughout treatment.

Determining the Feasibility of Using the Instrument

Since the instrument takes only about five minutes to complete, is self-administered, and is easy for college students to reliably complete, implementation is quite feasible. In fact, it would be possible to include the instrument in a self-administered informational questionnaire given to students before the first assessment interview. The social workers and director of the counseling center are also considering investing in computer stations with which clients could complete their intake questionnaire, including the GCS. The intake worker could then use the applicants' ratings to inform the first interview.

EXERCISES

1. What would be the advantages and disadvantages for the counseling center clinicians, in the example above, if they decided to measure a broader range of mental disorders instead of measuring depression alone? What instruments are available to measure a broader range of psychopathology? Which would you choose for use in the student counseling center and why?

2. Locate two instruments that can be used to assess a problem common to many of the clients seen in your practice setting. Evaluate each instrument in terms of the dimensions discussed in this chapter. Compare their relative advantages and disadvantages in relation to your practice and the setting in which you work.

SELECTED BIBLIOGRAPHY

Beck, A. T., Steer, R. A., and Brown, G. K. 1996. *Manual for the BDI-II.* San Antonio, TX: Psychological Corporation.

Bloom, M., Fisher, J., and Orme, J. G. 2003. *Evaluating practice: Guidelines for the accountable professional.* Boston: Allyn and Bacon.

Combs-Orme, T., and Thomas, K. H. 1997. Assessment of troubled families. *Social Work Research, 21,* 261–269.

Corcoran, K. 2004. Locating measurement tools and instruments for individuals and couples. In A. R. Roberts and K. R. Yaeger (eds.), *Evidence-based practice manual,* pp. 463–470. New York: Oxford University Press.

Corcoran, K., and Fisher, J. 2000. *Measures for clinical practice.* Vols. 1–2. New York: Free Press.

Hudson, W. W., and McMurtry, S. L. 1997. Comprehensive assessment in social work practice: The multi-problem screening inventory. *Research on Social Work Practice, 7,* 79–98.

Richter, L., and Johnson, P. B. 2001. Current methods of assessing substance use: A review of strengths, problems, and developments. *Journal of Drug Issues, 31,* 809–833.

Roberts, A. R., and Yeager, K. R. (eds.) 2004. *Evidence-based practice manual: Research and outcome measures in health and human services.* New York: Oxford University Press.

Tran, T. V., and O'Hare, T. 1996. Congruency between interviewers' ratings and respondents' self-reports of self-esteem, depression, and health status. *Social Work Research, 20,* 43–51.

Tutty, L. M. 1995. Theoretical and practical issues in selecting a measure of family functioning. *Research on Social Work Practice, 5,* 80–106.

Urbina, S. 2004. *Essentials of psychological testing.* Hoboken: Wiley.

Table 2.1

Collections of Measures Useful for Clinical Social Work Practice

American Psychiatric Association, Task Force for the Handbook of Psychiatric Measures. 2000. Handbook of psychiatric measures. 1st ed. Washington, DC: American Psychiatric Association.

Corcoran, K. J., and Fischer, J. 2000. Measures for clinical practice: A sourcebook. 3d ed. New York: Free Press.

Lyons, J. S. 1997. The measurement and management of clinical outcomes in mental health. New York: Wiley.

Paniagua, F. A. 1998. Assessing and treating culturally diverse clients: A practical guide. 2d ed. Thousand Oaks, CA: Sage.

Roberts, A.. R., and Yeager, K. R. (eds.) 2004. *Evidence-based practice manual: Research and outcome measures in health and human services.* New York: Oxford University Press.

Spies, R. A., and Plake, B. S. (eds.) 2005. *The sixteenth mental measurements yearbook.* Lincoln: Buros Institute of Mental Measurements.

Streiner, D. L., and Norman, G. R. 2004. *Health measurement scales: A practical guide to their development and use.* 3d ed. Oxford: Oxford University Press.

Tansella, M., and Thornicroft, G. (eds.) 2001. *Mental health outcome measures.* 2d ed. London: Gaskell.

Touliatos, J., Perlmutter, B. F., and Straus, M. A. 2001. *Handbook of family measurement techniques.* Vols. 1–3. Thousand Oaks, CA: Sage.

Yoshioka, M. R., and Shibusawa, T. 2004. Psychosocial measures for Asian Pacific Americans. In A. Roberts and K. Yaeger (eds.), *Evidence-based practice manual,* pp. 488–496. New York: Oxford University Press.

Table 2.2

Web Sites with Purchasable Measures Useful for Clinical Social Work Practice

Organization	Web address	Tests available
Buros Institute	http://buros.unl.edu/buros/jsp/search.jsp	Searchable database of over 4000 measures, including reviews and availability.
Harcourt Assessment, Inc.	www.harcourtassessment.com	Broadband and specific clinical assessment tools for children, adolescents, and adults.
Pearson Assessments	www.pearsonassessments.com	Broadband and specific clinical assessment tools for children, adolescents, and adults; includes projective personality tests
Psychological Assessment Resources, Inc.	www.parinc.com	Broadband clinical assessment tools for adults
Western Psychological Service	www.wpspublish.com	Broadband and specific clinical assessment tools for children, adolescents, adults, and families
Multi-Health Systems, Inc.	www.mhs.com	Broadband and specific clinical assessment tools for children, adolescents, adults, and elderly; includes the Structured Clinical Interview for DSM-IV disorders
M.D. Angus and Associates Limited	www.psychtest.com	Wide variety of specific clinical assessment tools for children, adolescents, adults, and families

Systematic Observation | THREE

Direct observation is one of the most natural methods for gathering information. All of us observe phenomena continually and make decisions based on our observations. Similarly, in their practice clinical social workers routinely observe clients and base diagnostic and treatment decisions upon what their clients say and do. In the context of social research, however, observation is conducted more systematically than in daily life or in much of clinical practice.

In its most structured form, systematic observation is a method of quantitative data collection that involves one or more observers, observing events, or behaviors, as they occur, and reliably recording their observations in terms of previously structured codes or numerical categories. In some observational studies the events or behaviors to be observed are first preserved on video or audio recordings. Observations may take place through one-way mirrors as well. Whatever the means of access to the observational data, systematic observation is sufficiently structured to allow testing of research hypotheses or, in the case of practice, to allow for assessment or evaluation.

At the other end of the observational research continuum, unstructured or nonsystematic observation involves one or more observers recording narrative or qualitative accounts of their observations without employing previously structured numerical categories for describing events or behaviors. In social science research this method is used to generate rich descriptions of phenomena or to propose theory. Clinical social workers, however, engage in this form of qualitative observation all the time. Their training and practice experience enables them to make highly refined use of these observations for diagnostic and treatment purposes. Observation for qualitative analysis will be discussed more in chapter 8.

In this chapter the focus is on systematic observation, a procedure with great potential to contribute to diagnostic and treatment decision making. More specifically, we concentrate on the use of systematic observation to study individuals interacting in families, groups, or other social institutions. Our intent is to provide clinical social workers with systematic observational principles and techniques that can assist in diagnostic assessments of these individuals. For those readers interested in the assessment of goals and outcomes for a group or a family, however, we recommend several articles listed in table 3.1 and referenced in the selected bibliography at the end of the chapter.

SYSTEMATIC OBSERVATION AND CLINICAL SOCIAL WORK

In social research observational techniques are frequently used to measure research participants' behaviors in "natural" settings such as at home or school. Often they are utilized along with other more obtrusive approaches such as self-administered questionnaires or interviews in order to provide direct measurement of behaviors that may be difficult to reliably capture through the use of self-report instruments. For instance, in some situations research participants may be unaware of the behaviors of interest to the researcher or they may be unable to accurately share information related to the behavior or concept of interest. Systematic observational techniques are useful in such situations. Likewise, clinical social workers can employ systematic observation to generate practice-relevant information that facilitates accurate assessments of clients' behaviors in natural settings. For instance, systematic observational techniques can be valuable diagnostic tools in schools, hospitals, work with developmentally delayed persons, and more.

Systematic observational techniques are potentially useful in all phases of clinical social work practice. In diagnostic assessment, for example, observations of individuals referred for treatment can be made by social workers, other professionals, or significant others in the referred individual's environment. The contents of these observations can include both the problems and the strengths the individual brings to social situations. For instance, observational techniques can be used to assess the frequency of provocative behavior within the family, disruptive classroom behaviors, or physically self-destructive behaviors in an institutional setting. Alternatively, these techniques can supply information about positive expressions of affection in a family, cooperative behavior in the classroom, and self-caring behaviors in an institutional setting.

Systematic observation can also be employed to validate information obtained by other, less rigorous procedures. For example, a mother may consult a social worker in a community family service agency for help with her child. A discussion with the mother reveals that she is troubled by her child's "immature behavior." The mother is unable to be very specific, however, about the nature of these behaviors or their frequency. In addition, it is unclear whether these behaviors are "abnormal" in frequency and kind when compared to the behaviors of other children of the same age. By visiting the home, and using systematic observation, the social worker can better assess the specific nature and frequency of the behaviors that are problematic to the mother. The social worker can also observe the mother's efforts to reduce the occurrence of these behaviors. In this way the social worker can determine whether the "problem" is with the child or with the mother's expectations.

Systematic observation can be used as well to monitor the extent to which clients follow treatment plans. In fact, the monitoring can be done by clients themselves. Thus, for example, marital partners may be instructed to follow a relaxation procedure for five minutes before dinner each evening. The objective of this is to reduce tension and angry outbursts during dinner. Both partners may be asked to record on a simple form the number of times during the week that they followed this procedure as well as the number of arguments they had during dinner. Such systematic recording will give the social worker an indication of the extent to which the clients are complying with treatment and whether the procedures are having any positive effect.

Another way that systematic observation can be used is to assess or monitor the clinical process. A creative example of such use is provided by McDowell (2000), who describes the use of systematic observation to resolve a therapeutic impasse. In this case both clinician and client observed videotaped sessions and identified "helpful" and "nonhelpful" interventions. By comparing and discussing their observations, the pair was able to move forward in treatment.

Finally, systematic observation can be employed to evaluate the effectiveness of treatment. This would require recording problematic behaviors or mood states before, during, and after treatment to determine whether they have declined significantly and whether the benefits persist even after treatment has been terminated. For example, the parent of a twelve-year-old child currently in therapy because of school-related problems may be asked to record the number of times per week the child completes assigned homework. This recording is maintained for a while after treatment ends to determine whether treatment gains persist. If they do not, treatment may need to be modified and continued.

PRINCIPLES OF SYSTEMATIC OBSERVATION

Determining What Is To Be Observed

To observe a phenomenon reliably, one must decide upon the behaviors to include and to exclude from systematic observation. It is impossible to observe and record everything. Consequently, social workers should decide on the purpose of the observation before considering techniques of observation. In the context of clinical social work practice, observation-generated information should assist the social worker in carrying out practice-related tasks. In the assessment phase of practice, the information should be linked to diagnostic decision making.

The focus of observation may be either overt or covert behaviors. Overt behaviors are directly observable by others, for example, crying, laughing, or hitting. Covert behaviors, on the other hand, involve self-reported feelings, moods, or thoughts such as despair, sense of well-being, or feelings of anger. Covert behaviors are directly observable only by those experiencing the feeling states, and are only indirectly observable to others. As a result, systematic observation is often confined to observation of overt behaviors. Since more than one observer can observe the same set of overt behaviors, higher reliability in measurement can be achieved. However, covert behaviors such as thoughts and feelings can also be measured with systematic observation through the use of self-reported observations.

Assessing the Availability of Existing Observational Instruments

Referring to the principles for assessing available instruments presented in the previous chapter, social workers should determine whether instruments exist that can be used directly or serve as stimuli for the construction of new observational devices. Two observational instruments are mentioned here: the Behavior Assessment System for Children (Reynolds and Kamphaus, 1998) and the Behavioral Observation Instrument (Lieberman et al., 1974). The Behavior Assessment System for Children is a broadband instrument used to assess behavioral problems in children and adolescents. The Behavioral Observation Instrument can be used to classify the behaviors of individual clients in clinical settings such as psychiatric units in hospitals. Staff members may be trained in this method to systematically observe how and where patients spend their time.

If appropriate observational instruments do not already exist, an original instrument can be developed using the following principles.

Constructing the Observational Instrument

The basic task in constructing observation instruments is to provide well-defined, easy to understand dimensions and categories that can be reliably and accurately recorded. Attached to the instrument should be a set of instructions among which are included operational definitions of dimensions and categories, instructions regarding when observations are to be made, and instructions for making necessary tallies of observations. The number of dimensions and categories should not be excessive.

In an observational instrument each dimension refers to a single behavior or attribute that is to be observed, such as playing, crying, or laughing. Each dimension should be sufficiently specified by an operational definition so that observers can agree that the behavior is or is not taking place. In addition, a dimension can be recorded in terms of frequency, duration, magnitude, or some other quality of it. Thus, for example, playing can be classified in terms of the number of times it occurs in a specified time period, the length of time that it takes place over a specified time period, how actively it is engaged in, and whether it is solitary or involves others. As in the construction of forced-choice questions for questionnaires, observational categories should be mutually exclusive and exhaustive. Hence, whatever the classification scheme, categories should not overlap and, in addition, they should exhaust the range of possibilities along that dimension.

The actual recording of observations can be done on paper using a checklist, a tally sheet, a form, or a rating scale. On a checklist, behavioral dimensions are identified and observers indicate whether or not the behaviors are observed. For example, therapeutic technicians in a psychiatric unit of a hospital may be asked to indicate whether given patients appear depressed, anxious, or manic. Naturally, to use such a checklist properly, technicians must be trained to accurately and reliably observe patients in terms of the foregoing categories.

A tally sheet requires that the observer mark each time a specific behavior occurs within a specified time period. Space is left for tallying up the total number of times the behavior is observed. An observer in a classroom, for example, may be asked to record the number of times in an hour that a student speaks without permission or hits other children. The forms generally include a space for adding up the totals for each behavioral dimension observed.

Similarly, forms may be used to record the duration of a particular behavior. The observer would simply indicate the amount of time a specified behavior occurred over the course of a specified amount of time. A classroom observer, for instance, could record the length of time a child is on task over a duration.

Rating scales attempt to record the intensity or degree to which a dimension is exhibited. For example, an observer in a halfway house for clients recovering from alcohol or drug abuse may be asked to rate residents daily in terms of degrees of depression. The rating scale may be numerical, rating the presence of depression from 0 to 10, with 0 indicating no depression and 10, extreme depression. Or, specific non-numerical categories that are mutually exclusive and exhaustive may be provided, such as "not depressed," "mildly depressed," "moderately depressed," and "severely depressed." Many of the principles discussed in chapter 1 on questionnaire development apply to the construction of rating scales for systematic observation.

In addition to pen and paper methods, the recording can be done electronically using a notebook, laptop, or handheld computer. With appropriate software, portable and handheld computing devices have an advantage over forms in that the data can be downloaded directly into a database or statistical software package. Table 3.2 lists several available software packages for recording and analyzing observational data.

Whatever the method, it should be user friendly and as nonobtrusive as possible. If the method is not easily utilized by observers, in all likelihood, it will not be carried through. As Bloom, Fisher, and Orme (2003) point out, some observers do well with one of many low-tech nonpaper methods such as dropping a poker chip in a basket each time a particular behavior is observed. After a specified amount of time, the observer simply counts the chips and records the number on a form. This type of method may be particularly useful for busy observers such as parents and teachers.

Determining the Sample of Observations

For reasons of economy, in most clinical situations observations must be made on a selective basis. For example, it might be clinically useful, but prohibitively expensive, to observe a child with a behavioral disorder all day, every day, for a month. As a result, it is necessary to select a sample based on time or situational factors. A time sample involves making observations at previously designated periods of time to obtain what is hopefully a representation of typical behavior. The times chosen for observation may be selected randomly or systematically, for instance, every twenty minutes. Alternatively, the choice of times may be based on situational factors, that is, on some strategic sense of the times that are most critical to the expression of the behavior to be observed. For example, observation of a child's social skills may take place only at recess and lunch since those are the only unstructured times with peers during the school day.

As much as possible, the number of dimensions observed should be small enough and the number of observations made should be large enough to ensure the reliability and validity of the observations made. However, if observers are not full-time observers but must perform other roles, the number of observations should not interfere with management of their other roles. If the demands of these other roles are not taken into account, the result will be fatigue, resentment, and errors in judgment and in recording.

Overall, the observations should be spaced broadly enough so that recording them need not be overly laborious, yet they should be spaced narrowly enough to provide a fairly reliable representation of the situation to be observed. In a family situation, for example, recording parent-child conflicts on a weekly basis would lead to highly unreliable recording. Alternatively, monitoring conflicts every five minutes would be exhausting and unnecessarily precise. As with many other research issues, some balance must be struck between precision and practicality in constructing the instrument.

It should also be noted, in the case of observing behavior within a family or other group, that the social worker must decide how many and which of the individuals to observe. The sample chosen should be unbiased and representative of the group overall. (See chapter 12 for a more in-depth discussion on sampling.)

Choosing the Observer

As indicated earlier, any number of individuals may be involved in the collection of observational data. What is important, however, is that the observer has familiarity with the situation being observed and with the dimensions and categories that are to be recorded. Consequently, only a trained clinician should be used to make complex clinical judgments. Alternatively, if the categories of behavior to be recorded are simple and part of everyone's day-to-day language and experience, nonexperts may be used. Accordingly, only trained clinicians should make judgments about whether a patient appears "manic." It does not take a professional, however, to record when someone is laughing.

Whatever their usual role in the situation to be observed, the observers should try to refrain from projecting their own biases and values on the behaviors observed. This is often difficult. It is facilitated, however, by an instrument that includes clear instructions for making and recording observations and is composed of simple, behaviorally specific dimensions and categories. Valid and reliable observational data are also greatly facilitated with training. Even experienced clinicians may require training in order to do systematic observation.

Training the Observers

To properly use an observational instrument, observers must be adequately trained. The purpose of such training is to standardize the use of the observational instrument, to reduce the number of errors and ambiguous recording of observations, to increase reliability, and to promote objectivity. The amount of training necessary depends on the complexity of the instrument and the clarity and specificity of dimensions, categories, and instructions. The more complex or abstract the dimension, the more training is required.

In training observers, they should first be instructed about the purpose of the instrument, how it is to be used, and the definitions of dimensions and categories. Each dimension to be observed should be clearly and specifically defined so as to avoid confusion among the observers. This can be accomplished through written instructions, oral presentations, and discussion for clarifying ambiguities or misunderstandings. Role-plays also can be helpful for simulating the situations to be observed and trying out the instrument.

Observers should be instructed to observe and record behaviors in as unbiased a way as possible. Ideally, observers should not be aware of the expected changes in behavior. In clinical practice, however, observers' expectations and levels of optimism (or pessimism) about the effectiveness of interventions are likely to bias their observations such that they will support their expectations of success or failure. The use of more than one observer may help to compensate for this bias. Often, however, only one observer is available. Moreover, the observer is frequently the clinician who developed the instrument, requiring a high level of self-control and objectivity so that the instrument is not used in a biased fashion to support a predetermined conclusion.

Pretesting the Observational Instrument

Before actually implementing an observational instrument, it should be pretested so that reliability estimates can be made and ambiguities in procedures can be corrected. This can be accomplished by using the instrument on a trial basis in actual clinical situations or with videotapes, audiotapes, or role-plays of them. In pretesting, one should establish whether instructions are clear, whether the observers can use the instrument reliably and accurately, and whether use of the instrument causes undue fatigue or boredom. The latter elements, if present, will reduce reliability over time.

Having two independent observers pretest the instrument is a useful procedure to help ensure reliability. However, that may not be practical in many clinical situations. If only one person is used for observing many events over time, it is desirable to have another observer do spot checks of small segments of events occasionally to test reliability. If that is not practical, and events are recorded on video or audiotape, observers can spot-check their own reliability by recoding an event and comparing the two data sets. If events are not recorded, observers should, of course, be instructed to do the coding while the event is taking place. Coding done after the event is likely to be inaccurate and distorted.

Assessing the Validity of the Observational Instrument

In the context of systematic observation, validity refers to the extent to which the observational instrument measures what it claims to measure. The two types of validity that are particularly relevant to observational instruments are content and concurrent validity. Here, content validity refers to the logical connection between the observational instrument and the information pertinent to diagnostic assessment. This relationship can be established by having two or more experts review the dimensions and categories of these dimensions in the instrument to determine whether they constitute appropriate indicators of the clinically relevant information sought. For example, observation of a child at play would not be a valid way to measure that child's ability to stay on-task in the classroom.

Concurrent validity refers to the extent to which the information generated by the observational instrument is consistent with information generated by other means. Thus, one would expect observational data regarding a child's level of social skills to correspond with the level indicated by the score on a questionnaire completed by the child's teacher. Although concurrent validity may be difficult to demonstrate and may not be practically obtainable in many instances, we recommend, at minimum, that an observational instrument exhibit a high level of content validity before using it to make diagnostic assessments.

Determining the Reliability of the Observational Instrument

To ensure a high degree of reliability in the observations, observers should be trained to make and record their observations in a nonbiased, nonintrusive manner. When a number of observers are used, training and practice are necessary until a high level of interobserver reliability is achieved. Here, interobserver reliability refers to the extent to which two or more independent observers, observing the same situation without mutual consultation, using the same form, agree in their judgments and coding of the event. A simple index of interobserver reliability is a percentage based on the number of agreements between the judges, relative to the total number of judgments that they make, multiplied by 100. In other words, the number of agreements would be divided by the total possible number of agreements and then multiplied by 100. A score above 80 percent is generally regarded as fairly high. Thus, two judges who agree in eight out of ten judgments exhibit an 80 percent index of interobserver reliability.

It should be noted, however, that the larger the number of categories employed, the more difficult it is to reach such a high level of agreement. In other words, the greater the number of choices available for coding observations, the greater is the probability of disagreement. Thus, if there are two categories for recording a dimension, by chance alone, observers are likely to agree 50 percent of the time. If there are three categories, chance observations would lead to agreement 33 percent of the time even if they were both blindfolded during observation sessions. The probability of chance agreement would decrease with each additional response category.

In order to take the probability of agreement into account, interobserver reliability can be tested in two ways. The first involves collapsing contiguous categories of observation so that there are only two. Thus, if a rating scale includes four categories of anxiety (no anxiety, low anxiety, moderate anxiety, and high anxiety), and observations are roughly equally distributed among the categories, the no and low anxiety categories can be added together and treated as one category and the moderate and high anxiety categories added together and treated as another single category. Agreement will then be calculated on the basis of the two newly constructed categories. If the observations are not equally distributed among the categories, the split between the two should be done in such a way that roughly 50 percent of the observations fall into each of the newly constructed categories. Thus, if almost all the observations fall into the moderate and high anxiety categories, the no, low, and moderate anxiety categories should be collapsed and added together, and the high anxiety category should be kept intact.

Another procedure for roughly estimating reliability is used when there are more than two categories within a dimension and when the distribution of cases within categories is relatively equal. This procedure is based on the difference between the results that one would expect based on chance alone and an arbitrary standard set at 20 to 30 percent higher. So, for example, if a dimension has three categories, the expected agreement by chance alone would be 33 percent of the observations. By adding an additional 20 to 30 percent, a rough criterion of 53 to 63 percent agreement could be established as an acceptable standard of interobserver reliability. Likewise, if there were four categories, agreement in 45 to 55 percent of the observations could be established as an acceptable standard of interobserver reliability. A formula for more precisely calculating an estimate of interobserver reliability, the Kappa coefficient is often used in research. An acceptable Kappa score is at least .60, with higher scores being more desirable.

An important principle for estimating interobserver reliability is that the observations are made independently, without the mutual collaboration of the observers. Under these conditions, high agreement among the observers indicates that they understand the dimensions and categories of observation, that the instructions for recording observations are clear, and that the format for recording the observations works. An observational system that is unreliable should not be used. An unreliable system should either be discarded or the reasons for unreliability should be identified and modified until acceptable levels of reliability are attained.

For each observer used, a high degree of intraobserver reliability is also desirable. In this context, intraobserver reliability refers to the extent to which a single observer repeatedly records the same event in the same way. With videotaped or other electronically recorded events, this is computed relatively easily by viewing or listening to the taped events twice, observing and coding them, and computing a percentage based on the number of agreements in observations relative to the total number of observations made, multiplied by 100. Here again a 70–80 percent reliability is generally required. For observational dimensions in which more than two categories exist, the techniques suggested earlier for estimated interobserver reliability can be used. In either case, there should be a sufficient time-lag between observational sessions, or a sufficient number of events to observe, in order that the observer does not reproduce the observations from memory.

Finally, one should not assume that once established, a high degree of reliability is easily maintained. Over time, observers get tired or bored and their reliability declines. As they become more familiar with the situation to be observed, they may become less attentive to new aspects or prejudge the course of events. To protect against these possibilities, spot checks should be done throughout the assessment or evaluation. If a high degree of reliability is maintained, social workers can have more confidence in the diagnostic or treatment implications drawn from the findings.

Making the Observations

In attempting to be as objective as possible, observers should avoid influencing those being observed. The observers' stance should aim for neutrality; they should refrain from intervening with the participants in the observed situation. Even if they say nothing, however, their mere presence may significantly affect the behaviors of those under observation. Because of this, it is sometimes helpful to give clients time to get used to the presence of the observer. Real data should not be collected until observers are relatively confident that the participants in the situation are able to ignore their presence and recording activities.

SYSTEMATIC OBSERVATION IN ACTION

Two school social workers who work in the elementary school setting frequently receive referrals from teachers of children who are described as "out of control," "immature," or "disruptive." Quite often the teachers are specific about neither the behaviors to which these labels refer nor their frequency. Due to the heavy volume of referrals that the social workers receive, they need to evaluate which of the children referred are most immediately in need of social work intervention. In addition, they suspect that some of the referrals may be from teachers who are either less tolerant of behaviors that are developmentally appropriate or may be scapegoating particular children. If this is the case, in-service training for the teachers may help increase classroom control and decrease referrals. They wish to have a better understanding of the behaviors and their frequencies.

The social workers decide to devise an observational instrument that will make it possible to record the frequency of the behaviors teachers find disruptive among those children referred. Such an instrument would make assessment of individual children possible as well as comparison of these children with some of their classmates. In addition, the instrument might indicate whether some teachers are less tolerant than others of normal levels of activity among children or are biased in other ways with regard to specific children.

Determining What Is To Be Observed

Social workers want to observe the classroom behaviors of children who have been referred to them for treatment. In addition they want to be able to compare these children's behaviors with the behaviors of some of their classmates. For a start, they are concerned about monitoring behaviors that teachers are most likely to describe as the bases for their referrals. These behaviors generally include speaking without permission, getting out of seat without permission, arguing with other children, and refusal to comply with teacher's instructions.

Assessing the Availability of Existing Observational Instruments

In the library the social workers discover a number of books and articles in the psychology and education field pertaining to "classroom management." Some of these publications contain highly complex observational instruments that would be overly time-intensive to implement. However, some components of a few instruments are suggestive of observational dimensions that seem relevant. The social workers decide to use these elements as a guide to developing their own observational instrument.

Constructing the Observational Instrument

After talking with teachers and reviewing available literature, the social workers decide that there are four behavioral dimensions they would like to include in their instrument: inappropriate talking, appropriate talking, being out of seat inappropriately, being out of seat appropriately. An "other" dimension is included to cover behaviors not included in the foregoing dimension. The social workers then begin to develop categories of behavior that fall into each of the dimensions. For example, inappropriate talking may include such things as answering questions without being recognized by the teacher or talking to a classmate when it is not permitted. Appropriate talking may include answering a question when called upon by the teacher or talking to a classmate during a free period. Being out of seat inappropriately may include running around the class or actually leaving the class without permission. On the other hand, running an errand for the teacher or going to the bathroom with teacher's permission are appropriate ways to be out of seat. Finally, "other" may include quietly working or reading.

Once the dimensions are specified and agreed upon, the social workers develop an observational form on which they can code, within specified intervals, the occurrence of behaviors of the children referred to them, as well as the behaviors of the neighboring children. Initially, they develop a form that is very simple, including only the five dimensions to be coded for each child. Later, a more refined version might be developed in which the categories within these dimensions could be coded as well. In its present state, however, the specific categories only serve as examples of indicators for coding each of the dimensions. The simplified form might look like this.

Recorder's Name:		Date:		
Time Start:		Time Finish:		
Referred Child's Name:				

	Interval (5 min.)			
Behavior	**1**	**2**	**3**	**Total**
Appropriate talking:	/			1
Inappropriate talking:		//	/	3
Appropriately out of seat:				0
Inappropriately out of seat:		/		1
Other:				

Child A (to the front)

Behavior				**Total**
Appropriate talking:	/	/		2
Inappropriate talking:				0
Appropriately out of seat:			/	1
Inappropriately out of seat:		/		1
Other: (Inappropriate gesture)	/			1

Child B (to the back)

Behavior				
Appropriate talking:	/			1
Inappropriate talking:	/	//		3
Appropriately out of seat:				
Inappropriately out of seat:				
Other (tipped chair back)		//		2

With this form individual observations are recorded by "hash marks," which are totaled for each dimension and for each child at the end of the specified length of observation.

Determining the Frequency of Observations

Based on other aspects of their workloads, the social workers determine that for pretesting purposes it would be possible for them to engage in three fifteen-minute observational periods on three successive days. On one day observation will take place relatively early in the morning at 9:30 A.M.. The next day observation will begin at 11:30 A.M. On the final day, observation will be conducted in the afternoon at 2:00 P.M.

At the beginning of each fifteen-minute observational period, the behavior of the referred child and the children immediately in front and behind him or her will be recorded on the form. Using a stopwatch, observers will repeat this process, every five minutes, resulting in three observations for each child during a thirty-minute observational period. At the end of each observational period, the results are tallied for each child. Then, at the end of the three-day period, these can be added together.

Choosing the Observers

During the pretesting stage of the instrument, both social workers observe the same children in the same classroom, at the exact same times. This common observation of the same events is necessary for checking interobserver reliability. In other situations it might be appropriate to have the teacher, a student teacher, or a teacher's aide conduct simultaneous observations. In any case, once observers become well-trained in the use of the instrument, they may be used to collect the primary information without the presence of a dual observer.

Training Observers and Pretesting the Observational Instrument

Since the social workers were themselves the authors of the observational forms and the observers, no additional training was necessary. However, after pretesting the form, they found a few instances of disagreement, primarily in the category of talking behaviors. Through discussion, they arrived at a more refined definition of what constitutes appropriate and inappropriate talking behavior.

In the future, if the workers decide to have others use this instrument, they will need to offer training sessions and conduct reliability tests of the new observers' use of the instrument. However, since they intend to use the instrument themselves, it is ready to be used by each of them for diagnostic assessment of the children referred to them.

Assessing the Validity of the Observational Instrument

The social workers judge the instrument to be valid based on the logical connection between the instrument and the behaviors that are of concern to the teachers and social workers. However, if there are vast discrepancies between teacher reports concerning specific children's behaviors and the information generated by the forms, the question of concurrent validity arises. Thus one possible explanation is that the form has low concurrent validity and needs to be refined further. The other possibility is that the teacher's reports are not valid and are, in fact, based on a biased perception of the particular child's behavior. To deal with this problem, the social worker may want to do another round of observations first, before changing the instrument. If the results based on the structured observations remain consistently at variance with the teacher's reports, then the teacher should be presented with this information and the social worker's interventions may be directed toward the teacher.

Determining the Reliability of the Observational Instrument

After the pretest of the observational instrument, the social workers compare their results on each of the dimensions for each of the youngsters observed, across all three observation sessions. By dividing the number of agreements by the total number of observations for each dimension and multiplying by one hundred, they establish an 80 percent or higher interobserver reliability for each dimension. Consequently, they assume that they can each employ the instrument reliably enough to use it independently for diagnostic-assessment purposes.

Making the Observations

In order to avoid influencing the situation as much as possible, the social workers first made arrangements with the teachers in whose rooms they would conduct their observations. In addition, they spent about twenty minutes in the classroom the day before they conducted their systematic observation. Also, before each set of structured observations were conducted, the social workers spent ten minutes in the classroom so that teachers and students would be accustomed to their presence and presumably behave in a natural manner when the systematic observations began.

EXERCISES

1. Based on the school social work example above, develop a sampling procedure and simple rating scale that could be used if the social workers decided that they wanted to measure the duration rather than the frequency of the behaviors they were observing.

2. With at least one colleague, observe fifteen minutes of a videotaped clinical interview. After the tape is finished, write a brief narrative statement describing the level of anxiety exhibited by the client. After each person has finished writing, discuss the indicators, such as client's statements or nonverbal behaviors, on which you based your decision about level of anxiety. Next, devise a systematic observational instrument for recording the number of times the client exhibits one of the agreed-upon indicators of anxiety. Replay and code the tape. Wait a day, view once more, and repeat coding. Compute the interobserver and intraobserver reliability of the instrument. How reliable is it? Which form of reliability is higher? Comment on the validity of your observation instrument.

SELECTED BIBLIOGRAPHY

Auerbach, C., La Porte, H. H., and Caputo, R. K. 2004. Statistical methods for estimates of interrater reliability. In A. Roberts and K. Yaeger (eds.), *Evidence-based practice manual,* pp. 444–448. New York: Oxford University Press.

Bales, R. F. 1999. *Social interaction systems: Theory and measurement.* New Brunswick: Transaction.

Bloom, M., Fisher, J., and Orme, J. G. 2003. *Evaluating practice: Guidelines for the accountable professional.* Boston: Allyn and Bacon.

Cabral, R. J., and Strang, M. 1984. Measuring child care: An examination of three assessment measures. *Journal of Social Service Research, 7,* 65–77.

Franklin, C., Cody, P. A., and Jordan, C. 2004. Validity and reliability in family assessment. In A. Roberts and K. Yaeger (eds.), *Evidence-based practice manual,* pp. 436–443. New York: Oxford University Press.

Gavazzi, S. M. and Anderson, S. A. 1988. The Family Health Scales (FHS): Review and critique. *American Journal of Family Therapy, 16,* 273–276.

Kuehne, V. S., and Collins, C. L. 1997. Observational research in intergenerational programming: Need and opportunity. *Journal of Gerontological Social Work, 28,* 183–193.

Lieberman, R. P., DeRisi, W. J., King, L. W., Eckman, T. A., and Wood, D. 1974. Behavioral measurement in a community mental health center. In P. O. Davidson, F. W. Clark,

L. A. Hamerlynck (eds.), *Evaluation of behavioral programs*, pp. 103–140. Champaign: Research.

McDowell, T. 2000. Practice evaluation as a collaborative process: A client's and a clinician's perceptions of helpful and unhelpful moments in a clinical interview. *Smith College Studies in Social Work, 70,* 375–387.

Reynolds, C. R. and Kamphaus, R. W. 1988. *BASC: Behavior assessment system for children.* Circles Pines, MH: American Guidance Service.

Table 3.1 Systematic Observation of Groups and Families

Type of Group	Dimensions	Authors
Wide variety of groups from task to therapeutic	Characteristics of members' participation, authority, and task orientation; group dynamics, such as subgrouping, scapegoats, and leadership.	Bales, R. F.
Community-based intergenerational support groups	Various interactions between older adults and children	Kuehne, V. S. & Collins, C. L.
Families	Overall functioning	Gavazzi, S. M. & Anderson, S. A.
Families	Functioning, competence, and style	Franklin, C., Cody, P. A., & Jordan, C.
Families, specifically related to child welfare	Various aspects of children's physical and emotional welfare within families	Cabral, R. J. & Strang, M.

Table 3.2 Systematic Observation Tools

Name	Description	Company	Web site
Behavioral Evaluation Strategy and Taxonomy (BEST)	Designed to facilitate direct observations in a wide variety of field-based, clinical, and experimental settings; either live or videotaped	Educational Consulting Inc.	skware.com

Observational Data Log (ODLog™)	Designed for accurate timing and recording of observational data; live or videotaped	Macropod Software	macropodsoftware.com
The Observer Basic and The Observer Mobile	Designed to set up coding methods, collect observational data, manage projects, and analyze results	Noldus Information Technology	noldus.com

Before conducting social science research, the variables of interest to the researcher must be clearly defined. This involves a process in which the researcher first defines the variable conceptually and then moves toward *operationalization* of the concept. An operational definition of a concept is precise and allows for measurement. The process is similar in clinical practice. Prior to moving into treatment planning and intervention, the clinician must specify and operationalize clients' problems, goals, and objectives that form the target of intervention. This process involves several steps in order to move from clients' description of the problem to a specifically defined problem as well as from broadly defined goals to measurable goals and objectives.

Once specified, some concepts or problems are easily operationalized using available measurement instruments. For example, clinicians and researchers alike may choose from a number of available measures of depression that have been shown to be reliable and valid. In this case the items on the scale operationally define the concept of depression. By completing the scale, clients or study participants measure their levels of depression. Some client problems or goals, however, may be somewhat unique or idiosyncratic, making the use of an available instrument difficult. In such cases, clinicians may choose to utilize goal-attainment scaling (GAS) or individualized rating (IR) scales, two techniques that have been developed and found to be useful for operationalization and measurement in clinical practice.

SPECIFICATION AND RATING OF PROBLEMS AND GOALS IN CLINICAL PRACTICE

In clinical practice, specification and operationalization of problems and goals serve many purposes. Specification of clients' problems is related to the concepts of *reliability* and *validity* discussed earlier. In order that an assessment of clients' problems is valid, that is, accurate; it must be based on observations that are logically connected to the diagnostic conclusions. Moreover, assessment should be reliable, that is, consistent. In other words, the problems must be described specifically enough that they can be consistently observed and linked to professional diagnostic conclusions. Careful description of clients' problems allow for such accuracy and consistency. Most clinicians actually engage in this process of specification at some level whether they are aware of it or not. Diagnostic conclusions are necessarily based on observations of clients, and, in some way, clinicians link those observations to their ideas about the clients' problems. Operationalization goes a step beyond specification in that it creates the ability to measure the extent, severity, and intensity of clients' problems, further aiding the assessment process.

Specifying and operationally defining goals is also an important process in clinical practice. Well-defined goals should be directly linked to the clinician's choice of interventions. In addition, operationalized goals provide a way to measure clients' progress toward the desired outcomes during the intervention phase of treatment. In short, valid and reliable assessment, the choice of appropriate interventions, and evaluation of social work intervention all require measurable problems and goals.

PRINCIPLES FOR SPECIFICATION AND RATING OF PROBLEMS AND GOALS

Specify the Problem

As discussed earlier, social workers gather information in the assessment phase in order to understand the problems for which clients seek help. Once those problems are generally understood and prioritized, the next step is to move toward greater specificity by operationalizing the chosen problems. That is, indicators of the problem must be selected that can, in some way, be observed.

Although important, operationalization of the problem is often overlooked in the clinical process. This may be because the problems that are seen by social workers are often complex and thought to be difficult to capture by particular indicators or observations. In addition, specification often requires an investment of time and thought, both of which are valuable commodities in the practice environment. There are, however, several guidelines outlined by Bloom, Fisher, and Orme (2003) that help to streamline the process. First, they suggest that social workers help clients to clarify their problems by requesting concrete examples, asking "when and where" questions, and performing functional analyses. A *functional analysis* requires an exploration of what precedes the problematic situation, details of the problem itself, and the consequences that follow the problematic event. Next, it is suggested that social workers consider the problem in terms of frequency, that is, how often and for what duration does the problem occur? Other suggestions include considering how others in the clients' lives may observe the problem or considering an increase or decrease of the problem. Each of these considerations pushes the client and social worker to become more specific. It is simply more difficult, for a problem that is vague and ill-defined, to consider what others would observe or what would change in frequency. Finally, Bloom, Fisher, and Orme suggest that social workers consider whether they are *reifying* a problem, that is, treating an abstract concept as if it were real. If that is the case, the problem can be easily specified by first thinking of the abstract concept as an adjective to describe behavior and then describing the behaviors related to the adjective. For example, John is *out of control*, a reified problem, may be specified by stating that John exhibits out-of-control behaviors such as yelling at his employer when frustrated and hitting his son when angry. For all of the suggestions provided above, details are the key to specifying the problem.

Specify the Goals and Objectives

While the operationalized problem describes what the client wants to experience less, the goals describe what the client hopes to experience more. Goals are often subdivided into objectives that represent either parts of the goal or milestones toward achievement of the goal. Goals and objectives should be stated in positive, measurable terms.

Goals and objectives must include several parts in order to be specified and useful as outcomes. First, the goal must *name who will be changed* in some way through the course of the intervention. Often goals are developed for individuals, but they may also refer to groups of people, for instance, a family or a group of volunteers in training. Next, the goal must *specify what will change*. This does not refer to the activity or intervention that will be utilized but to the desired outcome. For example, a client with a social phobia may decide that a beginning milestone toward the ability to participate freely during a meeting at work may be to introduce one friend to another. The goal must also *specify the conditions in which the change is expected to occur*. Continuing with the client with social phobia, the introduction of friends can be further specified by deciding that it will take place at lunch in a casual restaurant in which the client is very comfortable. This environmental condition is quite different, from, say, a formal dinner party at a five-star restaurant. Next, the goal must *specify a level of performance*, that is, what criteria will be used to indicate the outcome has been accomplished? Returning to our client, the social worker may use a scaling technique to establish a desired level of comfort during the introduction, so that the goal is a perhaps a comfort level of seven on a ten-point scale. Putting all the pieces together, the goal would be "the client will introduce one friend to another over lunch at a familiar, casual restaurant with a comfort level of at least seven."

Decide on Who, When, and Where to Rate the Problems, Goals, and Objectives

After operationalizing problems, goals, and/or subgoals; the social worker must make several more decisions related to their measurement. First, the social worker must decide *who* will do the rating. The determination of who should do the actual rating depends on the potential for objectivity, access to the client, and time available. When interested in change of subjective mood states such as "comfort level" used in the example above, there is little choice but to have the client do the rating. Other problems and goals, however, may be rated by others. For example, desirable and undesirable behaviors among children may be observed and rated by parents and teachers. Relational partners may be asked to rate each other's communication skills. Clinical supervisors may find it helpful to rate trainees' empathic clinical responses and vice versa. Ideally, of course, it would be better if more than one person rated the client. This would promote greater confidence in the ratings.

Another factor that affects the reliability of the ratings is the extent to which the rater understands the dimensions covered in the scale and the system for recording observations or perceptions. When social workers are not doing the rating, they should take the time to fully explain the use of the scale to those who are doing the actual rating. Moreover, social workers should make at least an informal assessment of the degree to which their own clinical observations of the client are consistent with the ratings provided by the client or significant others. Calling attention to such inconsistencies may provide useful clinical material as well as clarify the client's condition.

In addition to who will do the rating, decisions must be made about *when* and *where*, or under what conditions, the rating process will take place. Will teachers be asked to rate children's behaviors during free-time or during lessons? Will the client with social phobia be asked to rate comfort level at home watching television in the evening or only during particular social interactions? Primarily, the answers to these questions must correspond closely with the targeted problems and goals of intervention. In addition, as much as possible, the conditions under which the ratings are made should be standardized. Thus, the person doing the rating should be able to observe the client in regular intervals, in similar situations, which are relevant to the goals of treatment.

Decide on Measurement Tools

Next, the social worker must decide what tool will be used to measure the problem and the goals. The first choice is often to find and utilize a rating scale that has already been developed and standardized. The steps in this process have been discussed in chapter 2. For some problems seen by social workers, this is a relatively easy process. For example, there are many readily available instruments with which to measure the problem of depression. When a suitable rating scale cannot be found easily, however, there are at least two practical alternatives, including goal-attainment scaling and individualized rating scales. Before addressing each of these client-driven measurement tools in more depth, there are a few cautions about developing more complicated scales with which to measure client problems or goals.

While it may be tempting to some social workers to create an instrument, developing a scale that is reliable and valid is a time-consuming process. Without going into the many steps that are required to move from a construct, or idea of something to be measured, through the process of validating the instrument, suffice it to say that researchers often spend years to develop strong measurement instruments. The time and effort required for this process are not generally available to clinicians. For those who are interested, however, the first two references in the bibliography provide the necessary information. Another suggestion, if development of a scale is a priority, is to partner with a social work faculty member or other researcher to help with the project.

Although they do not require the developmental rigor described above, there are two types of scales developed for clinical use that can be very helpful in practice. Descriptions of each of them follow.

Goal-attainment scaling was developed by Kiresuk and Sherman for use in community mental health. It is useful for articulating goals, monitoring progress, and evaluating outcomes. In addition, it is tailored directly to the problems and goals of each client, is easy to administer, and can be administered repeatedly.

In GAS the client and clinician first define problem areas and potential outcomes for each area. Then, for each problem area, they construct a scale from -2 to +2, with 0 representing the level of the desired outcome at assessment. If

Table 4.1

Sample of Goal-Attainment Scaling for Client with Symptoms Related to PTSD

Goal attainment scale for _____ **Date:** _____
(Client's name)

Goal Attainment Level	Problem and Weight: Sleep Disturbance/.40	Problem and Weight: Concentration/.20	Problem and Weight: Avoidance/.40
+2 Best Possible Progress	Restful sleep through the night 90 percent of time	Able to concentrate at work when desired 100 percent of time	Able to talk with intimate partner and friend about the traumatic event
+1 Some Progress Level	Restful sleep through the night 75 percent of time	Able to concentrate at work 75 percent of time	Able to go to work and shop in pre-traumatic event locations
0 Level at Assessment	Restful sleep through the night 25 percent of time	Able to concentrate at work 25 percent of time	Able to go to work and shop only at locations distant to the traumatic event
-1 Some Decline in Level	Restful sleep through the night 15 percent of time	Able to concentrate at work 15 percent of time	Able to go to work and shop only in daylight
-2 Severe Decline in Level	Restful sleep through the night 0 percent of time	Able to concentrate at work 0 percent of time	Able to work and shop only in daylight with another person

the outcome is much worse than expected at the next point of measurement, -2 would be assigned; somewhat worse would be indicated by -1; some improvement would be indicated by +1; and great improvement by +2. Points on the scale are operationalized according to the desired outcome; they may be based on specific behavioral observations, ratings of subjective states, or even scores on rapid assessment instruments. For example, table 4.1 shows a goal-attainment scale for a client experiencing symptoms of post-traumatic stress disorder (PTSD). The table indicates the problems across the top row and the operationalized levels of goal attainment in each column.

Each of the GAS problem areas may be weighted according to the priority of the problem, or they may be considered to be of equal importance. In either case, the outcome scores for all the problem areas can be averaged to obtain an overall indicator of the client's accomplishments. If the GAS is used repeatedly to measure progress throughout an intervention, the scores can be graphed and used in single-subject designs.

Individualized rating scales can be developed by clinicians and clients to measure specific targets of intervention. They consist of one item that is measured across a specific dimension using a selected number of potential responses. Multiple individualized rating scales may be used with one client. The responses or measurement points must be clearly anchored by the client's potential behaviors, thoughts, or mood states. The anchors may be uniquely tailored to a client or they may be more generic. Figure 4.1 shows an individualized rating scale that targets a client's level of anxiety in social situations. The anchors on the top line are generic, while those on the bottom are uniquely tailored to the client.

Table 4.2 Individualized Rating Scale Examples

Level of Anxiety in Social Settings

1	2	3	4	5	6	7	8	9
"Not at all Anxious" OR "Feels perfectly at ease during events such as the office party"				"Moderately Anxious" OR "Feels manageable levels of anxiety in social settings"				"Extremely Anxious" OR "Anxiety interferes with attendance at social events"

In order to develop items for IR scales, the social worker and client must determine the dimension to be measured and develop the response scale. The item then is made up of two parts. First, it includes the dimension to be measured, called the stimulus; this is the question, set of instructions, or statement to which the rater responds. Stimuli can take the form of single sentences, phrases, words or questions. The second part of the item is the response scale that represents the format within which the ratings are made. These are similar to the response systems in closed-ended questions that were discussed in chapter 1. In the scale above, "level of anxiety in social settings" is the stimulus, and the numbers 1 through 9 are the response categories. The statements under scale steps 1, 5, and 9 are referred to as anchoring illustrations. They promote the reliability of the ratings.

Note that as with closed-ended questionnaire items, the response categories are mutually exclusive and exhaustive. Below are some generic stimuli and response systems for rating a client's level of anxiety using an IR scale.

(1) Frequency of symptom description
    How often is the client anxious?
        1-very infrequently
        2-infrequently
        3-frequently
        4-very frequently

(2) Severity of symptom description
    How anxious is the client?
        1-not at all anxious
        2-slightly anxious
        3-moderately anxious
        4-strongly anxious
        5-severely anxious

(3) Frequency of symptom by percentage
    About what percentage of the time is the client anxious?
        0–0 percent
        1–1-10 percent
        2–11–20 percent
        3–21–30 percent
        4–31–40 percent

(4) Frequency designated by time intervals

About how often does the client appear anxious?

1-once a month or less

2-once every two weeks

3-once a week

4-twice a week

5-every other day

6-daily

(5) Likert Scale (with or without neutral category)

The client appears anxious.

1-strongly agree

2-agree

3-uncertain

4-disagree

5-strongly disagree

(6) Comparative scale

Compared to when treatment began, which would you say the client is now?

1-much more anxious

2-more anxious

3-about the same

4-less anxious

5-much less anxious

The scales listed above are only a sampling of those available. The following principles will help to decrease *measurement error* and should be kept in mind when constructing IR scale items.

Avoid having too many or too few scale points. Too many scale points could lead to unreliability in the ratings. Too few could lead to a lack of discrimination of important differences. Typically, scales have between four and nine steps in the response system. Two measurement errors related to the response system are worth noting here. *Central tendency* errors are those that result from the raters consistently choosing noncommittal, neutral, or middle points on rating scales. These errors can be minimized by response systems that do not have "uncertain" or "undecided" response categories or by increasing the number of response categories that are close to neutral. Depending on the situation, a cruder or a more refined scale may be called for when ratings are consistently noncommittal.

A similar type of error results when respondents give relatively noncommittal responses to *avoid extreme alternatives*. For example, a scale that has three points on it, including "always," "sometimes," and "never," is likely to generate a high proportion of "sometimes" responses irrespective of the attitude, mood, or behavior that is being rated. Here, more refined categories between the midpoint and the two extremes would be called for.

Provide clear anchoring illustrations for several scale points, especially the ends and the middle of the scale. These promote interrater reliability. The response system anchors should be *balanced,* that is, the response categories should be weighted similarly in both directions. For example, a four-point scale of therapeutic progress that ranges from 1 (a small amount of progress) to 4 (a great amount of progress) would not entertain the possibility that the client makes no progress or even gets worse during treatment. A more balanced and less biased scale would provide an equal number of categories for these less desirable outcomes.

In attempting to measure a target that has several component dimensions, several separate IR scales should be used to measure each dimension. For example, the concept of social anxiety may involve the client's experience at work, with family, and in social settings. Each of these dimensions can be measured with a separate IR scale. An overall measure of social anxiety can be determined by adding the individual's score on the respective scales. To correctly perform this data manipulation, each IR scale must have the same response system and each set of responses must be scored the same way. So, if there are three component scales, each scoring from 1 (low anxiety) to 5 (high anxiety), by adding the scores for all the items one can compute an overall score of social anxiety. This is called a cumulative or additive index. On this index any individual can range from a score of 3 (which would indicate the lowest social anxiety possible) to a score of 15 (which would indicate the highest anxiety possible). It is also possible to compute an average or mean score by dividing the total score for all three IR scales and dividing by three.

When several different dimensions of client behavior are being rated, it is preferable to use only one response system. If more are used, it is important to remember that the greater the number of response systems used, the greater the likelihood of response error. An exception to this may be if there is great concern about a measurement error called the halo effect. Halo effects are response errors that result when the response to one scale or scale item is affected by responses to previous scales or scale items. This is most likely to occur when a series of nonspecific and socially desirable traits are being rated, such as trustworthiness, helpfulness, or kindness. Scoring an individual high on one is likely to lead to high scores on subsequent dimensions. Halo effects cannot be completely eliminated, but they can be minimized by varying response systems, by occasionally reversing positive and negative ends of bipolar rating scales, and by stimulus items that are sometimes positive and sometimes negative. The order of these variations in items should be random. In following these procedures, however, one must be careful to take into account these scoring reversals in accumulating and interpreting scores.

In our earlier social anxiety index, if "anxiety at work" and "anxiety with family" scales, scored from 1 (low anxiety) to 5 (high anxiety), are to be combined with a scale of "relaxed comfort in social settings," scored from 1 (low comfort) to 5 (high comfort); the values of the scores on the "comfort in social settings" scale would have to be reversed (5 = 1, 4 = 2, and so on) before being added to the other two scales. Failure to pay close attention to the directionality of the scoring systems can obviously lead to considerable error in computation and interpretation.

Finally, measurement error related to the stimulus may be decreased by providing clear, unambiguous instructions to raters and by avoiding value-laden terms in the stimulus items themselves. In addition, clients and other raters should be assured that accuracy is more important than pleasing the clinician or the client.

SPECIFICATION AND RATING OF PROBLEMS AND GOALS IN ACTION

A young woman, Clara, is referred to a clinical social worker in a small group practice by the employee assistance program of a large corporation. The referral indicates that the woman was sexually assaulted five months previously and is experiencing relationship issues, difficulty concentrating, and fatigue. Through the assessment process, the social worker wants to develop a clear understanding of Clara's problem and her goals for intervention.

Specifying the Problem

In order to specify the problem, the social worker asks for examples of the identified problems. Clara describes nightmares that disrupt her sleep, leading to fatigue; and intrusive memories of the assault when trying to concentrate at work, despite great efforts to avoid any reminders of the assault. Thinking about each of these problems in terms of frequency, Clara thinks that she has sleep disturbance about three-quarters of the time and is unable to concentrate at work at about the same rate. Exploring further, Clara describes feeling distant from close friends and her husband, but cannot bring herself to talk to them about the assault or its subsequent effects on her. The relationship problem is the one that worries Clara most, and the social worker decides to pursue understanding of it using functional analysis. The social worker learns that prior to disagreements, Clara's husband approaches her with affection from which she recoils. The ensuing argument generally focuses on her emotional distance and is followed by her retreating to solitude and deriding herself for "not being over it yet." Further, she thinks that her relationship difficulties are related to her efforts to avoid any and all reminders and memories of the assault.

Specifying the Goals and Objectives

Next Clara and the social worker work on defining goals for treatment. Moving on from the identified problems, Clara wants to increase her ability to tolerate memories and reminders of the assault, increase her nightmare-free nights, and increase her ability to concentrate at work. The use of goal-attainment scaling helps Clara to be specific about her ultimate and subgoals. As shown in table 4.1, Clara's ultimate goals are to return to pretrauma patterns in which she was able to sleep restfully through the night about 90 percent of the time, could concentrate when desired 100 percent of the time at work, and could comfortably share her life experiences with her husband and closest friend. The latter goal would involve being able to tell her husband and friend about the assault experience and aftermath.

Deciding on Who, When, and Where to Rate the Problems, Goals, and Objectives

The social worker and Clara next decide on whom and under what conditions the goals will be measured. Since the ratings require subjective judgments about the quality of her sleep, her ability to concentrate, and her level of comfort with reminders of the trauma, Clara will do the ratings herself. The detailed goals provide the conditions in which the ratings will take place, that is, concentration will be measured at work, etc. Clara agrees to complete a GAS form at the beginning of each therapy session.

Deciding on Measurement Tools

In addition to the GAS form, with which Clara's progress on her unique goals may be tracked, the social worker also decides to administer a standardized measure of PTSD. Using the method for locating available instruments outlined in chapter 2, the clinician easily finds a reliable and valid self-report instrument that can be administered at the start and end of treatment.

Thus, having operationalized Clara's goals and objectives, the social worker can move into treatment planning and intervention. In addition, the intervention can easily be evaluated through the use of the GAS and self-report instrument.

EXERCISES

1. Using the GAS provided in figure 4.1 as a template, think of an alternative way to operationalize Clara's goals for each of the designated problem areas.
2. Think about a problem frequently seen among the clients in your practice setting. Specify the problem according to the principles discussed above.
3. Using the same problem area, define and specify goals for a potential client.
4. Describe a method for measuring the client's progress toward the specified goals in question 2. Design an individualized rating scale for at least one of the goals.

SELECTED BIBLIOGRAPHY

American Education Research Association. 1999. *The Standards for Educational and Psychological Testing.* Washington, DC: Author.

Anastasi, A., and Urbina, S. 1997. *Psychological Testing.* 7th ed. Upper Saddle River, NJ: Prentice Hall.

Bloom, M., Fisher, J., and Orme, J. G. 2003. *Evaluating practice: Guidelines for the accountable professional.* Boston: Allyn and Bacon.

Garvin, C. 2002. Developing goals. In A. R. Roberts and G. Greene (eds.), *Social worker's desk reference*, pp. 309–313. New York: Oxford University Press.

Kiresuk, T. J., and Sherman, R. E. 1968. Goal attainment scaling: A general method for evaluating comprehensive community mental health programs. *Community Mental Health Journal, 4,* 443–453.

Litzelfelner, P., and Pierpont, J. H. 2001. Demystifying client-outcomes: Identifying, monitoring, and using client outcomes in child protection. *Professional Development, 4,* 25–31.

Pike, C. K. 2002. Developing client-focused measures. In A. R. Roberts and G. Greene (eds.), *Social worker's desk reference*, pp. 189–193. New York: Oxford University Press.

Proctor, E., Rosen, A., and Rhee, C. W. 2002. Outcomes in social work practice. *Journal of Social Work Research and Evaluation, 3,* 109–123.

Raines, J. C. 2002. Present levels of performance, goals, and objectives: A best practice guide. *School Social Work Journal, 27,* 58–72.

Vonk, M. E., Bordnick, P., and Graap, K. 2004. Cognitive-behavioral therapy with post-traumatic stress disorder. In A. R. Roberts and K. R. Yaeger (eds.), *Evidence-based practice manual*, pp. 303–312. New York: Oxford University Press.

Treatment selection and implementation is the second phase of clinical social work practice. Simply stated, treatment selection involves choosing a social work intervention plan that will effectively move clients toward their goals. Selection of a particular treatment or intervention for a client should be based on its evidence of effectiveness, compatibility with social work values, and suitable match with the client's values, needs, and desired outcomes.

Treatment implementation involves carrying out the chosen and agreed upon intervention plan. Monitoring is the process by which judgments are made about the extent to which the client is actually receiving the prescribed intervention in a manner consistent with prior planning, agency and professional standards, and the contractual agreement between client and social worker.

Effective treatment monitoring involves specifying treatment standards, gathering and analyzing data concerning the attainment of these standards, assessing any discrepancies between planned and actual performance on the part of the clinician and the client, and making decisions to continue, stop, or modify the implementation strategy depending on the foregoing assessment.

Assessment standards and sources of monitoring data vary. Standards for interventions, for example, can be based on practice guidelines from research literature, values and standards set forth by professional associations such as the National Association for Social Workers, or agency policies and procedures. Likewise, information about compliance with these standards may come from process recordings, social workers' clinical observations, client self-reports, or the observations of significant others in the clients' or the social workers' environments.

Through the process of treatment implementation and monitoring, judgments can be made about the quality, comprehensiveness, and continuity of treatment. These types of treatment assessments are particularly important for problem areas where the ultimate impact of treatment is difficult to assess. They are valuable, as well, in assessing worker performance in treatment methods that have proven to be successful and may not require outcome evaluation.

Wherever possible, treatment monitoring should be based upon valid, reliable, and representative information available to the social worker or the social worker's supervisor. Research concepts and techniques can facilitate the systematic collection, analysis and interpretation of this information. In addition, data that are collected systematically from a number of comparable cases can be aggregated for the purpose of making generalizations about treatment with certain types of cases.

In this overview we describe the tasks and decisions associated with the treatment selection and implementation stage. Next we discuss several relevant issues related to diversity and professional ethics. Finally, we point out ways in which research concepts can inform this stage of practice. The four chapters in part 2 describe in detail the use of specific research concepts and techniques for treatment selection and monitoring.

Before proceeding, however, we should remind the reader of two things. First, the research concepts and techniques discussed in this section are not solely applicable to the intervention phase. They are useful also in diagnostic assessment and in the evaluation of treatment outcomes. Second, the reader is reminded that our phase model of clinical practice is only a heuristic device. Actual practice is not nearly as logically distinct or linear. Thus, for example, in practice initial diagnostic assessments and treatment formulations are likely to be strengthened, modified, or totally revised based on developments and information that arise during treatment implementation. As a result, treatment goals and contracts may have to be renegotiated. On the other hand, treatment monitoring and evaluation may take place simultaneously, with early indications of failure leading to changes in treatment implementation. Our purpose in logically distinguishing three phases of practice is to promote an understanding of the different functions and tasks involved in clinical practice rather than to definitively describe it. With these caveats behind us, we will describe the practice tasks and decisions associated with treatment implementation and its monitoring.

TASKS

Treatment implementation requires that the clinical social worker accomplish a number of practice tasks and make a number of decisions. What follows are descriptions of the necessary steps :

First, the social worker must determine the kind and extent of social work intervention or treatment that is called for. We use the term *treatment* here in its broadest sense to include any of a number of possible helping strategies. These strategies include *therapy*, helping clients achieve desired psychosocial changes in term of attitudes, behaviors, and moods; *case management,* accessing and coordinating services for clients from several resources; *education,* increasing clients' knowledge and skills; *advocacy,* locating and securing resources for clients or representing the clients in attempts to change their environment; *concrete services*, helping clients to seek and secure basic human needs such as housing, food, or employment.; and *referral*, helping clients to seek appropriate services from other health and social service resources.

The choice of an intervention is based on many factors, including those related to clients and their goals as well as those related to social workers' professional values, knowledge, and skills. With the development of evidence-based practice (EBP) in social work, there is increasing recognition that the choice of interventions should be based in large part on knowledge about the effectiveness of interventions, developed through empirical practice research. While social workers have an ethical obligation to utilize research-based knowledge, this does not rule out the importance of *clinical judgment*, that is, the use of knowledge gained through prior practice experience and empathic understanding of a particular client's values, needs, and desired outcomes.

In addition, whatever the intervention, it should be described in precise enough language so that it would be possible to determine whether the client is actually receiving the kind and amount of treatment contracted for. The specification of the amount and kind of treatment required to move clients toward their goals makes treatment monitoring possible.

With the intervention strategies tentatively chosen, the social worker can establish a "contract" or working agreement with the client concerning treatment goals and mutual role expectations in seeking these goals or objectives. In some social agencies this contract is a formal written statement of treatment goals and mutual expectations; in others the contract is oral and informal. Nevertheless, if treatment is to be successful, the client and social worker must arrive at a mutual understanding of goals, rights and role expectations. This consensus between worker and client may require renegotiation about goal priorities and means for achieving them. Thus, for example, the parents of a child with behavioral problems may want the child to behave better in school before they are willing to confront their own relationship difficulties. The social worker may prefer it the other way around. In any case, once the contract has been agreed upon, role expectations can be operationally defined (that is, stated in measurable terms) in order to be used for monitoring worker and client compliance with it.

Next, treatment procedures are implemented. In principle, these procedures are thought to be the most effective and efficient means for achieving the treatment goals specified in the diagnostic assessment and treatment formulation stage. In addition, they must be practical, ethical, and acceptable to the client. In actual practice situations, however, circumstances in the practice environment may limit the extent to which ideal treatment conditions can be realized. For example, although treatment may work best with voluntary clients, social workers employed in a correctional facility cannot ignore the element of coercion that is implied in any treatment contract with an inmate. Likewise, a school social worker, doing a social skills group with shy children, cannot ignore teachers' desires to maintain orderly behavior in the classroom. Thus, during treatment implementation, the clinical social worker should be sensitive to those factors that may interfere with the successful implementation of treatment plans.

Once treatment procedures are implemented, worker, client, and possibly significant others' compliance with the treatment contract is monitored. This is accomplished by the collection of data concerning the extent to which these individuals are living up to the expectations enumerated in the treatment contract. For example, the social worker may suggest that a couple join in quiet conversation or relaxation techniques before engaging in physical intimacy. The clinician may instruct the couple to report back at the next session the number of times compliance did and did not take place. A social worker's performance as a cognitive therapist may be monitored by tape recording the worker's interviews with clients. Standards of appropriate therapeutic technique could be applied by the social worker's supervisor to an analysis of actual interview behavior. Finally, a residential employee of a halfway house for severely emotionally disturbed clients could be asked to monitor the treatment-relevant behaviors of a resident, such as compliance with a medication regimen or participation in group therapy.

Based on the foregoing analyses of treatment implementation and contractual compliance, judgments are made about whether treatment procedures should be continued, modified, or replaced by other procedures. While attempting to implement group treatment with behavior-disordered children, for example, a social worker may observe that one group member's fearful and withdrawn behavior interferes with participation. The worker may decide to work individually with that child to increase appropriate assertiveness skills before returning to work in the group. The important point here is that diagnostic assessment and treatment formulation is a continuing process that is aided by treatment implementation and monitoring. Though logically distinct, the two phases work together closely.

DECISIONS

Clinical social workers make many crucial decisions during treatment selection and implementation. These decisions are implied within each of the above-mentioned tasks, but they can be specified by indicating some of the questions that social workers should ask themselves during this phase of practice. Since clinical practice is a dynamic process, the questions are interrelated. They are related as well to questions of diagnostic assessment and treatment evaluation. Hence the impact of a given treatment intervention cannot be evaluated unless one knows that the treatment intervention was faithfully implemented. The following are some of these questions:

1. What intervention strategies and techniques should be employed? Has the selection been based on evidence of effectiveness, professional values, and compatibility with clients' cultural identification?
2. Are the social worker and client in agreement about treatment objectives and the means to achieve these?
3. Are the expectations of the client, social worker, and significant others clearly specified? Are they stated in understandable and measurable terms?
4. Have treatment procedures been implemented in accordance with practice guidelines, professional values and standards, agency procedures, and the treatment contract?
5. What barriers to successful implementation exist within the practice situation? Can these be overcome in any way?
6. To what extent do client, clinician, and significant others fulfill their contractual obligations? If they don't, how and why not?

7. Are there reasons to revise the initial diagnostic assessment or treatment formulation based on contractual noncompliance?
8. What changes, if any, should be made to the intervention based on intervention monitoring?

DIVERSITY AND ETHICAL CONSIDERATIONS

Several diversity and ethical issues should be considered in the treatment selection and implementation phase of treatment. The following table summarizes the diversity considerations related to each of the tasks. In addition to the many factors relevant to selection of intervention that have already been mentioned, clients' identification with a particular culture must also be considered. Without an understanding of clients' worldviews and cultural norms, social workers cannot be sure that particular interventions will be accepted by a client. In addition, social workers may overlook potentially helpful interventions that are related to a different way of viewing such things as spirituality or interdependency among family members. Similarly, a contract with a client, whether written or oral, must reflect the same sensitivity in order that the client is able to fully agree to the plan. Finally, social workers must have the ability to form genuine and empathic relationships across cultures. Without this ability, social workers will be ineffective in their attempts to implement and monitor interventions.

Ethical issues are summarized in the next table. While the issues have been paired with particular tasks in the table, all three issues could be applicable to all four tasks. Social workers have an ethical responsibility to continually update their store of knowledge and their skills through the use of research reports, professional workshops, and clinical supervision. In addition, they must be aware of and adhere to basic social work values, including self-determination and autonomy for the client. Without all three—knowledge, skills, and values—

Diversity Issues in the Intervention Phase

Task	Issue
Selection	Selecting culturally compatible interventions
Contracting	Developing contract that is culturally compatible
Implementation and monitoring	Ability to form genuine and empathic relationships across cultures

Ethical Issues in the Intervention Phase

Task	Issue
Selection	Informed practice
Contracting	Awareness of and adherence to social work values
Implementation and monitoring	Competence to implement variety of intervention types

social workers will be disadvantaged in their ability to select and competently utilize interventions that are known to be effective with their clients.

RESEARCH CONCEPTS AND TECHNIQUES

As with diagnostic assessment and treatment formulation, the concepts of validity, reliability, and representativeness of information are central to effective treatment monitoring. In addition, research techniques such as standardized interviewing and systematic observation, which were introduced in the context of diagnostic assessment and treatment formulation, are applicable to treatment monitoring as well.

In the following four chapters we introduce more research concepts and techniques applicable to selecting and monitoring interventions. We begin in chapter 5 with a discussion of the principles for choosing among many available intervention strategies. These principles include EBP and the research concepts of efficiency and effectiveness. In this context reliability, validity, and representativeness also play a role in making judgments about which intervention strategies to employ. In chapter 6 we introduce content analysis, a research technique for systematically analyzing written documents and other preserved forms of communication such as films or videotapes. We illustrate the use of content analysis of process records by supervisors to monitor worker performance.

Chapter 7 is devoted to form construction. Clients can be taught to use specially constructed forms to monitor their own therapeutically relevant activities. This kind of self-monitoring is particularly useful in providing systematic information about what is happening between therapeutic sessions when direct observation by the clinician is not possible. In addition, forms can be used by the social workers themselves to monitor their own behaviors related to integrity of interventions. Finally, chapter 8 provides an overview of qualitative research methods that can be used to gather information pertinent to monitoring clients' and social workers' subjective responses to interventions. Qualitative methods rely on observation of phenomena in their natural settings. They allow for description and interpretation of observations or responses to open-ended questions. Since the method does not use systematic observation guides or standardized questions with response sets, the range of potential results is broad and may include unexpected results.

SELECTED BIBLIOGRAPHY

Anastas, J. 2004. Quality in qualitative evaluation: Issues and possible answers. *Research on Social Work Practice, 14* (1), 57–65.

Gilgun, J. F. 2005. The four cornerstones of evidence-based practice in social work. *Research on Social Work Practice, 15,* 52–61.

Hepworth, D. H., Rooney, R. H., Larsen, J. A. 2002. *Direct social work practice: Theory and skills.* 6th ed. Pacific Grove, CA: Brooks/Cole-Thomson Learning.

Lum, D. 2005. *Cultural competence, practice stages, and client systems: A case study approach.* Belmont, CA: Thomson/Brooks/Cole.

Manoleas, P. 1994. An outcome approach to assessing the cultural competence of MSW students. *Journal of Multicultural Social Work, 3,* 43–57.

Meares, P. A. 1985. Content analysis: It does have a place in social work research. *Journal of Social Service Research, 7,* 51–68.

NASW. 1999. *Code of Ethics.* Silver Spring, MD: National Association of Social Workers.

Rosen, A., Proctor, E. K. (eds.) 2003. *Developing practice guidelines for social work intervention: Issues, methods, and research agenda.* New York: Columbia University Press.

Rothman, J. C. 2002. Developing therapeutic contracts with clients. In A. Roberts and G. Greene (eds.), *Social workers' desk reference,* pp. 304–309. New York: Oxford University Press.

Rubin, A., and Babbie, E. 2001. *Research methods for social work.* 4th ed. Belmont, CA: Wadsworth/Thomson Learning.

Once a diagnostic assessment has been made, the clinical social worker is faced with the task of selecting a treatment or intervention strategy. Some social workers rely completely on their previous training and practice experience as a basis for their selection. Others may base their decisions on the treatment traditions of the agency in which they are employed. An alternative and increasingly accepted method for guiding the selection of interventions can be found in *evidence-based practice* (EBP).

EBP includes selecting, implementing, and then evaluating interventions related to the client's specified problems and goals, based on the best available information or evidence of effectiveness. Evidence about effective social work interventions can be found at professional workshops as well as in several types of research literature sources. Ideally, evidence is gained through practice research in which hypotheses about the effectiveness of specific intervention techniques and the conditions under which they work best are tested empirically. Although the methodological rigor of practice research varies greatly, social workers can learn to evaluate its quality or strength using basic research principles outlined later. In effect, EBP requires the social worker to find reliable sources of information and then judge the quality of that information in order to inform selection of interventions.

This chapter provides principles for evidence-based intervention selection, including locating and critically reviewing practice research. It focuses on the sources of available evidence for practice, guidance for evaluation of the quality or strength of the evidence, and assessment of issues related to the utility and implementation of selected interventions.

PRINCIPLES FOR SELECTING INTERVENTIONS

Specifying the Problem

Practice research literature may be utilized for guidance at any phase of clinical social work intervention, for example, social workers may seek instruments with which to measure signs and symptoms to aid in the diagnostic process. However, the use of literature is perhaps most often considered by clinicians at the point of choosing the best possible treatment for a specific client's clinical problem. This may be particularly true if the client presents a problem or confounding condition that is unfamiliar to the clinician.

Whatever the source of the need for new knowledge, the search should begin with a specification of the problem, its pervasiveness, its frequency of occurrence, as well as the conditions under which it is likely to occur. In addition, there should be a complete understanding of the characteristics of the client involved, the client's goals, the treatment techniques that have been tried in the past, and any evidence of success that may have been achieved. Specific information will make it possible to locate relevant literature and to assess whether alternative treatment strategies described in the literature are potentially better than those that may have already been considered by the practitioner.

Locating Relevant Research Literature

Having specified the problem, the next step is to locate research literature relevant to social work or related clinical efforts to treat the problem. There are at least four sources of evidence-based knowledge for practice; they are systematic reviews, practice guidelines, expert consensus guidelines, and self-directed search of the literature. The last of these four sources involves a much more time-consuming process, but one that may be necessary for problems about which information has not been previously synthesized. Table 5.1 provides resources for locating systematic reviews, practice guidelines, and expert consensus guidelines.

Systematic reviews provide an excellent source of information about specific clinical problems in that they summarize all of the available relevant practice research. Systematic reviews utilize stringent criteria, generally based on the methodological rigor of research, to guide the search for and inclusion of information. In addition, the process of critically analyzing and synthesizing the information follows an explicit procedure. When the review includes only knowledge gained from randomized, controlled studies, the procedure of *meta-analysis* is often used. Meta-analysis is a statistical procedure that combines information from many studies to provide information about the effect of a particular treatment. Systematic reviews may be found in a number of ways, including searches of databases such as *Social Work Abstracts or PsycINFO*, Web sites, and books.

Practice guidelines are another excellent resource. Practice guidelines provide clinicians with organized information about effective interventions for particular client problems or goals. Often they include recommendations relevant to intervention with clients under various specific conditions. They are based both on research findings and on the recommendation of teams of experienced clinicians who have studied, synthesized, and critiqued the available research. Practice guidelines are sometimes called *treatment protocols or manuals* and may be found in a number of sources.

Expert consensus is another source of knowledge for EBP intervention selection; however, it is not based solely on empirical research. Instead, this type of guideline is based on the consensus of experts who have been surveyed about the assessment and treatment of a particular clinical issue. Expert consensus guides may be very helpful for guidance with problems in which research has not clearly supported the effectiveness of particular interventions.

Finally, social workers may choose to do their own search of the literature. This may be necessary if none of the other three sources are available. In addition, even when one of the other sources is available, the social worker may want to check for new, recently published developments in treatment information. This process requires searching for, selecting, and evaluating research articles. Basic knowledge about research is needed in order to critique the quality of the information found in the articles.

First, the social worker will need to perform a search of relevant databases, such as *PsycINFO* and *Social Work Abstracts* to find applicable research studies. Key words related to the specified problems or diagnoses, along with terms such as *outcome, effectiveness, or treatment evaluation* are helpful for locating articles of interest. Before reading a research study in depth, however, the social worker should first skim it to get an overview of the material presented in order to determine whether the study deals with relevant problem formulations and intervention strategies. This is greatly facilitated by reading the abstract that appears at the beginning of most articles published in scholarly journals. Once relevant practice research has been identified, its level of evidence must be evaluated.

Assessing the Level of Evidence

The strength or level of evidence for EBP is based on the methodological quality of the research on which the knowledge is based. Several level systems exist, of which the following is a simplified blend. More information about EBP and evidence strength levels may be found in sources listed in the bibliography. The strongest evidence, at level 1, is based on meta-analyses of *randomized controlled trials* (RCT), or well-designed *experimental* studies in which hypotheses about the effects of particular interventions on specified client problems are tested among large groups of people. In level 2 are *quasi-experimental* or *nonexperimental* studies that provide information about statistical relationships between outcomes and interventions. Further decreasing in strength of evidence is level 3 that includes case studies, pilot studies, and the like that primarily describe intervention techniques, client characteristics, and agency settings. Finally, level 4, the lowest level of strength, includes opinions based on either clinical practice or untested theoretical hypotheses that predict relationships between practice techniques and client outcomes.

Clearly, the last level of knowledge is highly speculative. However, the knowledge becomes less speculative and more certain moving from level 4 up to level 1. Thus it is easier to hypothesize about the relationship between intervention and outcome than to demonstrate that the intervention has a clear and specific impact on the outcome. Nevertheless, information taken from all four levels can be used in the process of building knowledge for evidence-based practice.

In order to fully comprehend levels of evidence for practice, the criteria for evaluation of the quality of research methodology must be understood. With each step toward the strongest evidence at level 1, more stringent criteria for research methodology are added to those already in place at lower levels of evidence. For educated opinions or theoretical hypotheses (level 4), the internal logic and the extent to which hypotheses are consistent with previous theory and research must be considered. To assess descriptive studies (level 3), the extent to which measurement accuracy, reliability, and validity have been achieved also must be considered. Evaluation of correlational studies (level 2) must include the additional consideration of the evidence of statistical association. Finally, in assessing studies that provide evidence of cause and effect, in addition to the prior criteria, *internal* and *external validity* must be evaluated. Each of these criteria for assessment of research studies is discussed in subsequent sections of this chapter.

Assessing Measurement Accuracy, Reliability, and Validity

Whatever the level of evidence sought, the quality of a research study or report depends to a large degree on the accuracy, reliability, and validity of the measures it employs. In the context of studying the effectiveness of interventions, *measurement accuracy* refers to the degree of freedom from error in the process of measuring treatment effectiveness. There are several aspects of measurement accuracy. First, it refers to whether mistakes have been made in the process of recording, coding, or transferring the data. Although this type of error is not directly observable, researchers sometimes report their efforts to guard against such error.

Accuracy also pertains to whether measurement scales with mutually exclusive and exhaustive categories of effectiveness have been utilized in the research. In research on the effectiveness of treatment techniques, three kinds of scales are generally used in clinical research: nominal, ordinal, and interval. Nominal scales are the simplest. In nominal scales, data are classified into two or more mutually exclusive and exhaustive categories that imply no rank ordering or hierarchy. Thus a nominal scale item about case status following a given intervention might include two categories, "case active—client is still in treatment" and "case-closed—client has terminated." While the two categories do not necessarily imply a preferred outcome, the item can provide an important piece of information.

Ordinal scales present two or more mutually exclusive and exhaustive categories in an order or hierarchy of some kind. A scale describing clients as "not improved" or "improved" would be the simplest kind of ordinal scale. A slightly more refined ordinal scale might describe clients as "not improved," somewhat improved," and "greatly improved."

Interval scales are similar to ordinal scales except that they are even more refined. They are calibrated so that the units of measurement along the scale are equidistant from each other. These categories are also mutually exclusive and exhaustive. A scale describing the frequency of specific problematic behaviors such as drug use or incidents of child abuse may be expressed in the form of an interval scale. On this scale the distance between one and two incidents is the same as the difference between five and six incidents. A reduction of one unit at any point of the scale would be viewed as equally effective.

The type of scale employed in measuring both the intervention and its effectiveness will determine which statistical methods are most appropriate in correlating treatment techniques with outcomes. Interventions as well as outcomes can be expressed in nominal, ordinal, or interval scales. There are rules about the kinds of statistical measures that can be used in assessing their effects. For example, a *phi* correlation can be calculated if the intervention and the outcome are expressed in a *dichotomous* nominal scale, that is, a scale with only two categories. For nominal scales that have more than two categories, *Cramer's V* correlation is used. When both intervention and outcome are ordinal scales, a rank-order correlation, *Spearman's rho,* is most appropriate. *Pearson's r* correlation is most appropriate when both intervention and outcome are interval scales. A full discussion of these statistical measures and their uses is outside the scope of this book but can be found within any standard introductory text on statistical methods, some of which are referenced in the bibliography below.

Reliability of measurement, as discussed in earlier chapters, refers to the consistency with which an instrument measures something. It can be assessed in a number of different ways, including intraobserver, interobserver, split-half, and test-retest; and can be expressed in the form of percentage agreement or correlation coefficients. Just as in other contexts, one would expect reliability measures indicating 70 percent or higher agreement or .70 or higher correlations when comparisons are made utilizing scales with two categories. Lower reliability scores might be expected if the number of categories is higher; higher scores might be expected in split-half tests. In assessing the evidence of the effectiveness of treatment over time, however, it is essential that test-retest reliability be established. This provides assurance that indications of client improvement are the result of treatment rather than of the measurement instrument's lack of reliability.

The *validity* of the measurement instrument is equally important in assessing treatment effectiveness. The validity of a measure refers to whether the instrument is actually measuring the concept it claims to measure. Here what is most important is that the measures of outcome are as closely related to the treatment objectives as possible. Beyond the issue of content validity just raised, predictive validity is also important. Ideally, measures that show good predictive validity can be used to draw inferences about the extent to which successful treatment outcomes persist over time.

Taking the issues of accuracy, reliability, and validity together, it should be emphasized that studies that do not indicate sufficient attention to these issues should be treated as generating hypothetical knowledge rather than as being descriptive, correlational, or causal. In other words, unless measurement accuracy, reliability, and validity are reasonably demonstrated, the knowledge produced should be considered as hypotheses worthy of future testing.

Assessing the Empirical Relationship Between Intervention and Outcome

Only in correlational and cause-effect studies is it possible to test the strength of the relationship between treatment and client outcome. In assessing the knowledge generated in these studies, however, it is important to consider the strength, direction, and predictability of the relationship between the intervention strategy and the results obtained.

The strength of the relationship is determined by the degree of association between the treatment and desired outcome. It may be expressed in percentage differences, mean differences, or correlation coefficients. A study that employs percentage differences would indicate the strength of the relationship through one or more of the following comparisons:

- the percentage difference in desired outcome between those who received the intervention and a matched group that received no intervention (that is, a control group);
- the percentage difference in a desired outcome between groups that received different interventions (that is, contrast groups);
- the percentage difference in a desired outcome within a group before and after receiving the intervention (that is, a group serving as its own control); and
- the percentage difference in a desired outcome between a group that received an authentic intervention and group that received a placebo intervention.

On outcome measures that are expressed in numerical scores, for example, an anxiety scale or a reading score, comparisons may be made by showing the differences in the arithmetical averages or mean scores between the group that received the intervention and any of the comparison groups mentioned above.

The strength of the relationship between intervention and outcome may also be expressed in the form of a correlation coefficient. As we stated in chapter 2, most correlation coefficients can vary in strength from 0.0 to 1.0. However, in assessing the strength of a relationship between intervention and outcome one would not ordinarily expect correlations as high as one would for a test of reliability. A correlation of .25, though signifying a weak association, would be considered strong enough to justify the assumption that an intervention had some relationship with the desired outcome. A correlation of .50 would be considered medium, and a correlation of .70 or higher would be considered very strong.

Some correlation coefficients (for example, Pearson's r, Spearman's rho) are expressed in positive or negative terms. These measures range from -1.00 to +1.00 and indicate the direction as well as the strength of the relationship between intervention and outcome. A negative correlation would indicate an inverse relationship between the two. That would mean, the greater the amount of intervention, the lower the score on the measurement of client outcome. Alternatively, a positive correlation would indicate a direct relationship between intervention and the outcome measure. Thus, if treatment were designed to reduce feelings of depression, one would hope for a strong, inverse correlation between intervention and outcome. On the other hand, if an intervention was designed to increase assertiveness, one would hope for a strong direct correlation.

One advantage of correlation coefficients, as compared with percentage and mean difference data, is that with a correlation coefficient it is possible to approximate the percentage of the variation in the outcome that can be explained by the intervention. By squaring the correlation coefficient and multiplying by 100 one gets an approximation of the *explained proportion*. So, for example, if a study concluded that there was a correlation of .50 between participation in a conjoint therapy program and marital satisfaction scores, by squaring the correlation coefficient and multiplying by 100 one would find that approximately 25 percent of the change in marital satisfaction scores was explained by participation in the conjoint therapy program.

In outcome studies that use experimental designs, another statistic is used to test the strength of the relationship between treatment and client outcome; it is called the *effect size* (ES). Calculation of the ES allows for comparison of the results of one study with others by standardizing the difference in outcomes between the group that received treatment and the control group. ES statistics range from 0 to 1.0; an ES of .45 is similar to an r of .25 in terms of strength of association.

Assessing External Validity

Empirical generality refers to whether the findings of a study can be generalized to other comparable practice situations and to other populations of clients and practitioners. The use of random sampling techniques, increases the likelihood that findings can be generalized by making it possible to compute measures of *statistical significance* of the relationship between intervention and outcome. Statistical significance refers to whether the relationship between the intervention and the outcome found in the *population sample* studied reflects a true relationship in the *population* to which one would like to generalize and from which the sample population was drawn. This is important because the apparent success of an intervention may be the result of chance fluctuations. Assuming the study population was randomly selected, on the basis of the laws of probability, one can calculate statistical significance by means of various measures of association between intervention and outcome, for example, chi-square, for percentage differences and t-tests for mean differences, both of which are discussed more fully in chapter 13.

Social scientists have generally accepted findings that are significant at the .05 level or lower (.01, .001) as indicative of a statistically significant relationship. This means that the findings of the study were such that, given the size of the population studied, they could have occurred only 5 times in 100 by chance alone. Naturally, findings at the .01 level would be even more certain. That would indicate that the empirical relationship demonstrated between intervention and outcome could have occurred by chance only 1 time in 100. Statistical significance is often reported in research articles numerically, representing the probability of finding the results of the study purely by chance, such as $p < .01$.

Measures of statistical significance can be misleading, however, because of the manner in which they are calculated. The larger the study population is, the weaker the relationship between intervention and outcome needs to be to be judged statistically significant. For example, in a study with a sample of 100, a 35 percent change in an outcome measure may be required to attain statistical significance. In a similar study with a sample population of 1,000, a change of only 3 percent in the outcome measure may be required. In other words, with a large enough study population, a weak correlation may still be statistically significant. Consequently, measures of statistical significance tell us more about whether we can generalize from the sample studied to the population it represents than they tell us about the strength of a relationship between intervention and outcome. Thus the foregoing findings would tell us that in the study of 100 we can assume that, if the intervention were applied to the population from which the sample was selected, a moderate rate of success would be likely to occur. In the study of 1,000, statistical significance would suggest that if the intervention were applied to the larger population a low rate of success would be likely to occur. Therefore, statistical significance does not necessarily imply success but should be combined with a calculation of the proportion of variance or effect size in order to think about the effectiveness of the intervention.

Another way of assessing the level of external validity is to determine whether the findings of the study have been replicated elsewhere in other studies. Comparable studies that yield findings of similar strength and direction provide greater confidence in the results of a given intervention. In studies of a single subject or case, it has been suggested that there should be at least three successful replications with similar clients, clinicians, problem, and therapeutic intervention before empirical generality is inferred. In correlational studies there should be consistency with reference to the strength, direction, and statistical significance of the correlations.

Finally, in making decisions about whether study findings can be applied to another population, the extent to which the characteristics of practitioners, clients, setting, and intervention match those in the social workers' practice context must be considered. *Random sampling* in the study itself increases the likelihood that the findings can be generalized to the population from which the sample was selected. Similarity between the social workers' practice context and that of the study increase the likelihood that the study findings can be generalized to their own situation.

Assessing Internal Validity

In order to establish that a cause-effect relationship actually exists between an intervention strategy and a desired outcome, one must rule out alternative possible explanations for the outcome. This is accomplished through internal control procedures.

There are several questions that need to be asked to assess the adequacy of internal controls in a study. First, are the changes observed directly traceable to the intervention? Second, is there evidence that the changes followed rather than preceded the intervention? Third, is there evidence that changes are not simply the result of growth or maturity or other external factors influencing the research subjects or clients? Fourth, is it clear that observed positive changes are not a consequence of a desire for positive changes on the part of the researcher? In other words, are the measures of success fair and unbiased? Fifth, is there evidence that the observed changes are not a result of the clients' desire to please the research-practitioner, that is, to the *Hawthorne effect*? And, finally, is there evidence that observed changes are the result of an authentic intervention rather than a response to a falsely perceived intervention, that is, a *placebo effect*?

Many of these questions are dealt with in research studies through the use of control groups and statistical procedures for testing alternative explanations, some of which will be discussed in greater detail in chapter 13. Another way to rule out the possible confounding effects of age, gender, ethnicity, or social class on a given outcome is to limit the client population to single categories of individuals, for example, adolescents, females, African Americans, or middle-income clients.

Applying Appropriate Assessment Criteria

The foregoing assessment criteria should be applied differentially, depending upon the level of knowledge that a study is attempting to generate. The lower the level of knowledge produced, the less stringent will be the assessment criteria. Thus descriptive studies require a moderate degree of confidence in measurement accuracy, reliability, and validity; whereas cause-effect studies require relatively high confidence in the criteria.

Second, the ability to generalize the results to people outside of the population sample will determine whether study findings should be treated as strong evidence or simply as interesting hypotheses for future testing. When the external validity is low, the knowledge produced should be treated as hypothetical. Only when external validity is high can the inference be made that a comparable cause-effect relationship may exist between intervention and outcome for comparable populations and practice situations.

Studies in which both external validity and relationship strength are high provide trustworthy support for cause-and-effect knowledge, such that the intervention described may be successfully applied to one's own practice population. At the very least, clinical social workers should require correlational knowledge before applying a technique discussed in a research study. Interventions discussed in studies that generate descriptive or hypothetical knowledge should be applied with caution. Moreover, these applications should themselves be carefully evaluated. Strategies for evaluating practice interventions are discussed in part 3.

Assessing Utility of Intervention and Implementation Issues

After effective interventions have been identified, social workers must decide whether that intervention is relevant and useful for the particular client, problem, and practice setting. Regardless of how well research supports a particular intervention, clinical knowledge about clients and their situations, as well as constraints related to the setting and funding, must be considered in the choice of interventions. In addition, social workers need to consider professional values and ethics in the choice. The following issues and questions should be considered in light of the evidence presented in the research literature.

Issues Related to the Intervention

Concerns related to the intervention itself include how well the identified treatment is specified, whether it is an ethical way to work with clients, and whether it is compatible with social work values of self-determination and autonomy. Intervention techniques that are not specified but described in a vague, ambiguous way are not easily duplicated and therefore are not likely to be successfully adopted. If, on the other hand, the techniques are clearly described, social workers must then consider whether interventions are compatible with professional values and ethics. For example, does the identified intervention allow clients to remain in the least restrictive setting possible while assuring their and others' safety? Does the intervention allow for clients' right to determine their own goals?

Issues Related to the Client

The intervention must also be a good fit for the client in terms of cultural compatibility, that is, in order to be effective, an intervention must be acceptable to the client's worldview, religious beliefs, and cultural values. In addition, the expected results of the intervention must be acceptable to the client and, although not always possible, to the client's significant others as well. Some important related questions follow. What are the characteristics of the clients with whom the techniques have been used in the past? What obligations or expectation does it put upon clients? Under what conditions has it been employed?

Issues Related to the Social Worker and Practice Setting

There are several issues related to the social worker and the practice setting that must be considered in the choice of interventions. First, social workers must have the training and ability to provide the identified intervention. Even the most empirically supported interventions are not a good choice if the clinician is not skilled in its use. Next, the intervention must be suitable for the practice setting. For example, if a known effective intervention is expected to take thirty sessions or more, it is not a good choice in settings where sessions are limited to ten.

In addition, social workers should consider the extent to which information is provided about the effectiveness of the technique as compared with other techniques. Furthermore, to what extent does it provide information about the cost of achieving a given level of effectiveness? A technique may be highly effective but prohibitive in cost, a large concern in most practice settings and for most managed care entities. Finally, one should ask how the efficiency of the technique, that is, the relationship between effectiveness and cost, compares with the efficiency of other intervention strategies.

SELECTION OF INTERVENTIONS IN ACTION

A social worker in a faith-based counseling center does an intake with a couple who are worried that their marriage may soon end in divorce. They both identify the husband's symptoms of obsessive-compulsive disorder (OCD) as the primary problem. He has lived with OCD since childhood. Although his wife knew about his symptoms prior to marriage, it was not until they were married that she realized the extent to which the problem would impact their daily life. His compulsions include checking and ordering; his most prominent obsession concerns hurting others while driving. The social worker has never worked with a client with this diagnosis previously, and, although the couple is requesting marital counseling, the social worker is not sure this is the best choice.

Specifying the Problem

The primary problem is defined as identifying the most effective way to treat OCD. A secondary problem is defined as identifying the most effective way to intervene with significant others.

Locating Relevant Research Literature

Unable to locate a systematic review, the social worker finds practice guidelines (www.psychguides.com) based on research and expert consensus. The guidelines show that a combination of cognitive-behavioral therapy (CBT) and medication has been shown to be effective for treating OCD. In addition, the guidelines provide information that is relevant for helping family members cope with the disorder, including becoming educated about OCD and, at times, participating in therapy to learn how to respond to her husband's symptoms in a way that will help rather than hinder his progress.

Assessing the Level of Evidence

Expert consensus guidelines are not as strong as practice guidelines. Because of this, the social worker also checks the *Evidence-Based Practice Manual* for practice guidelines. There the social worker finds similar information that is supported by research published in reputable journals. The social worker does not have resources available with which to conduct a search of the literature, but moves ahead with the information she has at hand.

Assessing Utility of Intervention and Implementation Issues

The social worker is very familiar with CBT, and finds that the techniques are adequately specified in the practice guidelines. In addition, CBT is compatible with social work ethics and values and is utilized frequently in the agency. The social worker still has two questions to think about. First, should the husband be seen alone or with his wife? Second, should CBT be used alone before referring him to a psychiatrist for a medication evaluation? Relying on knowledge about this specific couple, and utilizing clinical judgment, the social worker decides to see the couple together initially in order to help them both understand OCD and the two recommended interventions. This decision is based on the social worker's concern about imminent crisis in their relationship. Finally, following the steps of EBP, the social worker makes a plan to assess the clients' progress.

EXERCISES

1. Search the research literature for information related to effective interventions for OCD. Choose one article that evaluates a relevant intervention and critique the strength of the knowledge produced in that study. Would the evidence in your article change the social worker's decisions in the example above? Why or why not?
2. Identify a practice problem for which you are unsure of the most effective treatment method. Search for information about effective interventions for the identified problem. What is the strongest level of evidence you can find? Where did you locate it? Based on the results of your search, can you make a recommendation about the most effective intervention? Why or why not?

SELECTED BIBLIOGRAPHY

Barlow, D. H., and Hersen, M. 1984. *Single-case experimental designs: Strategies for studying behavior change.* 2d ed. New York: Pergamon.

Campbell, D. T., and Stanley J. C. 1963. *Experimental and quasi-experimental designs for research.* Chicago: Rand McNally.

Dudley, J. R. 2005. *Research methods for social work: Becoming consumers and producers of research.* Boston: Allyn and Bacon.

Gambrill, E. 1999. Evidence-based practice: An alternative to authority-based practice. *Families in Society, 80,* 341–351.

Hanrahan, P., and Reid, W. J. 1984. Choosing effective interventions. *Social Service Review, 58,* 244–258.

Neuman, W. L., and Kreuger, L. W. 2003. *Social work research methods.* New York: Allyn and Bacon.

Roberts, A. R., and Yeager, K. R. (eds.) 2004. *Evidence-based practice manual.* New York: Oxford Press.

Smith, D. (ed.) 2004. *Social work and evidence-based practice.* Philadelphia: Jessica Kingsley.

Thyer, B. (ed.) 2001. *Social work research methods.* Thousand Oaks, CA: Sage.

Weinbach, R. W. 2005. *Evaluating social work services and programs.* Boston: Pearson/ Allyn and Bacon.

Table 5.1 Internet Resources of Evidence for Effective Practice

Name	Location	Content
Agency for Healthcare Research and Quality	www.ahrq.gov	Database of reviews, guidelines, and information for the public (AHRQ) related to healthcare.
Campbell Collaboration	www.campbell collaboration.org	Database and research articles related to the effects of treatments in social welfare, education, and criminal justice.
Cochrane Collaboration	www.cochrane.org	Contains several databases with information for EBP in health. Full-text systematic reviews require subscription; abstracts are free.
Expert Consensus Guidelines Series	www.psychguides.com	Guidelines for numerous and varied mental health–related problems.
Internet Mental Health	www.mentalhealth.com	Database of research articles related to treatment of numerous diagnoses.
Medline Plus	http://Medlineplus.nim. nih.gov/medlineplus/	Health related information from the U.S. National Institute of Health
Task Force on Community Preventive Services	www.thecommunity guide.org	Systematic reviews and EBP recommendations for prevention of problems in mental health, social problems, and more.

Content analysis is a research procedure for obtaining systematic, quantitative, descriptive information from written documents, audio and video recordings, or other forms of media. The principles of content analysis are similar to those involved in systematic observation. The major difference between these two research techniques is that content analysis is applied to data already available to the researcher, whereas systematic observation is generally conducted in vivo. Content analysis, then, has the advantage of being *unobtrusive*; that is, by examining data that already exist, the researcher does not have to worry about people's responses being influenced by their reaction to being observed.

Content analysis may be used to analyze and draw inferences from a variety of communication documents routinely available in clinical social work settings. These include verbatim written "process" recordings of interviews with clients, summary written reports, audio or video recordings of individual or group counseling sessions, diaries or logs kept by social workers or clients, among others.

Although content analysis may be used to analyze *latent content* related to the meaning of the material; *manifest content* will be the focus in this chapter. Qualitative analysis of latent content will be discussed in chapter nine. In this chapter, we will focus on the use of content analysis in monitoring the extent to which clinical social workers implement treatment in accordance with treatment planning. The major data source considered will be case records, the most commonly available description of worker-client interaction in clinical settings.

CONTENT ANALYSIS AND CLINICAL SOCIAL WORK PRACTICE

Content analytic techniques can be usefully applied to every phase of clinical social work practice. For example, a social worker might use this technique to identify themes that emerge in the interactions between partners in an intimate relationship during assessment sessions that are recorded or are reported verbatim in process records. Similarly, content analysis can be employed during the treatment implementation phase to determine whether the treatment behaviors of social workers are consistent with agency policy or the specified treatment plan. Finally, content analysis may be used to evaluate the success of treatment. Thus, by comparing the frequency and intensity of the mention of problematic themes at the beginning and termination of treatment, progress before and after treatment can be assessed.

Still other uses of content analysis in clinical social work include building knowledge, either specifically for use in the practice setting or for more general application to social work practice. In the practice setting, trends may be identified through content analysis of records over time. For example, by analyzing clients' stated presenting problems over a period of time, practitioners may identify unmet needs among clients or the need for continuing education concerning intervention with an emerging problem. Content analysis may also yield knowledge useful to a broad spectrum of practitioners. For example, through analysis of records, clinicians in a practice setting that serves a specific cultural group may find that a particular intervention for a problem, though found to be effective with other demographic groups, does not generalize well with their clients. This kind of information, derived from practice, can add to the base of knowledge related to evidence-based practice.

As a technique, content analysis is potentially valuable to clinical supervision as well. This is because supervisors rarely have direct access to the interactions between clients and the social workers they supervise. As a result, supervisors are usually totally dependent upon process records or audio/video recordings and supervisory discussions with line social workers for information about worker-client interactions. With experience, many supervisors become remarkably skilled at reading and analyzing process records or listening to segments of session recordings. Their approach, however, is largely intuitive. The principles of content analysis, applied to such records, could conceivably make this effort more systematic and enhance the validity and reliability of the inferences drawn from these records of practice.

Although the following steps of content analysis are related to treatment monitoring, they can easily be applied to any of the other uses of the technique outlined above. Regardless of the purpose for conducting content analysis, the steps always include category development, definition of the units of analysis, sampling, attention to reliability and validity, and analysis and presentation of the results.

PRINCIPLES FOR CONTENT ANALYSIS IN TREATMENT MONITORING

Category Development

Category development involves deciding on the dimensions of interest within which data should be sorted. Social workers engaged in content analysis utilize theory, professional standards, research literature, and practice wisdom to begin their thinking about categories. In the case of treatment monitoring, category development involves specifying monitoring standards. Monitoring standards refer to dimensions that reflect expected intervention techniques, behaviors, and content to be exhibited by clinical social workers. These constitute the ideals against which actual worker performance is assessed. These standards may vary among clinicians and clients, depending on many factors including the experience level of the clinician and the treatment needs of the client.

Irrespective of what the standards are, they should be stated as clearly as possible, they should be adjusted to the individual clinician's treatment style and approach, and they should be reflective of content related to the implementation of treatment plans. In clinical supervision with a particular worker, the ideal may be that the worker becomes less didactic or directive in sessions. With another worker the ideal may be that the worker effectively utilizes cognitive therapy. With the former, categories or standards might include 1. directive interactions, 2. empathic interactions, and 3. supportive interactions; with the latter, one category might be "educates client about cognitive therapy." In each case, the more specific the standards, the more easily they are monitored. In addition, the particular indicators of these ideal dimensions most often emerge from the records themselves. For example, in attempting to monitor "directive interactions," the supervisor cannot anticipate the many specific ways in which such interactions may be displayed.

Defining the Units of Analysis

In the context of content analysis, the unit of analysis refers to the informational units that will be categorized or coded. Identifying the unit of analysis involves specifying the information the content analyst should pay attention to in developing categories for analysis. The unit of analysis may be as detailed as every word in a document or as broad as whole sections of documents. Sentences, paragraphs, or thematic content areas can all serve as units of analysis.

Naturally, the more detailed the content analysis, the smaller will be the unit of analysis. However, the more detailed the analysis, the more time-consuming and expensive it will be. Consequently, the unit of analysis should be small enough so that it provides reliable and valid information pertinent to the purpose of the analysis, but not so small that it requires excessive amounts of time and money for processing and analyzing the data. For example, in the supervision example concerning directive interactions, little would be gained by characterizing an entire recorded session as either "empathic" or "directive." Neither would it be helpful to try to code each word in the session. An appropriate unit of analysis might be the content of the clinician's speech in response to each of the client's contributions to the dialogue. Each of the worker's responses could be characterized accordingly.

Operationally Defining Analytic Categories

Once units of analysis have been broadly defined, the materials that are to be analyzed are reviewed for the purpose of identifying dimensions of variables that are relevant to the purpose of the study and that are translatable into nominal, ordinal, or interval scales. For example, a therapeutic interview may be examined to determine which type of therapeutic intervention predominates. The therapeutic interview is the unit of analysis, the predominate type of intervention is the variable to be analyzed, and the categories of types of interventions represent a nominal scale whose categories are based upon what emerges from studying a sample of interviews. Likewise, a therapeutic interview might be divided into three fifteen-minute units of analysis. The variable to be analyzed may be type of therapeutic intervention, but it may be represented as an ordinal scale in which each type of intervention within a time unit is ranked in terms of whether it appears most frequently, sometimes, or never. Finally, the unit of analysis may be as detailed as every sentence uttered by the social worker. The variable to be measured may be an interval scale in which the frequency of empathic statements is counted.

Just as in other efforts to operationally define variables, the categories for analysis should be mutually exclusive and exhaustive. In content analysis, however, the categories and their behavioral referents will come primarily from studying the documents to be analyzed themselves rather than from categories that are fully formed before the documents are reviewed. Once these are identified, specific instructions should be written concerning which information to consider and which to ignore, what code categories are to be used, and, finally, what are the empirical referents for assigning code categories to units of analysis. Illustrative examples of each code category are helpful as well. The more detailed these instructions, the more reliable the classification scheme.

Specifying Sources of Data and Sampling

In order to conduct content analysis, the social worker must specify sources of data as well as their availability. For treatment monitoring, data should be drawn from available documents or recordings that adequately reflect worker-client interactions. Audio or video recordings are usually the best sources of such information. Ideally, such recordings should be consistently available over time, across cases, and across workers. In order to monitor treatment of a single case, adequate recordings of each worker-client interview should be available. In order to compare treatment done by a single worker with clients who required comparable treatment, adequate records would have to be available for each of these clients. Finally, in order to compare the performance of social workers, each would have to make available adequate recordings for comparable clients over a period of time.

Another aspect of availability is whether recording of sessions is done systematically. In order to make comparisons of clinicians' work over time, for example, each interview must be recorded. Otherwise, as treatment proceeds, selective bias could become a problem, particularly if clinicians fail to record or save or, in some other way, "lose" recordings of sessions that are perceived to be problematic. When data are not consistently available or have been collected unsystematically, treatment monitoring through content analysis requires that social workers begin to record their practice routinely and systematically. Although perhaps viewed as burdensome, it is the only way in which valid and reliable inferences can be made.

The materials containing data for content analysis can be defined in terms of their sources, dates, and contents. In addition to recordings, sources include written notes and reports in the client's file, process notes written for supervision, and client logs, among others. If only one source is used, it is important to establish that it gives an authentic and comprehensive picture of the phenomenon to be studied. Thus, for example, a content analysis of progress notes in the client's file would not necessarily provide reliable data about how well the client understands the cognitive therapy model. Additional data from the client's log would be helpful. When multiple sources are employed, it is important to establish how authentic and comprehensive each of them is.

Dates refer to the different times for which materials are available. When multiple sources are used, there may be different dates for each source. For instance, a school social worker's process records may describe ten interviews with a child, two interviews with the child's parents, and one interview with the child's teacher over the course of a semester. Each of these sources of information may be analyzed. In the final report of such a study, information regarding the dates and frequency of the interviews should be provided so that proper interpretations may be made in relation to study findings. For example, a study based on records of weekly interviews over the course of a semester would be more reliable than one based on a single interview at the end of a semester.

Contents refers to the actual communications data that are to be analyzed for each source, for each date. Here, again, it is important that the contents of the materials to be analyzed constitute as authentic a representation of the phenomenon to be studied as possible. A study based entirely on the contents of memos from a social worker to a supervisor would be a poor source of information about what transpires between worker and client.

Sampling is sometimes used in content analysis when the amount of data is so large that analysis of it is impractical. Sampling refers to systematically choosing a subset of data, called a *sample,* to represent all of the relevant data under consideration, called the *population* or *universe.* The method for sampling data in content analysis is similar to the steps outlined in detail in chapter 11. For now, it is important to know that a sample can not be chosen at whim or by ease of access. Instead, a specific method must be followed to help control bias and allow for inferences or generalizations to be drawn about the population, based on the data in the sample.

Determining the Reliability of Analytic Categories

The procedures for determining the reliability of measures in content analysis are identical to those described in chapter 3 on observational techniques. In content analysis test-retest and interrater reliability are particularly relevant. Test-retest reliability should be established when content analysis of documents is to take place over a long period of time. This will ensure the fact that the one or more people who are rating the documents are not changing the bases of their judgments over the course of the study. Interrater reliability, on the other hand, is important to establish in order to ensure that different raters are consistent in their judgments of the same materials.

Once the categories for content analysis have been selected, the following guidelines should help to promote the reliability of coding procedures:

- Make sure the basic dimensions or variables to be identified are clearly defined and understood by the raters.
- Make sure instructions for categorization of the variables are clear. This is promoted by basing categories on behavioral manifestations that are closely related to the overt content of the documents to be analyzed. Thus a count of the number of times a client used the word *angry* is likely to be more reliable than a count of the number of times the client "appeared hostile."
- On a small but varied sample of the documents or recordings to be analyzed, have raters make independent ratings on the key dimensions of interest. Calculate the interrater reliability on these dimensions. If the reliability is too low (say below 70 percent agreement), discuss those instances in which there were differences in judgments. Then refine the rules for categorizing dimensions. Conduct ratings on a second sample to determine whether reliability has been brought to an acceptable level.
- Once interrater reliability has been established, actual data collection may begin. However, it is important to establish that the reliability is maintained over the course of the study. Ratings, therefore, should be spot-checked against the documents on which they are based throughout the study.
- Finally, reliability is likely to decline when raters are fatigued, bored, or under great time pressure. It is important, therefore, that work schedules and conditions be such that these negative conditions are minimized.

Estimating the Validity or Authenticity of the Documents or Recordings

Whether for treatment monitoring or one of the many other uses of content analysis, inferences drawn from recorded or written materials are valid only to the extent that the documents are a true representation of the phenomenon of interest. In the context of social work intervention, documents are authentic to the extent that they represent what actually transpired during the intervention process. Naturally, then, an audio- or videotape of an interview is more likely to be authentic than a process record based on the social worker's memory of the interaction with the client. When process recordings are used, their authenticity can be increased by making sure they are written immediately after the interview has transpired and are based on note taking during the intervention. In addition, process recording should be behaviorally specific including descriptions of client's and social worker's behaviors. Inferences or generalizations such as "the client appeared defensive" should be replaced with actual behaviors and dialogue.

Collecting, Tabulating, Presenting, and Utilizing the Data

Once the materials that contain the relevant information have been collected, raters should be meticulous in recording and counting data. Spot checks of reliability will help to decrease inaccuracies and sloppiness in recording. Awareness of the spot checks themselves often keep raters alert and promotes accuracy.

After recording and tabulating the data, results should be presented in a form that is easy to read and relevant to the purpose of the analysis. Since many of the findings of content analyses are in the form of simple counts or percentages, bar graphs and line graphs are quite useful for presenting the findings. Graphs may be easily produced using statistical or spreadsheet software programs.

In a bar graph the bars may be either horizontal or vertical. The area within each bar represents 100 percent of a particular dimension, for example, total time involved in an interview. Within the bar different colors or symbols can be used to represent different categories and their relative frequency within a given dimension. For example, in monitoring changes in client-worker interaction over time, a bar may represent each interview. Within each bar the medium gray area may represent the relative amount of silence, the dark gray area may represent the relative amount of time the therapist spoke, and the light area may represent the amount of client talk time. By constructing the bar graph for each recorded interview and placing them side by side, changes over time are easily seen.

Figure 6.1 shows that there has been a sizable reduction in therapist talk time over the course of five interviews and a corresponding increase in client talking. In addition, the periods of silence have declined. The same findings may be represented in a line graph, as in figure 6.2, in which the percent of interview time is represented on the vertical axis, the interviews on the horizontal axis, and the different data categories by variously shaded and marked lines.

It should be clear from figures 6.1 and 6.2 that the bar graph is better for representing relative amounts of each category of worker-client communication, whereas the line graph is better for representing absolute amounts of each category. Each, however, offers the findings in a manner that is easy to read and interpret.

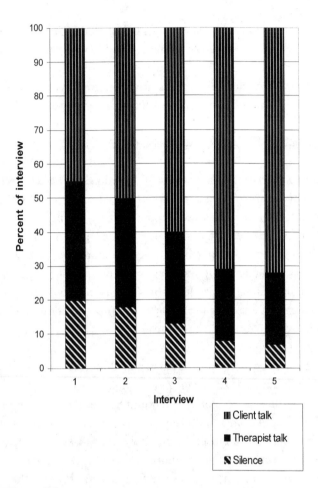

Figure 6.1

The final step in any treatment monitoring study involves comparing the findings against standards for worker performance. These standards may be derived empirically, that is, based on the performance of other clinicians. They may be based on agency rules, professional norms, or specific treatment plans. Whatever their origin, guidelines should be established for determining what constitutes a serious departure from the standard of acceptable performance. This is often a matter of judgment based on previous experience and taking into account such considerations as the level of the clinician's training and the experience or the severity of clinical impairment of the client. If serious discrepancies are noted

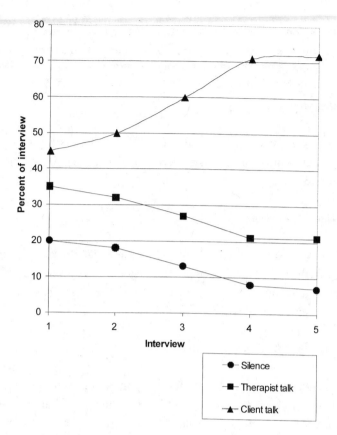

Figure 6.2

between actual worker's performance and standards, the documentation of these discrepancies can serve as a useful tool for supervisory intervention.

CONTENT ANALYSIS IN ACTION

A supervisor of MSW students in a mental health center discovers that one of her four students is having difficulty getting clients to return for service after the first two interviews. The clinic is located in a public housing community and serves a low-income clientele. The program offers short-term supportive treatment, accompanied by assistance with money management, and referrals for help with medical problems, child care, and employment. In supervisory conferences the student appears intelligent and perceptive and seems to accept instruction readily. The supervisor decides to do a content analysis of the audio recordings in an attempt to locate the problem.

Category Development

The general standard for treatment in this unit is short-term treatment geared to altering the client's situation through referral, problem solving, advocacy, and emotional support.

Defining the Units of Analysis

The supervisor decides that each recorded interview will constitute a unit of analysis. Since each student has had approximately four cases, and each of these has had from one to four interviews, the total number of interviews is small enough that sampling procedures are not necessary.

Operationally Defining Analytic Categories

The supervisor determines that she wants to compare the treatment activities of each student social worker in their recorded interviews. Taking a single interview from each student, she listens to the tapes to get a general sense of the kinds of student-initiated behaviors revealed in these records. Four kinds of student-initiated behaviors immediately become apparent. They are asking questions, providing alternatives, making empathic/supportive statements, and making interpretive statements. She then goes back to the recordings to identify the behavioral bases for her intuitive judgment about these dimensions. These will serve as guides for subsequent analysis of all the process records. Questions are easily discernible in the process records where students clearly ask the client something. Provisions of alternatives are those statements in which the student offers suggestions or resources to the client. Empathic statements are those in which the student expresses compassion, understanding, or support of the client's situation and feelings. Interpretive statements are those in which the student attempts to explain the client's attitudes, feelings, or behaviors based on previous information that the client has volunteered.

By simply counting the number of times each student takes each of these actions and dividing by the total number of actions the student has recorded, one can get a relative picture of the differences between students in each of these dimensions.

Specifying Sources of Data and Availability

The supervisor decides to do a content analysis of the audio recordings of all the students in the unit. Students are required to provide audiotapes of all sessions with their clients. The supervisor collects all these and notes which tapes come from each student as well as the date of the recorded interview. She is then ready to compare the performance of the student in question with other students.

Determining the Reliability of Analytic Categories

Since the supervisor is the only one that will be rating student behaviors, she is concerned only with intrarater reliability, that is, the extent to which her ratings are internally consistent. After coding the first four interviews, she re-codes them to determine that her ratings are consistent. There is a high level of agreement in her ratings for each of the student-initiated activities.

Estimating the Authenticity of the Documents Used

By using audio recordings, the representation of the actual interviews is considered to be quite good. Lacking a visual record, however, there is a slight possibility that it is the students' nonverbal behaviors that are related to client return rate. An easily accessible, additional outside source of information will be the rate of client return. High-quality interviews, as assessed by content analysis of audio recordings, which are highly associated with a nonreturn rate, would indicate that audio recordings do not provide a valid way to understand the student's nonreturn rate.

Collecting, Tabulating, and Presenting the Data

The supervisor proceeds to tally the number of times each student asked a question, provided alternatives, demonstrated empathy/support, and made interpretive statements. By dividing by the total number of student-initiated statements in the process recording of a given student, the supervisor converts these findings into percentages and displays them in a bar graph. Figure 6.3 shows the relative proportion of each of these types of student-initiated interventions for each student.

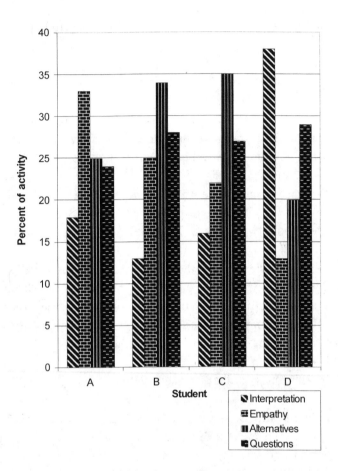

Figure 6.3

Figure 6.3 shows that Student D, the one who was having difficulty getting clients to return, is lowest in providing alternatives and empathic statements and highest in asking questions and providing interpretations to the client. This high level of interpretive activity and relatively low level of empathy and alternatives is also inconsistent with treatment standards of the agency as a whole.

Using the bar graph for illustrative purposes, the supervisor discusses these findings with the student, who acknowledges a preference for providing nondirective psychotherapy with clients. Having identified the problem through systematic monitoring of the student behavior with clients, the supervisor can proceed to work with the student on this issue.

EXERCISES

1. What would be the advantages and disadvantages if the supervisor in the example above decided to do content analysis using only the tapes of the student who was experiencing the return-rate problem?

2. Select a process recording or an audio or video recording of one therapeutic interview from your own or someone else's clinical practice. Identify three types of interventions. Divide the interview into three parts, beginning, middle, and end. What is the incidence of each of the three types of interventions within each segment of the interview? Does the incidence of each of these interventions change from segment to segment? Illustrate your findings with a graph.

SELECTED BIBLIOGRAPHY

Allen-Meares, P. 1985. Content analysis: It does have a place in social work research. *Journal of Social Service Research, 7,* 51–68.

Berry, Kenneth J., and Mielke, Paul W. Jr. 1997. Measuring the joint agreement between multiple raters and a standard. *Educational and Psychological Measurement, 57*(3), 527–530.

Deal, K. H., and Brintzenhofe, K. M. 2004. A study of MSW students' interviewing skills over time. *Journal of Teaching in Social Work, 24,* 181–197.

Evans, William. 1996. Computer-supported content analysis: Trends, tools, and techniques. *Social Science Computer Review, 14*(3), 269–279.

Graybeal, C. T., and Ruff, E. 1995. Process recording: It's more than you think. *Journal of Social Work Education, 31,* 169–181.

Krippendorff, K. 2004. *Content analysis: An introduction to its methodology.* Thousand Oaks, CA: Sage.

Kronick, J. C., and Silver, S. 1993. Using the computer for content analysis. *Journal of Social ServiceResearch, 16,* 41–58.

Neuendorf, K. A. 2002. *The content analysis guidebook.* Thousand Oaks, CA: Sage.

Neuman, K. M., and Friedman, B. D. 1997. Process recordings: Fine-tuning an old instrument. *Journal of Social Work Education, 33,* 237–243.

Sheppard, M. 2004. *Appraising and using social research in the human services: An introduction for social work and health professionals.* Philadelphia: Jessica Kingsley.

Table 6.1 Notable Web Sites

Title	Address	Contents
The Content Analysis Guidebook	http://academic.csuohio.edu/ kneuendorf/content/	Links to bibliographies, as well as information about coding, reliability, and computer software.
Overview:	http://writing.colostate.edu/ references/research/content/ index.cfm	Introduction to content analytic methods.

When designed and used properly, forms can be highly efficient devices for generating systematic, objective, treatment-relevant information about clients. Client monitoring forms are sometimes called *client* or *personal logs, journals, diaries;* or *critical incident records.* By whatever name, client self-monitoring forms provide information that is not otherwise easily or reliably captured.

Client monitoring forms are particularly useful in social service settings such as family service or community mental health agencies where clients are treated intermittently and observed only in interaction with the social worker. In such settings the client's subjective memories are generally the primary source of information concerning client problems, efforts to deal with these, and success or failure in resolving them.

For improving the quality of client self-reporting, forms can be used for systematically and routinely recording information related to clients' behaviors, attitudes, and moods. The recorded information may focus on problems, solutions, or compliance with the treatment contract. In addition, the information can come from client monitoring forms completed by the clients themselves or by their significant others. Moreover, the information may be in the form of quantitative or qualitative data. In this chapter we focus on how client self-monitoring forms can be used to monitor interventions as well as to monitor clients' behaviors and activities in between contacts with their social workers.

Although the construction of forms is not, strictly speaking, a "research technique," good forms make use of concepts and principles that are basic to all research instruments. Thus concepts and principles for constructing observation instruments, questionnaires, rating scales, and other research instruments are relevant to form construction. Accordingly, other chapters in this book also provide relevant information about the potentials and requisites of good forms.

CLIENT SELF-MONITORING FORMS AND CLINICAL PRACTICE

Client self-monitoring forms are potentially useful in all phases of clinical social work practice. In the diagnostic assessment phase, for example, they can be used to understand and define clients' problems within their situational context. In some instances self-monitoring may provide a "baseline" of the occurrence of problematic behaviors, attitudes, or moods at regular intervals prior to intervention. Such systematic monitoring of problems and the dynamics that effect their expression can greatly aid clinical assessment.

Forms also can be used to systematically assess treatment outcomes. Accordingly, a series of postintervention measures taken by the client or by significant others can determine the effects of treatment and the persistence of these effects. Interrupted time series designs (discussed in chapter 10) make use of both pre- and postintervention measures in evaluating clinical outcomes.

Finally, forms can be used in the treatment monitoring phase to determine how well the client is following the intervention contract, to find out whether situational factors are enhancing or hindering progress, or to track relevant behaviors or activities between meetings with the social worker. Again, this monitoring can be done by clients themselves and/or by significant others in their environment. Most important is that the information generated in this monitoring process is part of a regular, systematic, and objective effort to describe client behavior.

Although not a focus in this chapter, it should also be noted that self-monitoring forms also can be used by clients as a form of intervention and by clinical social workers as a professional learning tool. Clients and social workers alike may benefit from the increased self-awareness that comes from systematic self-monitoring. Such use is described more fully by Swenson (1988) and by Kopp (1988), referenced in the bibliography.

PRINCIPLES FOR DEVELOPING AND USING FORMS

Determining the Purpose of the Form

In considering the potential usefulness of a client self-monitoring form, it is important to consider two questions. First, what kind of information is sought? In the context of treatment implementation, three different kinds of information can be secured through the use of client self-monitoring forms: 1. information concerning client adherence to treatment procedures and/or time schedules that have been agreed to in a verbal or written contract with the social worker; 2. information concerning situational factors that facilitate or obstruct client compliance; and 3. information concerning client behaviors, attitudes, or moods during the treatment process.

For example, figure 7.1 shows a form that could be used to determine the frequency with which a client in a job counseling program contacts potential employers, the conditions under which the client does so, and the client's attitude following these contacts. Likewise, a parent in a child-abuse prevention program could be asked to record the frequency with which physical punishment is used versus alternative means, the factors that precipitated the use of physical punishment, and the client's self-attitude following these events.

Table 7.1 Form to record job-seeking behaviors and attitudes

ID # 65 Week of March 2, 2005

Time & Date of Contact	Information Source	Company and Name/Title of Contact	Result	My Reaction
10am March 1	Newspaper	Acme Agency Receptionist	Already filled	I'll never find anything! Why do I bother with this?
3pm March 6	Friend told me about job opening where she works.	ABC, Inc. Sue Jones / Human Resources	Need to mail resume.	Job's not my top choice, but maybe it could work out.
3:30pm March 6	Web site of professional organization	Omega Hospital Ken Smith / Dept. Head	Email resume ASAP.	Only temp. (cover maternity leave), but good fit... hope I get it!

A second question to ask when considering the use of a client monitoring form is whether the desired information is already available through some other, less intrusive means. If the client, for example, appears to have sufficient insight, distance, and objectivity to reliably report this information, a form may not be necessary. Alternatively, a form may be unnecessary when the information can be secured from significant others who can provide reliable and valid information based on existing observational or standardized research questionnaires. Specifying the purpose of and information needed from the form helps determine whether the information is already available through other means.

Setting Treatment Monitoring Standards

Treatment implementation cannot be adequately monitored without first specifying expectations or standards of social worker and client behavior. Whether monitoring worker or client, the more specific the standards, the easier the monitoring. For example, overweight clients could be asked to "keep track of their weight" during a one-week period. This lack of specificity would probably result in sporadic, self-monitoring efforts on the part of the client and unreliable information for the clinician. On the other hand, clients asked to weigh themselves daily, at the same time of day, unclothed; and to record the weight on a simple weekly form will produce much more reliable information. In addition, the information does not only indicate the success or failure of weight-reduction efforts; the client's compliance with the self-monitoring instructions also represents a measure of the client's commitment to and fulfillment of the treatment contract.

Just as with treatment expectations, monitoring expectations should be as specific as possible. How often and under what conditions is the form to be filled out? When are the forms to be returned to the social worker? Questions such as these should be clearly answered in the monitoring instructions.

Determining Who Fills Out the Form

In this chapter we are emphasizing client self-monitoring. However, the person who uses the form may be anyone who regularly observes the client's treatment-relevant behaviors. It may be a relative, friend, nurse, teacher, coworker, employer, among others. When client self-monitoring is the primary source of information, any of the above may be used to determine the reliability of the client's self-reports. Such external checks are particularly useful when there is reason to think that the client's self-reports might be biased. In self-monitoring, clients may be prone to many of the same types of bias discussed in earlier chapters, including bias due to social desirability, desire to please the clinician, and others.

In deciding who should use the form, it is important to consider who can follow the monitoring instructions and respond in a reliable, unbiased manner. Naturally, for forms to be used, a minimum degree of literacy is necessary. Instructions must be understandable and geared to the user's level of knowledge and sophistication.

Constructing Treatment Monitoring Forms

In many respects, the principles that apply to the construction of interview questionnaires discussed in chapter 1 and observation instruments in chapter 3 are equally applicable to the construction of treatment monitoring forms. Information should be operationally specific, valid, and reliable. Categories within an informational dimension should be mutually exclusive and exhaustive. Each question should relate to a single category of information about client behavior, attitude, mood, and/or the conditions affecting these.

The information generated may be quantitative, including numerical counts of client behaviors, ratings of client attitudes or moods, and duration of particular symptoms or events. Alternatively, information may be qualitative, based on narrative descriptions of client behaviors, interpersonal exchanges, or the conditions affecting these. The former are appropriate when the clients' problems, treatment goals, and target behaviors are highly specified. When such specificity is lacking, qualitiative information gathering is preferable. In the course of treatment the clinician may begin with qualitative monitoring and, based on this, develop more specific standards and a more quantitative from. Or a form may have a combination of qualitative and quantitative questions. In general, monitoring well-defined interventions with clear target behaviors should be registered in simple quantitative categories of one kind or another. On the other hand, if questions arise related to treatment plans that are difficult for a client to implement or that do not result in expected change, qualitative information may provide ideas about obstacles to treatment that were not anticipated.

Whether quantitative, qualitative, or a mixture of both, treatment monitoring forms should be constructed with the following principles in mind:

- The information gathered by the form should have a clear relationship to treatment monitoring objectives. In other words, the information gathered should reflect directly on issues of client commitment to the treatment contract and/or factors that facilitate or obstruct the client's ability or willingness to fulfill the contract.

- Each form should contain identifying information and indicate the dates on which the monitoring took place. This will make it possible to analyze clients' behaviors, attitudes, and so forth, over time. It may be preferable to use a code to identify clients' forms in order to protect confidentiality and privacy.

- Duplication of information should be avoided. Information that is already available in agency records should not be requested on monitoring forms. If, in the future, an attempt is made to correlate self-monitoring information with other client characteristics, the latter information can be retrieved easily enough from the case records.

- For each category of information a precise operational definition or set of instructions should be given to facilitate classification and tabulation of the data and to promote validity and reliability of the data.

- Operational definitions should be consistent on all forms given to a single client. If a number of clients are engaged in similar treatment efforts, operational definitions should be consistent in the forms given to all of these clients. This is particularly important if the client data are to be combined (see chapter 12) to make generalizations about overall client performance within the program as a whole.

- Forms should be simple, clear, efficient, and easy to use. When they are complicated or time-consuming, they result in fatigue and unreliability. Ideally, a client self-monitoring form should not require more than ten minutes to complete.

- Where possible, validating procedures should be built into the monitoring efforts. The social worker should discuss the results of clients' self-monitoring regularly. In addition, significant others in the client's environment may be asked to validate the client's self-monitoring.

- When qualitative descriptions are called for, instructions for recording these should be as specific as possible. If "critical incidents" are to be described, definitions and examples should be provided as well as instructions for how much information needs to be provided.

Pretest of the Form

Before using any form for systematic data collection, it should be tried out. The social worker should first discuss the form with the client, giving instructions and providing examples to illustrate how it should be used. Between treatment sessions the client will be asked to fill out the form and to consider ambiguities in the instructions, how much time it took, whether it was fatiguing, whether important question or answer categories were left out, and so on. The experience of the pretest and quality of the feedback should then be used by the social worker to make up a final version of the form for future use.

Collecting the Data

To ensure the collection of accurate, high-quality information, procedures should be worked out so that clients record their behaviors, attitudes, or other specified information at regular intervals during the day or at the end of each day. In the case of multiple recordings in a day, the form should be kept in an easily accessible place to facilitate its use. For forms that are filled out at the end of the day, the client should be encouraged to do so, rather than letting them go until the next day. Leaving them until the next day promotes unreliable information. Whatever the timing, client self-monitors should be praised and rewarded for completing the forms, for providing accurate information, and for taking such a direct role.

Analyzing the Data

At regular intervals the social worker and client should analyze the collected data together. This process should begin with noting and clarifying obvious inaccuracies or inconsistencies in the data recorded. Once it is established that the information gathered is accurate and complete, the findings are tabulated (see chapter 13) and compared against the expectations specified in the treatment contract. Is the treatment contract being carried out as planned? If not, why not? If the intervention is progressing as planned, are there indications of positive change with regard to the treatment objectives? If this appears to be so, the intervention and monitoring can continue. If not, further assessment and treatment formulation may be called for.

Naturally, no precise formula can be given for answering the questions and making the decisions described in the preceding paragraph. This is an area in which judgments must be made about whether discrepancies between ideal client behavior and actual client behavior are within reasonable limits. Here there is no substitute for practice wisdom based on clinical experience. It is our contention, however, that systematic monitoring of client participation and progress in treatment can facilitate the clinician's judgment process. And it may have beneficial treatment effects as well by giving the client a more concrete role in the treatment process.

FORMS FOR CLIENT SELF-MONITORING IN ACTION

A married couple of twenty-five years request therapy at a nonprofit family therapy agency. The problem that led them to seek treatment was that the wife was spending more and more time out of the house working, while the husband, newly retired, became more and more depressed. After some initial diagnostic interviews with the couple, the social worker felt that there was a dual problem. First, the husband was experiencing an adjustment disorder related to his recent retirement. The rewards as well as the obligations attached to his role as a successful attorney were absent and missed. As a result, for the first time in their married life, he became more dependent on his wife for social and psychological support. This led to the problem that brought them to treatment: frequent and growing conflicts about how to spend their time in the evenings and on weekends.

The social worker determined that two courses of treatment should be undertaken. In individual sessions with the husband, the worker helps explore potential interests and encourages him to actively pursue dormant interests in art and volunteer work with a literacy program during the day. He also considers whether he would like to use his expertise in law in a volunteer capacity. In conjoint sessions the worker teaches husband and wife techniques of negotiation and conflict resolution. No direct effort is made to limit the time the woman spends outside the home. Both husband and wife agree to participate in self-monitoring during the course of treatment. Two forms for monitoring will be constructed, one for the husband and one for the wife.

Determining the Purpose of the Form

The forms are intended to serve a number of purposes. They are intended to monitor 1. the husband's efforts to pursue his interests, 2. the incidence of marital conflict between the couple, 3. the use of negotiation techniques taught by the social worker, 4. the man's feelings of depression, and 5. the frequency with which the couple engage in leisure activities together or separately.

Setting Treatment Monitoring Standards

It is determined that the forms should be filled out daily. The man and woman are asked to fill out their forms separately, without consultation with each other. The man is instructed to complete the activities in the pursuit of his interests section each day before starting dinner. Both are instructed to complete the remaining items before going to bed.

Determining Who Fills Out the Form

Both husband and wife will each have their own form to fill out. His form will require information about seeking activities related to his interests; as well as about the incidence of marital conflict, the use of negotiation techniques, rating of depression, and frequency of leisure activities. Her form will have questions about everything but seeking activities. By having each fill out a separate form, without consultation with each other, it will be possible to assess the reliability of their self-monitoring, as well as to observe whether their perceptions are similar or different.

Constructing Treatment Monitoring Forms

The forms will combine quantitative and qualitative questions. Quantitative questions will be asked to record simple factual data such as the number of activities related to his interests made in a day. Qualitative questions will be asked about the issues over which the couple came into conflict and the conditions under which negotiation techniques did not seem to work.

The husband's form would look something like this:

Name_____ **Day**_____ **Date**_____

Activities related to my interest in art and volunteer work:

Time of Day   Activity

_____

_____

_____

Marital conflicts:

List each issue over which you came into conflict today.

_____

Were negotiation techniques used? (yes/no) _____

Did they help? (yes/no) _____

Husband's mood:

Which of the following best describes the way you felt today? (check one)

Very happy _____

Moderately happy ＿＿＿

Neither happy nor depressed ＿＿＿

Moderately depressed ＿＿＿

Very depressed ＿＿＿

Leisure activities:

Time of Day	Activity	With or without spouse

Pretesting the Form

Before fully implementing the self-monitoring, the social worker explains the purpose of the form and gives instructions to the couple on how to record information relevant to the conflict section of the form. When both seem to understand the purpose, how to complete the form, and express willingness to do so, they are asked to try it out for a day or two. Their experiences with this pretest will be discussed at their next session and ambiguities will be clarified, questions changed, or instructions given, as necessary.

Collecting the Data

Both the man and the woman have been relatively compliant in completing the forms during the first week of self-monitoring. The social worker praises both for their efforts and their obvious commitment to making the most out of their involvement in the therapeutic process.

Analyzing the Data

By looking at the data the social worker determines that the man has done little, during the first week of monitoring, beyond occasional searching on the Internet for information about art classes. This will be pursued further in individual sessions. The information regarding marital conflicts indicates that both husband and wife show a fairly high level of agreement about the number of conflicts and the issues over which they conflicted. Negotiation techniques were successfully used on a few occasions. On others, though the techniques were unsuccessful, information about why they failed generated content for further discussion and clarification of the techniques of negotiation. There was further indication that, on a few days, the husband indicated he was neither happy nor depressed and on one occasion both he and his wife engaged in leisure activities together. All these factors were taken as positive signs by the social worker. As a result, both treatment and treatment monitoring are continued.

EXERCISES

1. Consider the following questions in relation to figure 7.1.
   a. Write instructions to guide the client's use of this form.
   b. Imagine reviewing with the client information from several weeks of these completed forms. Devise a plan to analyze and utilize the information collected.
2. Devise a form to monitor some specific treatment plan you have completed with one of your clients. Ask the client to self-monitor treatment relevant behavior for a week. To what extent are the data obtained from the forms useful to you? Do the data generated by the form coincide with what the client tells you verbally about the preceding week? Do they coincide with information gathered from significant others in the client's environment? What do the data add to your understanding of the client, the problem, and the treatment plan?

SELECTED BIBLIOGRAPHY

Barber, J. G., and Crisp, B. R. 1995. Social support and prevention of relapse following treatment for alcohol abuse. *Research on Social Work practice, 5*, 283–296.

Bloom, M., and Orme, J. G. 1999. *Evaluating practice: Guidelines for the accountable professional.* 3d ed. Boston: Allyn and Bacon.

Galovski, T. E., and Blanchard, E. B. 2002. The effectiveness of a brief psychological intervention on court-referred and self-referred aggressive drivers. *Behavior Research and Therapy, 40*, 1385–1402.

Kolko, D. J. 1996. Clinical monitoring of treatment course in child physical abuse: Psychometric characteristics and treatment comparisons. *Child Abuse and Neglect, 20*, 23–43.

Kopp, J. 1988. Self-monitoring: A literature review of research and practice. *Social Work Research and Abstracts, 24*, 8–20.

Swenson, C. R. 1988. The professional log: Techniques for self-directed learning. *Social Casework, 69*, 307–311.

Qualitative research techniques rely on direct or indirect observation of phenomena in their natural settings from the viewpoint of the researcher or the respondent. Rather than striving for objectivity through its method, qualitiative methods attempt to provide in-depth understanding of participants' subjective experiences. Data are unstructured, including participants' behaviors and words as opposed to numerical coding. Instead of a fixed methodology for collecting data, qualitative data collection is more flexible, allowing for modifications as the study progresses. Since the method does not use quantitative techniques such as systematic observation guides or standardized questions with response sets, the range of potential results is broad and may include unanticipated results.

Qualitative research questions are generally broadly defined and are not based on specific hypotheses. The research questions are of several types. First, qualitative methods provide in-depth description and understanding of experiences or processes. Further, qualitative methods may help to understand the meaning attributed to experiences by study participants. In addition, qualitiative methods help to create theory, that is, hypotheses about the relationship between variables may be proposed based on the qualitative data. This is particularly useful in topic areas that have not been previously studied. As an example, qualitative methods could be used to examine the experience of child protective services (CPS) workers during their first year of employment. Qualitative data could provide an in-depth description of new workers' experience as well as the process of moving from trainee to worker status. The meaning of the work to the participants could also be explored. Potentially, the researcher may identify themes that could contribute to a theory about characteristics of those who continue in CPS work for the duration of a year.

It should be noted that qualitative methods are not particularly useful for answering questions related to" how much" or "how many." So, in the preceding example, quantitative methods would need to be used to determine the proportion of new workers who continue in CPS for the duration of a year. Also, it is possible to convert qualitative data into quantitative data through a process of numerical coding, at which point the principles of quantitative data analysis would apply. For example, if three characteristics were identified among CPS workers through qualitative analysis, the characteristics could be numerically coded and subsequently counted to see which appeared most frequently among those who stayed in the field longer.

A wide variety of qualitative methods exist, a few of which are listed below. All share the basic characteristics described above but vary in their purpose or data collection and analysis techniques.

- Narrative case studies provide an in-depth narrative analysis of a single case. The case unit of analysis may be an individual, family, social work agency, or any other single unit. Case studies have been used throughout the history of social work to highlight clinical themes, processes, and potential solutions to dilemmas.
- Ethnographic research provides a comprehensive analysis of a specific culture and its people. Described in detail by Lowery (2001), ethnographies are generally created through the use of participant observation. They describe people's characteristics, relationship patterns, and roles. Ethnographies may be used to describe entire societies or specific subcultures that may be of particular interest to social workers.
- Grounded theory, described in greater detail by Rubin and Babbie (2001) is a particular form of inductive research that was originally developed by Glaser and Strauss. In this method observations are collected by interviewing participants and then analyzed using the *constant comparison* method. This analysis method requires the researcher to search for hypothetical patterns and themes in the data and then continue to add observations from selected participants. The new observations are then compared with all previous data for the purpose

of modifying or specifying the patterns. This process continues until further interviews produce no new information.

- Qualitative content analysis involves using data collected either from existing records or from interviews to identify themes or patterns in the latent content. Unlike content analysis of manifest content discussed in chapter 6, analysis of latent content does not involve counting particular words. Instead the researcher looks for the underlying implications and meanings in the narrative data that can be categorized by themes.

QUALITATIVE TECHNIQUES AND CLINICAL SOCIAL WORK PRACTICE

Qualitative research methods are very compatible with clinical practice. In fact, it might be argued that clinical practice is similar to qualitative research in several ways. To start, clinicians gather information based both on observations of clients' behaviors and on narratives collected through interviewing. Clinicians then synthesize and analyze this information in order to locate themes, make interpretations, and find meaning in the information. These interpretations are then used as the starting point for implementing or modifying interventions. Thus the methods of both share similarities.

In addition to similarities in method, qualitative research is a good fit for clinical practice because of the types of questions it can answer (Oktay, 2002). Clinical social workers seek to fully understand peoples' experiences and cultural context. In addition, clinicians need to understand processes, oftentimes within complex service delivery systems. Moreover, clinicians often encounter new problems and populations for which in-depth understanding is required. Qualitative research methods suit these needs well.

Qualitative research methods can be used in any of the three phases of clinical practice. In the assessment phase, qualitative methods might be used to identify clinical themes important to individual clients or to groups of clients. It could also be used to better understand the needs of new populations or problems. Narrative case studies might be useful to better understand the experience of those with specific problems. Ethnography could lead to increased knowledge and understanding of clients' cultural context.

In the evaluation phase qualitative methods can be utilized to examine service delivery questions. For example, how is the service being implemented? What are some of the expected and unexpected effects of the service? How do clients and others perceive the service? Are there any identifiable phases or patterns in service delivery?

In this chapter, however, qualitative techniques will be discussed in relation to gathering information pertinent to monitoring clients' and social workers' subjective experiences during the treatment implementation and monitoring phase. Such information provides an understanding of how the intervention is experienced both by the recipients and the providers. It may also provide greater understanding of the process of the intervention. The information gathered can then be used to modify and strengthen the intervention and its delivery.

PRINCIPLES FOR QUALITATIVE TECHNIQUES IN TREATMENT MONITORING

Determine the Research Question

Several decisions must be made in relation to the research question. First, social workers should determine the purpose of the study, that is, whether they wish to describe, interpret, or build theory about a particular phenomenon. Quite often, the research question and ensuing study are multipurpose. The next decision is related to the focus of the study. Will the study focus on experiences, processes, or their meaning? Last, a decision must be made about who will be studied. Will the study look at individual clients, families, clinicians, or others?

A research question related to treatment monitoring might be How do first-generation Latino immigrants experience the resettlement services provided by Agency ABC? In the process of describing and interpreting the selected group of clients' experience, the study may also suggest hypotheses about how service could be tailored to improve compliance with the interventions. Or, from the social workers' perspectives, how well are the resettlement services meeting the needs of recent immigrants from Eastern Europe? Again, the results of this study might describe, interpret, or suggest hypotheses.

Determine Data Collection Source and Method

In general, three data collection methods are utilized in qualitative research methods. One method is to assume the role of the *participant-observer*. Described in greater detail by Grigsby (2001), the participant-observer engages in observation of the group being studied by participating in the life of the group. Some participant-observers participate in the role of researcher while others participate more covertly. Data may also be collected from *available records*. Progress notes, clients' journals, minutes from community meetings, or taped therapy sessions are examples of records that may provide enough detail for qualitative analysis. Finally, *in-depth interviewing* is probably the most widely used data collection method for qualitative research on social work clinical practice. Interviews may be implemented with individuals or with small groups of participants in *focus groups.*

Select Sample

Sampling for qualitative research is *purposive*, that is, the researcher selects participants based on their availability and their ability to provide information that is highly relevant to the research question. Because the purpose of qualitative research is to provide depth and breadth of understanding rather than to generalize to all similar cases and situations using inferential statistics, *nonprobability sampling* methods are preferred. This does not mean that the researcher doesn't have to think about how to obtain a sample. On the contrary, the sample should be chosen based on specific characteristics of participants related to the question under study. There are numerous purposive sampling techniques, many of which are reviewed by Rubin and Babbie (2001, pp. 399–403). Three of these, described below, may be useful for social work practice.

Quota sampling, discussed in greater depth in chapter 11, involves selecting cases based on particular characteristics in order to make sure that all relevant information is represented. For example, the workers who want to better understand clients' subjective experience of agency service provision may want to interview clients who have used each of the different types of service offered. Or the workers may want to interview some clients who used the agency before a particular date, when service provision changed dramatically, as well as some who used the agency after that date. The quota would be based entirely on characteristics relevant to the question under study.

Snowball sampling begins by identifying a few participants specifically chosen because of their ability to provide information useful to understanding the research question. These participants are then asked to refer others who would be good informants and who might be willing to participate. For example, a social worker who wants to know about the social service needs of a growing immigrant group in a metro area might begin by identifying a few members of the community through a local church group and then asking those participants to refer others. The worker could continue to add information in this way until a full, deep understanding of the community's needs was reached.

Intensity sampling involves making sure that at least a few participants are included who are involved in the experience under examination at different levels. So the worker interested in clients' subjective experience would be sure to include interviews with some clients who make use of the agency only once a month, on average, as well as some clients who utilize the agency on an almost daily basis. Intensity sampling allows the researcher a wide range of information while helping to maintain homogeneity in the sample.

Determine Data Analysis Method

Data analysis in qualitative research is narrative rather than mathematical. It relies on the use of *inductive* logic, that is, it moves from the use of very specific information to the formation of a generalization about that information. While there are many methods, they all involve immersion in the textual material in order to systematically synthesize and interpret the information that has been gathered. One such method, useful for social work practice, is qualitative content analysis. While this method may seem overly quantitative to some, it can be structured in a step-by-step process that makes use of an inductive method to identify themes, categories, and underlying ideas accessible to practicing social workers.

Interviewing for Data Collection

Interviewing for the purpose of conducting qualitative research may be structured in several ways. At the most highly structured end of the continuum, the interviews may be standardized using open-ended questions. This may be the choice for those who are new to interviewing or in situations when it is important to obtain particular types of information. However, most qualitative research interviewing is structured loosely around themes or issues of interest. The loose structure allows the interviewer to both maintain focus in the interview and follow up on unexpected but relevant subject matter. This type of in-depth interviewing is presented more thoroughly by Goodman (2001), who describes a few general guidelines for developing and implementing them.

Start by informing the respondents about the purpose and expected content of the interview. Not only is this an efficient and polite way to begin such an interview, it is also the ethical way. This initial statement should introduce the topic, clarify how the information will be used, describe protection and limits of confidentiality, explain how the interview will be recorded, and request signed consent to proceed.

Begin the actual interview with a broad question that introduces the topic. For example, "As I said earlier, I am interested in how the services at our agency have been useful to you. Could you tell me what services you have used from our program?"

From this broad question, begin to focus more narrowly on topics of interest. A sample question from an interview guide follows. Note that the topic areas are followed by potential *probes*, or follow-up questions, designed to elicit more detail.

3. English as a second language (ESL) classes
   a. How did you find out about this service?
   b. What was your first impression?
   c. Like/dislike?
   d. Helped/not helped in what ways?
   e. What makes it easy/hard to use?
   f. How would you describe to friend?
   g. Any suggestions to improve the service?

It may not be necessary to use all the probes because some interviewees are more forthcoming than others. In addition, interviewers will need to decide when to follow up on information that is unexpected. For example, if the respondent begins to talk about feelings of inadequacy when attending the program's ESL classes, the interviewer may choose to find out more about this even though there is no specific probe related to affective responses.

Finally, the interview should be recorded. Generally this is done through the use of audio- or videotape. The interviews are then transcribed to computer from the recorded tapes prior to data analysis. While it is essential to record and transcribe interviews, most interviewers also find it crucial to take *field notes* during the interview. The notes may include observations as well as the interviewers' thoughts, insights, or questions that come up during the interview. The handwritten notes should be typewritten as soon as possible after the interview, at which time the interviewer can add details and make clarifications.

Analyze Data

As stated previously, qualitative data analysis involves interpreting narrative data. For qualitative content analysis the process can be divided into four steps. It should be remembered, however, that the process is fluid, and, in reality, the researcher moves back and forth between the steps until a satisfactory conceptualization of the data has been developed. Qualitative researchers often keep a journal nearby to note questions and thoughts as they analyze data.

Identify Themes or Topic Areas

The first step in any qualitative analysis involves reading through the data in order to begin to identify topic areas or themes. The topics may at first be largely descriptive, based on the research question and the interview schedule. However, immersion in the textual data provides an opportunity to identify underlying patterns that may provide a richer understanding. Many patterns have been suggested (Rubin and Babbie, 2001, pp. 413–415). For example, searching for similarities and dissimilarities in the data may help the researcher begin to understand the text in a deeper way. Also, examining the data from a standpoint of curiosity and questioning is helpful. In any case, the themes should provide a framework for meaningful division of the information.

Identify Main Ideas Within Each Theme

Once themes or topic areas have been identified, the next step is to identify the main ideas within each area. This requires rereading the material and assigning each separate idea, as expressed in a phrase or sentence, to a topic area in which it fits. While this may sound relatively simple, it actually requires a great deal of thought. In addition, it often requires modification of the themes. For example, the researcher may find an idea that doesn't fit into any of the existing themes. Or, an idea may seem to fit into several of the themes, indicating that the conceptualization needs to be reconsidered and possibly modified.

Subgroup or Categorize the Ideas

The next step involves examination of the ideas assigned to a particular theme in order to identify potential categories of ideas. For example, perhaps in a study of clients' experience of agency services, the researcher identifies the theme, "Entry into the Agency." Many ideas are contained within this theme. Studying those ideas, the researcher identifies expressions of varying comfort levels about making the first contact with the agency. "Level of comfort" could then become a category of ideas within the topic of "entry into the agency." Again at this step, the researcher may decide to make modifications to an earlier one. This is the flexible nature of qualitative data analysis and is an expected part of the process.

Calculate Frequencies or Percentages

Finally, if the analysis is part of a qualitiative content analysis study, the number of individual cases that contributed an idea to a category and theme should be counted. For example, in the example above, the researcher would count how many interviews (cases) included a comment related to comfort level when starting at the agency. This could be refined further if the researcher determined how many of the interviewees expressed comfort, discomfort, or both.

Procedures to Increase Reliability and Validity

Standards for judging the worth of research studies involve the concepts of *reliability*, that is, consistency of measurement and ability to replicate findings, and *validity*, accuracy of measurement and ability to generalize findings. In qualitiative research, however, due to the subjective nature of the process, reliability and validity are defined differently from their definitions in quantitative research. Instead, reliability refers to whether similar themes and categories were constructed by more than one person involved in the study or if a similar construction would emerge from others not involved in the study using the same data. Validity refers to whether the findings actually represent the "truth" of the experience under study and whether the method and descriptions allow others to transfer the findings to other similar cases.

In spite of modified definitions, some qualitative researchers do not use the terms *reliability* and *validity* at all, preferring to ask instead whether their work is *dependable* and *trustworthy*. Several references in the selected bibliography furnish detailed procedures commonly used to increase the dependability and trustworthiness of qualitative research (e.g., Anastas, 2004; Oktay, 2002; Shek, Tang, and Han, 2005; Franklin and Ballan, 2001; and Padgett, 1998). A few of those procedures will be described briefly here. It should be noted that not all of them are used in every study. In addition, although they are presented here after selection of method and data analysis, their use should be considered in the planning stage of the study.

- *Explication of personal bias* is important in qualitative research because of the subjective nature of the process. The social workers involved in such a study should clearly state their personal interest and preconceptions about the research question and potential findings. In addition, the relationship between researcher and participants should be described in terms of its potential effect on the interviewing process. While it is not expected that personal bias will be eliminated, it should at least be described.

- *Documentation of methods* refers to the importance of carefully recording the procedures used in the study. Starting with conceptualization of the research question, memos related to procedural decisions should be kept and organized in such a fashion that the method can be clearly documented. This documentation should include information about the rationale for the sample selection, data collection procedures, and data analysis procedures.

- *Cross-checking* involves the use of more than one researcher to analyze the data independently of one another. This may be done with some or all of the data, using a second analyst who is an integral part of the study or one who is involved only as a cross-checker. The results are then compared for similarities in the way that they are interpreting the data. Often discussion of the comparisons is then used to modify definitions of constructs and to improve reliability of continued analysis. In other cases researchers discuss their differences until they arrive at consensus.

- *Audit trails* are records that detail the path of the results to the data itself. Audit trails may document the process as well as the development of particular concepts, providing for the possibility of checking to see if procedures were justified and if the conclusions fairly capture the data. Field notes, memos, transcripts, and journals are sources of information that can be used for audit trails.

- *Triangulation* refers to any of several ways of collecting data from multiple sources or methods to increase the validity of the conclusions drawn from the data. For example, data may be collected using two or more methods, such as interviews and standardized instrument. Other techniques include using more than one interviewer, using more than one analyst, each of whom have differing perspectives of that being studied, or using more than one source of data, such as interviews and available records.

- *Peer debriefing* involves discussing data collection and analysis with trusted colleagues who are not intimately involved in the project. This allows the researcher to hear new perspectives about the data as well as to check for ways in which personal bias may be affecting the research process.

- *Member checking* involves asking participants for their views of the interpretation of the information gathered. It is important to know if participants think that the essence of their experience has been captured by the researcher's conclusions.

- *Negative evidence* refers to carefully considering how the information from cases that are different from others fits into the conceptual interpretation of the data. In some situations this may involve adding participants until questions are resolved and an interpretation emerges that accounts for all of the information gathered.

Write Report

One of the biggest challenges in writing a report based on qualitative study is to provide enough detail that the method and results are communicated well while keeping the report at a reasonable length. The parts of a report, described in greater detail in chapter 14, include an abstract or summary, literature review, methods section, and discussion or implications section. The literature review must present a summary of background literature related to the topic of study as well as a well-defined research question that is suitable for qualitative examination. In addition, due to the subjectivity involved in qualitative method and analysis, the literature review should include a description of the researchers' interest and potential bias related to the question.

The methods section must provide enough detail that readers can understand the research process including selection of the sample, data collection procedures, and data analysis techniques. This includes not only a statement about the type of method or analysis utilized but also details about the actual steps that were taken. The use of field notes, or any other procedures to increase the dependability and trustworthiness of the findings, should be described.

The results section may take the form of a narrative description of participants; identification of themes, categories, and ideas; or hypotheses about relationships between the identified concepts. Whatever the form, care should be taken to include original data, that is, quotes from participants both to illustrate the concepts and to deepen the readers' understanding of the findings. Due to the length of qualitative results sections, they must be organized to aid the readers' understanding. The use of subheadings is often useful in this respect.

The discussion section of a qualitative report should relate the new findings to the background information discussed in the literature review. In addition, limitations of the current study and ideas for future research should be described. Perhaps more important in a practice setting, specific implications about practice related to the original research question should be proposed. The researcher, however, should keep in mind that the implications should be directly related to the data in order to avoid overreaching the study results and moving into speculation. Well supported implications may then be considered for modifying practice or policy.

QUALITATIVE TECHNIQUES IN ACTION

Social workers from an employee assistance program (EAP) provide counseling and other supports to people who have been laid off from jobs because of company mergers. Part of the program involves requesting clients to keep a log that includes listing their behaviors related to job training or seeking and at least briefly examining their thoughts and feelings about the process. One client, who had been making steady progress toward a new career until a few weeks ago, suddenly and inexplicably stopped moving forward with the training. In an effort to help the client as well as the worker gain insight into the situation, the clinician asked the client for permission to "analyze" the process part of her log. In addition, the worker spent time focusing on the client's thoughts and feelings about the process in the next interview, after which she wrote detailed process notes. The social worker hoped that a qualitative analysis of the process log and notes from the session would illuminate the situation.

Determine research question

The social worker decided that the focus of the analysis simply should be an examination of the client's thoughts and feelings about the experience of retraining for a new career.

Determine data collection source and method

In this case the data source will be process notes of an unstructured in-depth interview and the client's log entries. The data collected is both multimethod and multisource.

Select sample

Since the process part of the log and session notes are not of extreme length, the social worker decides to use all the data from both. It is a purposive sample in that the worker selected data that would most logically provide information relevant to the question of interest.

Select data analysis method

The worker decides to use a modified analysis of latent content. The worker is interested in discovering themes or ideas that may increase understanding of the client's experience of job retraining. The number of times that concepts appear in the log or session notes is not important to the worker.

Interviewing for data collection

The worker does not create a detailed interview guide but has a few questions in mind to keep the focus of the interview on the client's experience of job training and seeking over the time that the client has been involved with the EAP. Immediately after the session, the worker writes detailed process notes.

Analyze data

The worker discovers several themes in the data, including the client's fluctuating level of hope about her future career. Another theme focuses on her perception of support from the social worker through the EAP, a close friend who experienced a similar layoff, and her young adult children. In particular, the worker notices what seems to be a downward shift in the client's level of hope soon after one of her children moved back home upon completion of a graduate degree.

Reliability and validity

Dependability and trustworthiness of the worker's findings is increased in several ways. First, through the use of two sources of data and two methods for its collection, the worker has used the technique of triangulation. In addition, after receiving permission from the client, the worker asks a colleague to read over the log and process notes in order to share ideas about identifiable themes or concepts, thus engaging in cross-checking. Finally, the worker shares her ideas with the client, a form of member checking.

Write and utilize report

In this case the worker feels no need to write a formal report. Instead she shares her new insights with the client, fostering further discussion to explore the meaning of the daughter's return home in relation to the client's hope about career development.

EXERCISES

1. Base these exercises on the example above.
   a. Write a few questions or comments that could help guide an in-depth interview with the client.

b. Describe other methods than those mentioned for increasing the trustworthiness and dependability of the worker's findings.

c. If written as a formal report, are the results of this study important to share with other social workers? Why or why not? How would you strengthen the study if you planned to publish the report?

2. Think of a question related to your practice, either with one client or a group of clients, that could be examined using qualitative methods.

a. Describe how you would go about implementing such a study using the first four steps above.

b. If possible, carry out your design on a limited basis using the final four steps above. Collect a small amount of data and analyze it to identify themes.

SELECTED BIBLIOGRAPHY

Anastas, J. 2004. Quality in qualitative evaluation: Issues and possible answers. *Research on Social Work Practice, 14,* 57–65.

Denzin, N. K., and Lincoln, Y. S. (eds.) 2000. *Handbook of qualitative research.* Thousand Oaks, CA: Sage.

Fetterman, D. M. 1998. *Ethnography.* Thousand Oaks, CA: Sage.

Franklin, C., and Ballan, M. 2001. Reliability and validity in qualitative research. In B. A. Thyer (ed.), *Handbook of social work research methods,* pp. 273–292. Thousand Oaks, CA: Sage.

Gilgun, J. 1994. A case for case studies in social work research. *Social Work, 39,* 371–380.

Glaser, B., and Strauss, A. 1967. *The discovery of grounded theory: Strategies for qualitative research.* Chicago: Aldine.

Goodman, H. 2001. In-depth interviews. In B. A. Thyer (ed.) *Handbook of social work research methods,* pp. 309–319. Thousand Oaks, CA: Sage.

Grigsby, R. K. 2001. Participant observation. In B. A. Thyer (ed.), *Handbook of social work research methods,* pp. 333–343. Thousand Oaks, CA: Sage.

Huberman, A. M., and Miles, M. B. 1994. *Qualitative data analysis: An expanded sourcebook.* Thousand Oaks, CA: Sage.

Lofland, J., and Lofland, L. 1995. *Analyzing social settings.* 3d ed. Belmont, CA: Wadsworth.

Lowery, C. T. 2001. Ethnographic research methods. In B. A. Thyer (ed.), *Handbook of social work research methods,* pp. 321–332. Thousand Oaks, CA: Sage.

Oktay, J. S. 2002. Standards for qualitative research with exemplars. In *Social worker's desk reference,* pp. 781–786. New York: Oxford University Press.

Padgett, D. K. 1998. *Qualitative methods in social work research.* Thousand Oaks, CA: Sage.

Rubin, A., and Babbie, E. 2001. *Research methods for social work.* 4th ed. Belmont, CA: Wadsworth.

Shek, D. T. L., Tang, V. M. Y., and Han, X. Y. 2005. Evaluation of evaluation studies using qualitative research methods in the social work literature, (1990–2003): Evidence that constitutes a wake-up call. *Research on Social Work Practice, 15,* 180–194.

Straus, A., and Corbin, J. 1998. *Basics of qualitative research: Techniques and procedures for developing grounded theory.* 2d ed. Thousand Oaks, CA: Sage.

Evaluating Treatment   PART 3

Treatment evaluation is the third and final phase of clinical social work practice. It is the process by which treatment effectiveness and efficiency are assessed. In other words, treatment evaluation is necessary to determine whether treatment goals have been attained and at what cost. Moreover, treatment evaluation provides information that enables the clinical social worker to decide whether to continue, modify, or terminate treatment. Finally, treatment evaluation provides information about the efficacy of specific treatment strategies.

Treatment evaluation is one of the two basic foci of evaluation in social agencies or other practice settings. One focus, program evaluation, concentrates on the practice setting itself and attempts to evaluate the effectiveness and efficiency of whole programs. Treatment evaluation, on the other hand, focuses on evaluating the effectiveness and efficiency of a single social worker with a single client, family, or group. Program evaluation and treatment evaluation coincide, however, when the results of the work of more than one social worker, or treatment outcomes with more than one client unit, are aggregated and analyzed. Such aggregation of findings is only appropriate when treatment objectives and treatment strategies are the same for each social worker and client unit.

Within each level of evaluation a further distinction can be made between formative and summative evaluation. Formative evaluation involves the feedback of results within a program or for a client while the program or client treatment is ongoing. This information does not permit generalization of findings beyond that particular program or client unit. It does, however, permit program administrators or clinical social workers to make changes in the program or treatment plan.

Alternatively, summative evaluation provides information for feedback after a program or treatment cycle has been completed. While it permits generalization of findings beyond a particular program or client unit, what is learned from it must wait for a new program or client unit to be applied to practice. Thus summative evaluation provides more certainty about the causal links between intervention and outcome but less immediate applicability to practice.

In part 3 we emphasize formative evaluation of individual treatment units. This evaluation approach can be used by individual clinicians for assessing their own effectiveness with individual clients or with aggregates of their clients or client groups. Other resources listed here in the bibliography provide information about formative program evaluation.

Treatment evaluation can also be seen as a continuation of treatment monitoring. By providing valid and reliable information about treatment outcomes, the connections between treatment interventions and their effects can be clarified. Hence treatment evaluation can be located on a continuum of research activities between treatment monitoring and program evaluation.

TASKS

Treatment evaluation requires that the clinical social worker accomplish a number of practice-related tasks and make a number of decisions.

First, treatment strategies must be specified. Treatment evaluation makes sense only if the actual treatment that has taken place can be systematically described. This is true whether the intended treatment has been implemented as planned or if the plan was altered and another form of treatment has occurred instead. Careful treatment monitoring will help to provide accurate descriptions of interventions. In addition, for the purpose of monitoring and evaluation, it is helpful to indicate a time frame within which treatment objectives are to be achieved. This helps the task of evaluation considerably by indicating when systematic evaluation should take place. Accordingly, despite our heuristic distinction between treatment monitoring and treatment evaluation, the two are inextricably linked in practice.

Next, treatment objectives must be operationally defined, that is, translated into measurable terms by means of qualitative or quantitative evidence. This procedure should have been started in the assessment phase and continued in the monitoring phase for the purpose of collecting information about client progress. Specification of goals and objectives for treatment has been discussed in detail in chapter 5.

The measurement of operationally defined objectives continues through all three phases of treatment, but treatment evaluation most frequently takes place during the termination phase or, sometimes, after treatment has been terminated. For example, some treatment evaluation designs require that "outcome measures" be taken before treatment has begun and after it has been terminated. Another consideration is that not all variables will demonstrate change during the implementation phase of treatment, making it important to conduct evaluation in or after the final phase of treatment. Here, again, the connection between treatment monitoring and evaluation is very clear.

Once treatment objectives are operationally defined, evaluation objectives should be determined. Thus the purpose of the evaluation should be specified and the information necessary to achieve this purpose should be delineated. Evaluation objectives may be broadly or narrowly focused. A comprehensive evaluation would focus broadly on the extent to which numerous treatment objectives have been achieved, the relationships between treatment intervention and these objectives, the relationships between the objectives, and possibly the efficiency of the treatment. Alternatively, evaluation may focus more narrowly on the achievement of a particular, highly specific treatment objective.

Another component of evaluation objectives is the level of knowledge to be achieved. As discussed in chapter 5, research knowledge exists on four levels: hypothetical, descriptive, correlational, and cause-effect. In the context of treatment evaluation objectives, hypothetical knowledge would involve generation of hypotheses about the relationships between specific treatment interventions and outcomes. This is the least certain level of knowledge. Descriptive knowledge simply describes treatment outcomes without asserting a connection between the treatment interventions and these outcomes. Correlational knowledge demonstrates a relationship between interventions and outcome but does not firmly establish that one causes the other. Finally, cause-effect knowledge establishes the causal connection between intervention and client outcome. In so doing, it rules out other possible explanations for client improvement. As a result, it is the most certain form of knowledge.

The level of knowledge desired will determine the kind of evaluation design and methodology that is most appropriate. The next task, then, is to select an evaluation design and methodology that is likely to produce the level of knowledge required. The more certainty desired, the more comprehensive, time-consuming, and costly the evaluation is likely to be. Moreover, cause-effect knowledge requires rigorous experimental designs that frequently have serious ethical limitations. Therefore, formative treatment evaluation designs seek to maximize the level of knowledge produced while weighing the cost, available resources, and ethical limits.

Once the design and methodology have been chosen, the evaluation is implemented. This involves collecting and processing information from such devices as forms, observational instruments, and questionnaires. This information may be collected prior to and throughout the treatment process or only after treatment has been completed. The evaluation design will determine when the information is to be collected.

Next, the information must be analyzed in relation to the evaluation and treatment objectives. Based on this analysis, the clinician can decide whether there is evidence indicating that the treatment objectives have been fully, partially, or minimally attained. In some cases, in fact, the client's condition may have deteriorated.

Finally, the information must be used to decide whether treatment should be terminated, continued, or modified. If the treatment goals have been achieved, treatment may be terminated, with a follow-up contact with the client to determine whether treatment gains have been maintained. If treatment goals have been partially attained, treatment may be continued or modified in a new cycle of treatment. If there has been no improvement, or if the client seems to have deteriorated, the use of an alternative treatment strategy, a different clinician, a referral to another agency, or a clinical consultation should be considered.

TREATMENT EVALUATION DECISIONS

Clinical social workers need to make a number of important decisions in evaluating the effectiveness and/or efficacy of their treatment. Those decisions are implied within each of the foregoing tasks, but they can be specified by indicating some of the questions the clinical social worker should ask during this final phase of practice. Moreover, since clinical practice is a dynamic process, the questions are related to questions raised during diagnostic assessment, treatment formulation, and treatment monitoring. Some of these questions are as follows:

1. Are treatment objectives achieved? If so, to what extent? If not, why not? Were the objectives realistic for the client?

2. Was the treatment appropriate for the client? Should the treatment be modified? Should the clinician employ a different strategy?

3. Should the evaluation be reinstituted at some point in the future? Were the evaluation methodology and design appropriate for measuring treatment objectives?

4. If treatment objectives have been reached, is there evidence to indicate that the client will be able to maintain these gains without the clinician's continued involvement and intervention?

5. If treatment objectives have not been reached, should a consultation be sought? Should the client be referred to another social worker or to another agency?

6. Have appropriate measures been taken for client termination, referral, or continuation? Is the client agreeable to such action?

7. Has any knowledge been gained with this client that might be useful in working with other clients?

DIVERSITY AND ETHICAL CONSIDERATIONS

As in the previous phases of social work practice, ethical and diversity issues must be considered in tasks related to treatment evaluation. Relevant diversity issues are summarized in the following table. As discussed earlier, it is important that clinicians collaborate with their clients to determine treatment strategies and objectives that are compatible with clients' worldviews. This is just as important in evaluation as it is in the assessment phase; objectives and strategies that are not compatible will not likely result in measurable progress. Concerning the objectives of the evaluation, evaluation of practice with members of minority groups may be especially vital, particularly if

Diversity Issues in the Evaluation Phase

Task	Issue
Treatment strategies and objectives	Culturally compatible strategies and objectives
Evaluation objectives	Evaluating specific interventions with groups of people for whom effectiveness is unknown.
Design and methodology	Culturally compatible design and method.

the effectiveness of an intervention is untested or unknown. In such cases the information may be valuable, not just for the client at hand but also for other similar clients. Practitioners who have secured such information about practice effectiveness with particular groups of people can be of service to other clinicians by reporting their findings. In addition, the design and methodology of practice evaluations must be acceptable to clients, regardless of their gender, ethnicity, or level of ability.

Ethical issues that are relevant in the evaluation phase of social work practice are summarized in the next table. Concerning evaluation objectives, clinicians must be aware of their twofold responsibilities in this area. First, clinicians are responsible for evaluating their own practice for the sake of their clients. Second, and less often discussed, is the clinician's responsibility to contribute to the body of knowledge used to inform practice. While the idea of publishing a journal article may seem daunting, some clinicians contribute in this way. In addition, though, there are other ways to contribute knowledge developed through systematic evaluation of practice. For example, clinician's may share information with each other through peer supervision, in-service learning, or workshops. The purpose of collecting evaluation data must also be considered for the use of *informed consent*. Clients have the right to know exactly what data will be collected, for what purpose, and how data will be used. In addition, clients have the right to withdraw from research or evaluation procedures with no fear of penalty or loss of service.

Next, concerning design and methodology, clinicians are charged with the responsibility to do no harm either through the provision of an intervention or in the method of collecting evaluation data. For example, in some cases clients might be harmed with a research design that required a long baseline period before initiation of treatment. Another ethical concern, related to data collected during evaluation, is confidentiality. Clinicians must know how the clients' information will be safeguarded for privacy. A discussion of confidentiality with the client should always include an explanation of the limits of the clinician's ability to provide privacy.

Finally, the clinician is sometimes faced with ethical dilemmas related to resource allocation when it is time to make decisions, based on information derived from evaluation, about termination or further intervention. Current managed care organizations, other third-party payment systems, or agency policies often restrict availability of services. Consequently, this may place the clinician in an ethical bind when evaluation data indicate clients' needs for which there is inadequate availability of services.

Ethical Issues in the Evaluation Phase

Task	Issue
Evaluation Objectives	Responsibility for evaluating and researching practice. Informed consent.
Design and Methodology	Responsibility to do no harm.
Data Analysis, Use, & Storage	Confidentiality and its limits.
Use of Information in Decision-Making	Potential conflict between clinical needs and restrictions due to agency or 3rd party payment system.

RESEARCH CONCEPTS AND TECHNIQUES

As we implied earlier, for the purposes of treatment evaluation, all of the data-gathering devices that we have described in previous chapters can be used. Thus treatment evaluation data can come from standardized interviews, rating scales, systematic observation, monitoring forms, and qualitative or quantitative analysis of data from focus groups and records.

In part 3 we present some additional data-gathering and analyzing procedures. These are applied to evaluating the effectiveness of clinical interventions. We believe that the selected research concepts and techniques can be easily used by clinical social workers of different theoretical persuasions and with limited research background.

Single subject design, useful in both treatment and program evaluation, is discussed in chapter 9. In discussion of these designs, we indicate criteria for determining the extent to which the knowledge they generate is correlational or cause-effect.

Chapter 10 describes three single-subject designs that originated in behavior modification but can be employed to measure effectiveness of other intervention strategies as well. The advantages and limitations of these designs for evaluation of clinical practices are described.

In chapter 11 we discuss procedures for conducting follow-up surveys of client progress or client satisfaction. Several types of evaluations are considered, including face-to face or telephone interviews as well as mailed survey. In this context concepts and techniques of survey sampling are also discussed.

Simple group designs useful for program and practice evaluation are the topic of chapter 12. Along with describing procedures for conducting evaluations using pre-post test designs, threats to the validity of research findings related to pre-post designs are examined.

Chapter 13 concerns techniques of aggregating and analyzing data, from practice monitoring or evaluation, collected in a number of comparable cases. This set of techniques makes generalization possible across cases and across clinicians. Such generalizations can provide important information about the kinds of clients with whom particular techniques are most effective.

Finally, in chapter 14, we provide a wrap-up with a discussion of the use of research by social work practitioners, both for informing practice and for developing the social work knowledge base. The procedure of "clinical data mining" is described, along with a brief guide for writing reports about practice-based research.

SELECTED BIBLIOGRAPHY

Conrad, A. P. 1988. Ethical considerations in the psychosocial process. *Social Case-work, 69*, 603–610.

Dudley, J. R. 2005. *Research methods for social work: becoming consumers and producers of research.* Boston: Allyn and Bacon.

Lum, D. 2005. *Cultural competence, practice stages, and client systems: A case study approach.* Belmont, CA: Thomson/Brooks/Cole.

Manoleas, P. 1994. An outcome approach to assessing the cultural competence of MSW students. *Journal of Multicultural Social Work, 3*, 43–57.

Martin, J. I., and Meezan, W. 2003. Applying ethical standards to research and evaluations involving lesbian, gay, bisexual, and transgender populations. *Journal of Gay and Lesbian Social Services, 15*, 181–201.

Nelson, J. C. 1994. Ethics, gender, and ethnicity in single-case research and evaluation. *Journal of Social Service Research, 18*, 139–152.

Sheafor, B. W., and Horesjsi, C. R. 2003. *Techniques and Guidelines for Social Work Practice.* 6th ed. Boston: Allyn and Bacon.

Tripodi, T. 1994. A primer on single-subject design for clinical social workers. Washington, DC: National Association of Social Workers.

Weinbach, R. W. 2005. *Evaluating social work services and programs.* Boston: Allyn and Bacon.

Single-case design has been used frequently in all three phases of social work practice: assessment, intervention, and evaluation. Also referred to as single-subject designs, they are often used to evaluate a single client's progress from assessment through intervention and into follow-up. In addition, however, single-case designs can be used to evaluate progress of a single unit that is comprised of more than one individual. For example, the progress of a family's use of communication skills or a specified group's use of a new community resource may be evaluated with single-case design.

In a simple single-case design a series of measurements is made, before intervention begins, on a variable that the intervention is intended to influence. These measurements serve as a *baseline* against which measurements taken during and after the intervention are compared. Next, a series of measurements is taken during *intervention*. This series indicates the rate of improvement for the client who is receiving treatment and, possibly, the point at which treatment no longer seems to be having a beneficial effect. An additional series of *follow-up* measurements may be taken after treatment has terminated to indicate whether the beneficial effects of treatment are lasting. Visual or statistical analysis of the measurements is utilized to inform the practitioner about the client's functioning on the selected variable in each of the phases.

There are many types of single-case designs, ranging from those that are very simple to those that are more complex. The type described above can be referred to as an ABA design; where A represents measurements taken when no intervention is taking place and B represents measurements taken during the intervention phase. An extremely simple single-case design, the A design, involves a series of baseline measurements that may be used to demonstrate a growing, stable, or diminishing need for a particular social work intervention. The B design consists of measurements taken only during intervention and may be used to demonstrate the client's progress, or lack thereof, on a selected outcome while working with the clinician. The ABAB design is an example of a more complex design. It involves a baseline, followed by intervention, then withdrawal of intervention, and reestablishment of intervention. The ABAB design is one of several discussed in greater depth in chapter 10.

The design of the single-case study determines the type of knowledge produced. For example, in both A and B designs the information produced is purely descriptive. The ABA design also produces *descriptions* of the occurrence of the variable during baseline, intervention, and follow-up phases. In addition, however, the ABA design may also produce *associational knowledge* if a clear change in the occurrence of the variable can be demonstrated from baseline to intervention. Single-case designs may also be used to produce *causal knowledge*. However, the designs needed for this are more complex in order to provide assurance that the change in the variable can be attributed to the social work intervention.

Such assurance involves assessment of the *threats* to the *internal validity* of evaluation results, due primarily to evaluation design. Although this was discussed briefly in chapter 5, it is worthy of further consideration here because of its importance in planning for evaluation of practice. In their classic monograph, *Experimental and Quasi-Experimental Designs for Research*, Campbell and Stanley (1963) identified eight factors that can jeopardize the validity of the findings of a research study. Applied to treatment evaluation, these are 1. contemporary history—unanticipated events may occur while treatment is underway that change the character of the intervention, the client, or the client's situation; 2. maturation—during the course of treatment, clients may change simply as a function of time, developmental growth, or fatigue; 3. initial measurement effects—the process of measurement itself might affect client outcomes; 4. instrumentation—unreliability over time due to lack of standardization of the measure of effectiveness used; 5. statistical regression—the tendency of individuals or groups chosen for treatment on the basis of extreme scores on some measure of pathology or need tend to "naturally" regress to a more average score in subsequent testing regardless of the effects of treatment; 6. selection—differences among individuals receiving treatment can yield misleading generalizations concerning the effects of treatment; 7. subject mortality—certain types of individuals may drop out of treatment in disproportionate numbers, creating misleading generalizations based on those who remain; and 8. interaction effects—the combined effects of any and all of the above factors may be mistaken for the effects of treatment. These threats to validity are relevant to single-case design as well as group designs discussed in chapters 11 and 12.

The ABA single-case design does not then control for all threats to internal validity to which Campbell and Stanley referred. Nor does it produce knowledge that is indisputably causal about the effect of treatment intervention. In addition, it does not produce findings that are immediately generalizable to other clients. In spite of these shortcomings, the relatively simple ABA design can generate knowledge that is highly informative about the relationship of the intervention to change in the client from one phase to the next. Moreover, such information can be aggregated with other single-case evaluation data based on comparable interventions with comparable clients to provide evaluation information about client groups. Thus, even simple single-case designs are useful for practice evaluation, both for individual clients and for program evaluation.

SINGLE-CASE DESIGNS AND CLINICAL PRACTICE

Single-case designs provide systematic data concerning each phase of clinical social work practice. Such data may be generated through the use of forms, observational techniques, questionnaires, interviews, standardized instruments, and other types of data collection procedures. The data gatherer can be the client, the clinician, or significant others.

In situations where direct measurement is likely to be too intrusive or obstructive of treatment, data may be taken from agency records. For example, schools routinely keep records on attendance, grades, and disciplinary actions for all students. Social agency case records often contain repeated indications of client's social, psychological, and economic situations. These unobtrusive measures can also serve as the basis for a series of measurements before, during, and after treatment intervention.

In this chapter the principles for implementing single-case designs are discussed. In this context, simple graphing and statistical techniques are described, which indicate whether client change observed during and after treatment is statically significant. Single-case designs can be embellished in a number of ways to add to the refinement of the knowledge they produce. Some of these design refinements are discussed in the next chapter.

PRINCIPLES FOR IMPLEMENTING SINGLE-CASE DESIGNS

Specifying Treatment Objectives

As with every other treatment evaluation design, single-case designs begin with specification of treatment objectives. The difference between single-case designs and some of those discussed in subsequent chapters, however, is that in the former it is necessary to begin taking measurements on these objectives before treatment begins. As a result, the specification and operationalization of treatment objectives must occur early in the clinical process. Thus, single-case designs are best suited to treatment situations in which desired client outcomes are easily identifiable and measurable, such as in weight or smoking reduction, improving school attendance, or decreasing depression as measured with a rapid assessment instrument.

Operationally Defining Treatment Objectives

In single-case designs, as with other treatment evaluation designs, treatment objectives should be operationally defined in a manner that is consistent with the client's understanding of them. This is particularly important when the client is the data collector. When the data are drawn from records, the clinician must rely on the categories of information already available. Since this information was probably collected for other purposes, considerable ingenuity must be used sometimes to fit the categories of information that are available to the objectives of treatment.

As with other evaluation designs, measurement scales can be nominal, ordinal, or interval and should be subjected to tests of measurement reliability and validity as discussed in chapters 2 and 5. However, for a single-case design it is especially important that measures of treatment effectiveness have high test-retest reliability (a correlation of at least .80) since the research design requires repeated use of the same measures. If test-retest reliability is low, it is impossible to determine whether fluctuations on the outcome measures are reflective of the effect of the treatment intervention or of the instability of the measuring device.

Specifying the Treatment Strategy

Once treatment objectives have been delineated and operationally defined, the treatment intervention should be specified. A complete and behaviorally specific description of the intervention strategy is necessary for monitoring whether the client is, in fact, receiving the intended intervention. Without this it would be improper to infer that a particular intervention strategy was more or less effective. In other words, in order to test effectiveness of treatment one must first determine that the client has received it.

Such specification of the treatment is also necessary if one intends to aggregate those cases that have been treated by a single social worker and/or cases that have been treated by more than one worker. Aggregation requires comparable treatment means as well as comparable treatment objectives. Although single-case designs work best when the treatment intervention can be standardized from session to session, from client to client, and from clinician to clinician; the design is still useful for unique intervention situations.

Specification of the intervention strategy is also important in evaluating forms of treatment based on previous single-case studies. A new intervention may be shown to be much more effective than a previous approach, but if no effort is made to rigorously specify what the social worker did, the study is useless for describing and communicating the treatment innovation to others.

Taking Baseline Measurements

Before diagnostic assessment and intervention implementation, five or six measurements should be taken on the scales being used to assess client problems or treatment effectiveness. Such measures, taken at regular intervals before treatment begins, are called baseline measures. So, for example, following an assessment interview with a depressed patient in an agency or practice, the social worker may ask the client to complete a rapid assessment instrument at a specified time three specific days a week prior to initiating treatment. After the initiation of an intervention, the measures of depression would be recorded on the same schedule for the duration of treatment. After treatment, a follow-up evaluation would use the same measurement schedule for determining whether treatment gains appear to persist.

Under certain circumstances treatment begins with the first contact between client and social worker, and the foregoing mode of producing a baseline may be impossible. In these instances it may be possible to construct a baseline from records already available within the agency (for example, attendance records, medical reports, and parole reports, among others). Another possibility is to interview significant others in the client's environment to get an approximation of the frequency of problematic client behaviors, attitudes, or moods.

When it is possible to construct a baseline directly, an important consideration is when repeat measures should be taken. Unfortunately, there is no simple formula for this. Here, again, issues of validity, reliability, feasibility and cost enter in. It is a matter of judgment that depends on the variable to be measured, the intrusiveness of the measures, and the context within which measurement takes place. To monitor weight loss, weekly measures may suffice. For determining progress in resolving parent-child difficulties, daily measures of parent-child conflict may be necessary. Whatever the measurement interval, however, it is essential that baseline measures be taken at regular intervals and that the same intervals are used for measurement during and after treatment. This standardization of the application of the research instrument reduces the possibility that fluctuation in client scores are the consequence of different testing conditions.

Graphing the Baseline Data

Ideally, before treatment begins, stability in measures of client problems will have been established. If baseline stability has not been established before treatment begins, natural fluctuations on these measures may be incorrectly interpreted as treatment outcomes. Graphing the baseline data helps to determine whether stability has been established.

A graph is a visual device for describing regularities and irregularities in the data over time. Graphs for use in practice do not need to be complicated. In fact, social workers could easily create and make copies of a basic graph, such as in figure 9.1, that are ready to be completed when needed. In a baseline graph the horizontal axis is used to represent the time intervals between measurements. The vertical axis is used to represent either individual scores for one client or average scores for more than one client. A separate baseline graph should be constructed for each client measure.

Examples of stable baselines are shown in figure 9.2. Stability is established when the line connecting the scores on a particular measure runs parallel to the horizontal axis (9.2a), is not parallel but maintains a constant angle or slope with the horizontal axis (9.2b), or follows a regular and consistent pattern (9.2c).

By visually analyzing the baseline graph the pattern of client scores can be seen to be relatively high or low; increasing, decreasing, or constant; stable, cyclic, or unpredictable. It is important to keep in mind, however, that a graph is only a pictorial representation of client behavior, attitude, or mood over time. And,

Name_____   Treatment Objective_____

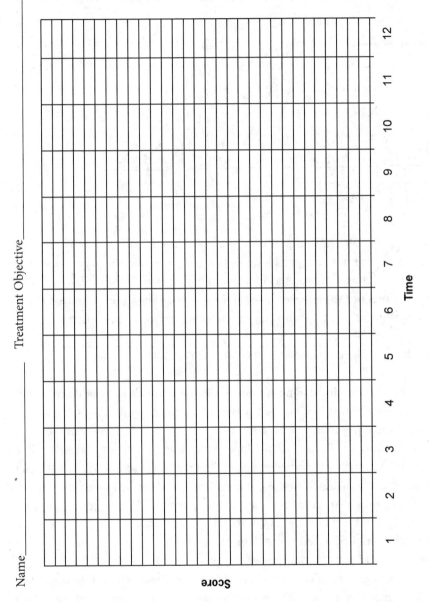

Figure 9.1 Sample Graph for Use in Clinical Practice

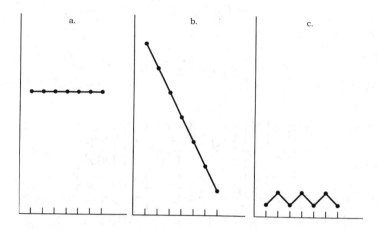

Figure 9.2 Examples of Stable Baselines

by altering the physical properties of the graph itself, stable patterns can look unstable, high scores can look low, and so on. As a consequence, graphs should be constructed and interpreted in a manner that is consistent with common sense and practice experience. Overall, the essence of baseline stability is that it is predictable, not that it is the same from time interval to time interval.

Assessing the Need for and Implementing Intervention

Using the baseline for diagnostic purposes, there are three conditions under which intervention would not be necessary: 1. if the magnitude of the problem or the frequency of its appearance is not great enough to indicate that there is a serious persistent problem; 2. if the slope of the baseline indicates a rapid decline in the problem without treatment; or 3. if group average scores obscure the fact that particular individuals in the group have no need for treatment.

In the first two instances the clinician should decline the request or referral for treatment. In the last instance, only those individuals in need of treatment should be asked to participate. Sorting these individuals out would require examining individual as well as group baselines. If the baseline data indicate that client problems are of a relatively low frequency or intensity, or the problems appear to be decreasing on their own or on the strength of the client's own efforts and resources, treatment might do more harm than good. Thus it might heighten the client's consciousness of a problem and thereby increase its frequency. Alternatively, it may interfere with natural internal coping processes or external support systems from which the client is already benefiting.

Once it has been determined that client problems occur with sufficient frequency or intensity to warrant clinical intervention, treatment should begin. The treatment itself should be consistent with the treatment plan and appropriate to the client's problem. In addition, it should be closely monitored as described in chapters 5 through 8. Treatment monitoring will ensure that the client is receiving the prescribed treatment, at prescribed intervals, in accordance with treatment planning and the treatment contract. Monitoring will also make it possible to determine the frequency and intensity of the intervention that accompanies different degrees of success. When interventions do not appear to be working, reassessment of the client's problem and reformulation of the treatment objectives might be required.

Taking a Series of Measures During Intervention to Evaluate Progress

From the time the intervention begins, a series of measures of client problems or progress should be taken at the same intervals and with the same measures that were used to establish the pretreatment baseline. The purpose of such data is to determine whether progress is being made in relation to the treatment objectives. The use of the same measurement procedures reduces the chances that measured "effects" are the product of random errors in the measurement process and increases the chances that the findings during the treatment phase are truly reflective of client progress. For program evaluations, average scores of all those who received the treatment should be graphed.

Comparing Pretreatment Baseline with Client Progress During the Intervention

The data collected during the intervention phase should then be graphed alongside the baseline data. In this chart the point at which intervention began should be clearly discernible.

After pretreatment and intervention phase data have been graphed, the trend lines can be compared visually, as is shown in figure 9.3. Is there a change in the magnitude of the client scores after intervention begins (9.3a)? Is there a change in the slope of the scores after intervention begins (9.3b)? Is there a change in the pattern of client scores (9.3c)? Is there a continuation of the same trend established prior to intervention (9.3d)?

In the first three graphs of figure 9.3, visual analysis shows a definite change in the client's score during the intervention phase. The fourth graph, however, could give an erroneous impression of change related to intervention. In fact, an inspection of the trend line in figure 9.3d strongly suggests that these outcomes

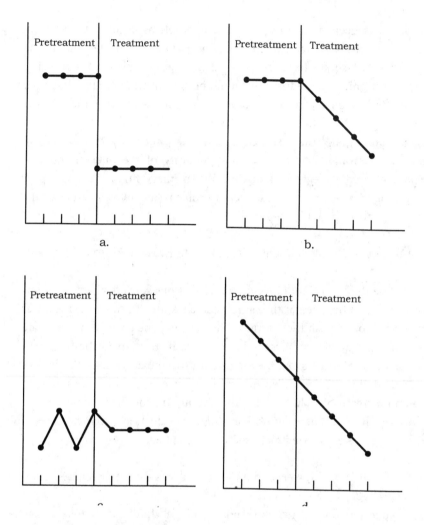

Figure 9.3 Comparing Baseline with Treatment Through Visual Analysis

would have occurred without any intervention at all as a result of factors already present in the baseline phase.

Unfortunately, visual analysis is not always so clear. In fact, often the interpretation of graphs is much more ambiguous. Bloom, Fisher, and Orme (2003) provides eight suggestions (pp. 564–566) for dealing with ambiguous patterns in single-case design graphs.

1. Acknowledging the ambiguity, make the best interpretation possible by seeking small patterns in the data and using all available evidence. This may include

discussion and consideration of events in the client's life outside the intervention as potential explanations for change.

2. Consider extending the phase until the measurements stabilize to the point that a pattern can be detected.

3. Think about modifying the intervention so that more stable, positive results may be produced.

4. Think about and discuss the meaning of the fluctuating measurements with the client. While difficult to interpret, the changes indicated by ambiguous results may be significant to the client.

5. Think about utilizing multiple measures. While intervention may produce ambiguous results on one, it may show a clearer pattern on another.

6. Consider the possibility of and correct for measurement error, including the use of an unreliable instrument and/or variability in measurement conditions.

7. Think about the fluctuating results as they relate theoretically to the client problem and intervention. Often the resolution of problems is nonlinear.

8. Apply more sophisticated visual analysis, such as that described by Nugent (2000).

In addition to visual inspection, tests of statistical significance are sometimes used to analyze single-case designs. If changes are discernible by visual inspection of the graph, confirmation that the changes are not the result of chance variations but are statistically significant can be determined using relatively simple statistical tests. Visually ambiguous results may be clearer as well if analyzed with statistical tests. Statistical significance, discussed more fully in chapter 13, is a mathematical estimate of the probability that the results are due to chance rather than to the intervention. Probability equal to or lower than five percent ($p < .05$) is an acceptable level.

One simple technique for determining whether changes discernible by visual inspection of the graph are not the result of chance variations but statistically significant was originally proposed by Gottman (Gottman and Leiblum, 1974). This technique, called the *two-standard-deviation procedure,* is only useful, however, when the data collected after intervention began do not indicate a continuation of the same trend line established prior to intervention. For example, the findings in figure 9.3d could not be analyzed with this method because of the clear trend line continuing from pre- to postintervention. The two-standard-deviation procedure also rests on the assumption that the measurements taken at each interval are not influenced by previous measurements—that is, they are independent of each other—and that measurements are taken at randomly selected times. Since neither criterion is likely to be met in a single-case study, our use of this technique yields only an approximation to statistical significance.

To illustrate the two-standard-deviation procedure, consider the following example. A clinician would like to systematically evaluate a new approach to counseling anorexic clients and their families. The goal is to stabilize a given client's weight twenty pounds higher than it was when counseling began. Figure 9.4 represents the client's weight taken at weekly intervals before and during treatment.

Visual inspection of the graph shown in figure 9.4 reveals a fluctuating pretreatment pattern and an overall increase in the clients' weight after counseling began. In addition, there is some indication of weight stabilization

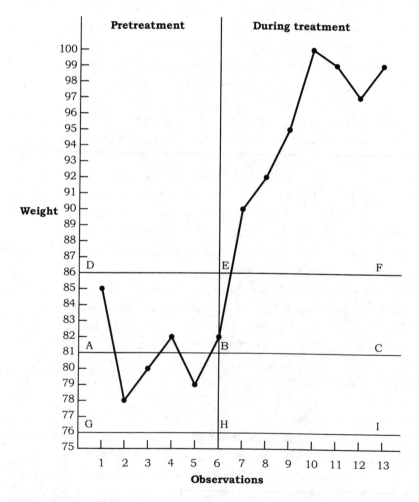

Figure 9.4 Two-Standard-Deviation Procedure

in the last four weeks of treatment. To determine whether the client's progress is statistically significant: 1. calculate the mean for the baseline data; 2. draw a line parallel to the horizontal axis representing the mean for the baseline data; 3. calculate the standard deviation for the baseline data; 4. multiply the standard deviation by 2; 5. add this figure to the mean; 6. subtract this figure from the mean; 7. draw lines parallel to the horizontal axis, two standard deviations above and below the mean. If the measures taken during treatment fall outside these lines, it strongly suggests that the client's progress is statistically significant at the .05 level of probability. Finally, a determination should be made as to whether the statistically significant results are in the desired direction. Thus they may indicate a statically significant loss of weight during treatment. This, of course, would be an undesired outcome of the intervention.

Following the foregoing instructions in our example, we calculate the arithmetic mean of the baseline data ($\bar{M}$) by taking the sum of the weekly pretreatment weights and dividing by the total number of weeks prior to intervention.

$$\bar{M} = \frac{85 + 78 + 80 + 82 + 79 + 82}{6}$$

$$\bar{M} = 81$$

Line ABC in figure 9.4 represents the mean of the baseline data.

To calculate the standard deviation (SD) of the baseline mean, we take the square root of the sum of the differences between each baseline measure and the baseline mean, square it, and divide by the total number of baseline measurements taken, minus one. Expressed as a formula, this is:

$$SD = \sqrt{\sum \frac{(each\ baseline\ measurement\ -\ baseline\ mean)^2}{total\ number\ of\ baseline\ measurements\ -\ 1}}$$

Substituting the baseline data in the formula, we get:

$$SD = \sqrt{\sum \frac{(85-81)^2 + (78-81)^2 + (80-81)^2 + (82-81)^2 + (79-81)^2 + (82-81)^2}{6-1}}$$

$$SD = 2.5$$

We then multiply the standard deviation by 2:

$$2\ SD = 5.0$$

Adding this to the mean gives us:

81 + 5 + 86 = 2 standard deviations above the mean.

Subtracting from the mean gives us:

81–5 = 76 = 2 standard deviations below the mean.

Line DEF in figure 9.4 represents the line two standard deviations above the mean. Line GHI in figure 9.4 represents the line two standard deviations below the mean.

Since all the observations during the intervention phase fall above line DEF, the increase in the client's weight during treatment is likely to be statistically significant at or below the .05 level of probability. If the observations during treatment had fallen below line GHI, they would have indicated a statistically significant decrease in weight. Finally, if most of the observations during treatment had fallen between DEF and GHI, they would have indicated that the intervention was having no statistically significant impact on the client's weight.

Moreover, if the social worker had been interested in evaluating the impact of treatment with several such clients, average weights of all the clients taken together would have served as the data base for the graph. To justify this, however, all clients would have had to receive the same diagnosis and the same intervention.

Collecting Supportive Data Regarding Contemporary History

The findings of single-case studies are not, strictly speaking, causal. This is due in large part to the absence of control groups or individuals who receive no treatment. There are, however, ways to increase the certainty of the inferences drawn from single-case studies about the effects of treatment. This is done by collecting supportive evidence regarding the extent to which events external to the treatment might have accounted for client outcome. External influences, including other concurrent treatments, situational factors, informal help sources, and other influences, must be ruled out to justify inferring more than a correlational connection between treatment and client outcomes. Even after these steps have been taken, the single-case study can be said to provide only an approximation of cause-effect knowledge.

Taking Post-treatment Measures

When treatment gains have been stabilized at an acceptable level, treatment should be terminated. However, single-case designs require that a series of follow-up measures be taken postintervention to determine whether treatment gains persist without further intervention. Here, again, the same measure and measurement procedures are used to ensure that postintervention fluctuations are not the result of random errors in the measurement process.

Comparing Client Scores During and After Treatment

To systematically compare post-treatment scores with those collected during treatment, the original graph should be extended to include post-intervention data. A visual interpretation of the graph will indicate whether treatment gains have improved, maintained at the level attained during treatment, or deteriorated. If they have deteriorated, the clinician should determine whether this decline is statistically significant. The statistical significance of the decline can be approximated by following the same two-standard-deviation procedure. In this instance, however, the data collected during the intervention phase are compared to the data collected after termination of the intervention. If statistically significant deterioration is found in the post-treatment measures, the intervention may be offered again to the client. No statistically significant difference in the measurements taken during the two phases indicates that the client's performance on the measure has stabilized.

Additional supportive data concerning "contemporary history during post-treatment" might be collected here as well. This would help explain any unexpected changes after treatment has ended. Moreover, it can provide information about the conditions during which stabilization of treatment gains takes place.

Comparing Client Scores from Each Clinical Phase

We have described three sets of data: 1. pretreatment data, 2. data derived during treatment, and 3. post-treatment data. A complete single-case study would involve statistical comparisons of all three. Thus, a comparison of 1 and 2 would indicate whether treatment gains during treatment were statically significant improvements over the pretreatment phase. A comparison of 2 and 3 would indicate whether there have been statistically significant changes after treatment has terminated as compared with the levels reached during treatment. Finally, a comparison of 1 and 3 would indicate whether there was a statistically significant difference between clients' condition prior to treatment and their condition after treatment has been terminated.

Whatever the outcomes, however, it is important to remember that interpretation of visual and statistical analyses should not be purely mechanical and based on numbers alone. The results should be considered in the light of their clinical significance, which is informed by common sense and practice wisdom. Statistically significant change on a measure that does not translate into a positive quality of life change for the client is not useful. Alternatively, change that is meaningful to clients may not always be statistically significant. The results can also be compared with colleague's experiences with similar clients and similar interventions. And, finally, results should also be considered in relation to research and practice literature.

SINGLE-CASE DESIGNS IN ACTION

A school social worker would like to try a group therapy approach with school phobic children. The worker identifies ten children between the ages of eight and ten who have consistently poor attendance records, no serious medical or learning problems, and whose parents have indicated that their children are extremely anxious about coming to school, complaining of frequent headaches and stomach aches.

Specifying the treatment objective

The social worker begins by choosing as the treatment objective, the reduction of the children's fears of school.

Operationally defining treatment objective

The school social worker's operational definition of the treatment goal is to achieve and maintain a statistically significant improvement in the mean attendance scores of these children within a two-month period.

Specifying the treatment strategy

A group therapy intervention is formulated based on a review of recent literature and a training workshop that the social worker recently attended. The group intervention will occur on a weekly basis, on the same day and time each week. An appropriate time has been negotiated with the children's teachers.

Taking baseline measures

Baseline measures of weekly school attendance for the past two months are taken for each child and for the group as a whole. All but one of the ten children shows remarkable regularity in their absence rates. The one child who does not clearly appears to be improving gradually as the school year progresses. This child is not included in the treatment group and a new baseline is computed for the group based on the attendance of the nine remaining children.

Graphing the baseline data

Ten baseline graphs are constructed, one for each child in the treatment group and one for the group of nine as a whole. The latter is based on the average attendance of the nine children prior to treatment.

Implementing treatment

Having established a need for treatment prior to start of the program, the social worker begins weekly sessions with the children. A detailed log is kept describing the techniques used each week, discussion topics, and the social worker's general impressions of how the children are responding to these. Attention is given to which techniques and topics of discussion seem to be most successful in generating group participation.

Taking measures during treatment

Weekly attendance records are then added to the graphs for the two-month treatment period. This is done for each of the nine participants and for the treatment group as a whole. The latter is based on average weekly attendance for the group of nine as a whole.

Comparing pretreatment attendance with attendance during treatment

The social worker then compares the pretreatment findings with those attained during treatment. This is done for each youngster and for the group as a whole. Using visual analysis, seven of the children show improved attendance rates. Further, improvement is statistically significant for four of those seven. The group taken as a whole, however, does not show statistically significant improvement in attendance.

Collecting supportive data

In a final session with the children, the social worker facilitates a discussion about their feelings about school and makes note of those youngsters who appear to be expressing less fearful and more positive attitudes. Phone interviews are also conducted with parents to corroborate these impressions. These interviews are also designed to determine whether the child or the parents are currently receiving any treatment elsewhere. Finally, information is gathered about the family's circumstances within the preceding couple of months.

The social worker discovers that the parents of three children, who have made statically significant improvements in attendance, are also in therapy. All the parents, however, indicate that their children seem to have a more positive attitude toward school.

Taking post-treatment measures

After treatment has terminated, the social worker keeps track of the individual and group weekly attendance scores for the following two months.

Comparing attendance scores during and after treatment

A visual and statistical comparison of the individual and group attendance scores during and after treatment reveals that those children whose parents are in therapy continue to improve, whereas there has been a slight decline for those children whose parents were not. This decline however, is not statistically significant. The post-treatment scores for the group as a whole appear to be stabilized and are not significantly different from the scores taken during treatment.

Comparing attendance records for each clinical phase

On the basis of comparisons made for each clinical phase, for each child, and for the treatment group as a whole, the social worker determines that the group technique is an effective one, but it is most effective when parents also receive therapy. As a result, the worker decides to try another similar group. In addition, however, parents of the children in the new group are simultaneously referred to a family service agency in the community.

EXERCISES

1. In the school social work example above, two of the children showed no improvement. Assume that the results for these children during the intervention phase varied widely from week to week with no discernable visual pattern. What steps would you take to try to make sense of their results?

2. Specify and operationalize one treatment objective for an individual or group that could be evaluated using a single-case design. Describe how you would implement such a design and the comparisons you would make to determine how effective treatment has been. Draw a graph that could be used to chart results for a client working toward the treatment objective, including baseline, intervention, and follow-up phases.

SELECTED BIBLIOGRAPHY

Bloom, M., Fisher, J., and Orme, J. G. 2003. *Evaluating practice: Guidelines for the accountable professional.* 4th ed. Boston: Allyn and Bacon.

Campbell, D. T., and Stanley, J. C. 1963. *Experimental and quasi-experimental designs for research.* Chicago: Rand McNally.

Collins, P. M., Kayser, K., and Platt, S. 1994. Conjoint marital therapy: A practitioners' approach to single-system evaluation. *Families in Society, 75,* 131–141.

Corcoran, K. 1993. Practice evaluation: Problems and promises of single-system designs in clinical practice. *Journal of Social Service Research, 18,* 147–159.

Gottman, J. M., and Leiblum, S. R. 1974. *How to do psychotherapy and how to evaluate it.* New York: Holt, Rinehart, and Winston.

Hersen, M., and Barlow, D. H. 1984. *Single case experimental designs.* New York: Pergamon.

Nugent, W. R. 2000. Single case design visual analysis procedures for use in practice evaluation. *Journal of Social Service Research, 27,* 39–49.

Reid, W. J. 1993. Fitting the single-system design to family treatment. *Journal of Social Service Research, 18,* 83–99.

Secret, M., and Bloom, M. 1994. Evaluating a self-help approach to helping a phobic child: A profile analysis. *Research on Social Work Practice, 4,* 338–348.

Thyer, B. 2001. Single-system designs. In B. Thyer (ed.), *Handbook of social work research methods,* pp. 239–256. Thousand Oaks, CA: Sage.

Tripodi, T. 1994. *A primer on single-subject design for clinical social workers.* Washington, DC: National Association of Social Workers.

Variations and Replications of Single-Case Designs

Although single-case designs vary in complexity, all of them use two basic components, the baseline phase and the intervention phase. These two phases are employed in a variety of combinations, three of which are described in this chapter along with their uses and limitations: the graduated design, the withdrawal design, and the multiple baseline design. In addition, we discuss the importance of replicating single-case studies. Each of these evaluative approaches is based on the single-case format detailed in chapter 9. As a result, we will not be describing in detail the step-by-step principles for their implementation. More extensive and detailed discussions of these and other variations on the single-case design can be found in Hersen and Barlow (1984) and Bloom, Fisher, and Orme (2003). In addition, published examples of each of the variations discussed in this chapter are listed in table 10.1, full references of which are found in the bibliography.

Since the evaluative approaches mentioned above are all based on the single-case design, they are subject to the requirements and limitations of the basic design. Thus, effective implementation depends on the extent to which valid and reliable data are employed in the measurement process, particularly on the demonstration of high test-retest reliability. In addition, the use of more complex design variations such as graduated designs, withdrawal designs, and multiple baseline designs involves additional effort in order to produce stronger support of causation. This extra effort may take more time or may make other demands on the social worker and client that are not practical in many clinical settings. However, these more rigorous designs need not be routinely implemented. Rather, they may be used when there is a desire for greater certainty about the effectiveness of clinical interventions and when practice conditions permit. Moreover, knowledge of these design variations and principles can contribute to systematic thinking about clinical social work practice whether or not the research designs themselves are ever actually implemented.

RESEARCH DESIGN VARIATIONS AND CLINICAL DECISION MAKING

As indicated earlier, the design variations to be discussed here are refinements of the ABA design. When using this basic evaluative design, a statistically significant improvement from baseline to the treatment implementation phase, with no significant deterioration in the follow-up evaluation, would suggest a positive association between treatment and effectiveness. Three refinements of the single-case design, including the graduated design, the withdrawal design, and the multiple baseline design are relevant to clinical decision making. So, for example, after an initial period of treatment, a clinical social worker may be faced with the option of continuing treatment in this present form, increasing the frequency or intensity of the treatment, adding a new intervention, or withdrawing treatment. In making these decisions the clinician could certainly benefit from systematic information about the effects of the original intervention, the effects of increasing intervention, and/or the effects of decreasing intervention. In addition, the clinician would be interested in whether the gains that a client has made are generalizing to other areas of the client's life. Finally, the clinician would want to know whether other comparable clients would make similar gains if they received the same interventions.

To assess the effectiveness of a continuous form of treatment, the ABA design would suffice. However, to systematically assess variations in treatment and to answer questions about the extent to which treatment gains can be generalized, one must turn to variations on and replications of single-case designs. Some of these design refinements, their uses, and their limitations are discussed below.

GRADUATED DESIGNS

The graduated design is logically similar to the ABA single-case design but meant to assess the effects of gradually changing either the treatment intensity or the criterion for client performance. In implementing this design, client stability or change is monitored during a baseline phase, during the initial treatment phase, and during the graduated treatment phase. Figure 10.1 represents an ideal data pattern for an AB^1B^2 design, with statistically significant decreases in the expression of client problems from baseline (A) to the first treatment phase (B^1) and from the first treatment phase to the graduated treatment phase (B^2).

Since the graduated design involves the assessment of two or more successive treatment phases, it is less likely that changes in the client's life due to contemporary history or maturation could account for the statistically significant shifts noted in figure 10.1. It does not, however, control for all threats to internal validity and therefore cannot establish a cause-and-effect relationship between intervention and outcome. However, the graduated design is very practical for clinical use because it allows the social worker to track changes in the intervention while measuring outcomes.

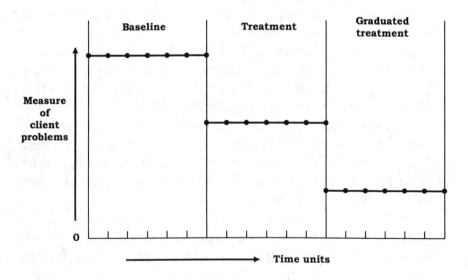

Figure 10.1

The graduated design is particularly useful when the clinician is interested in the effects of gradually changing either the treatment intensity or the criterion for client performance. Treatment intensity can be operationalized in terms of variations in the duration of treatment, the frequency of treatment, the degree of involvement by the clinician, and the degree of participation by the client. For example, an anxious client may be asked to practice progressive muscle relaxation for ten minutes a day in the first treatment phase, followed by a second treatment phase in which the client is asked to practice relaxation twenty minutes a day. Performance criteria can be operationalized as frequency or duration of a problem as well as other relevant steps toward a desired outcome. For example, a client who needs to develop an exercise routine may be required to walk a total of thirty minutes a week to earn a desired reward during treatment phase 1, sixty minutes a week during phase 2, and so on until the desired activity level has been reached.

The graduated design is least useful when the ideal data pattern referred to in figure 10.1 does not emerge, for example, when there are not statistically significant differences between the first and second treatment phases or when the pattern does not stabilize within the treatment phases. In addition, graduated designs are difficult to implement simultaneously with more than one client. Ideally, simultaneous implementation would make possible aggregation of client data and generalizations about treatment effectiveness. In clinical situations, however, client treatment goals and treatment itself are rarely the same from client to client and from therapist to therapist. In those unusual instances in which comparability does exist, however, graduated designs can be used to evaluate whole treatment programs.

WITHDRAWAL AND REINTRODUCTION DESIGNS

Another device for testing the relationship between clinical intervention and outcome is a design in which the intervention is systematically introduced, withdrawn, and then reintroduced. This variation, the $A^1B^1A^2B^2$ design, involves a baseline, introduction of intervention, and then withdrawal of treatment after a statistically significant improvement has occurred. The client's moods, attitudes, and and/or behaviors are then monitored to determine whether there has been a statistically significant regression to the baseline level during the period in which treatment is withdrawn. If this regression does occur, treatment is reintroduced. Then, if a statistically significant improvement takes place, one can assert that cause-effect inferences have been supported and that positive

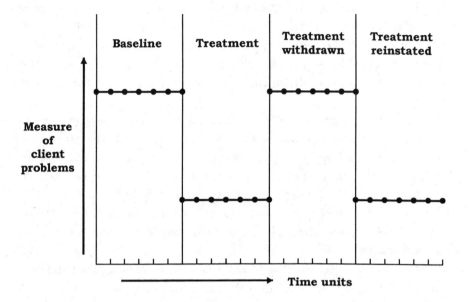

Figure 10.2

client outcomes are clearly related to treatment. If regression does not occur, the second nonintervention phase may be used as the follow-up phase as in the ABA design.

Figure 10.2 shows the ideal data pattern in a withdrawal design. Here again the likelihood is greater than in the ABA design that client outcomes are the consequence of clinical intervention rather than of contemporary history or maturation.

There are several limitations of the ABAB design. First, it depends on an ideal data pattern and cannot be employed unless there has been a statistically significant regression to the baseline level after treatment has been withdrawn. In many clinical situations client change begun during the initial intervention phase is not reversible, making it unlikely that the problem will return to baseline levels. Other limitations of this design are related to the demand placed on the practitioner and agency. The design requires extensive monitoring of the client's progress during the various phases of treatment and nontreatment. Such long-term monitoring is often difficult to achieve. Moreover, it cannot be employed if agency conditions or other factors make it impossible to reinstitute treatment. For selected clients, particularly those with recurring problems and long-term relationships with the agency, a withdrawal and reintroduction design may be feasible. For purposes of program evaluation, however, this design is impractical.

MULTIPLE BASELINE DESIGNS

Multiple baseline designs may be used to determine whether the beneficial effects of treatment with a client can be successfully applied to other areas of the client's life or to other clients receiving similar treatment. For example, a client may be receiving treatment primarily focused on improving relationships with coworkers. A baseline is constructed to monitor improvement in relationships on the job. In addition, however, a baseline is constructed to assess changes in the client's relationships at home. If there are statistically significant improvements

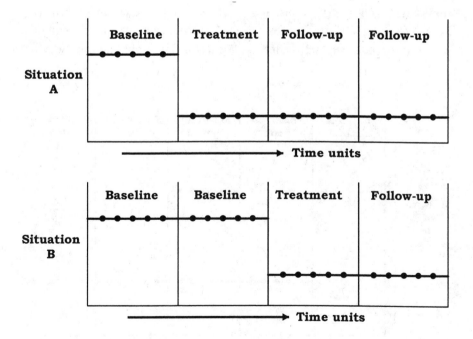

Figure 10.3

in relationships at work and at home then the assumption is made that the beneficial effects of treatment have generalized beyond the work site.

The ideal data pattern for a multiple baseline design of two situations with a single client is illustrated in figure 10.3. To properly employ this design variation, the clinician must first demonstrate that the two baselines are independent of each other. In other words, it would have to be shown that there was not a strong correlation between the clients' behaviors, attitudes, or moods in the different situations prior to intervention. Second, it must be shown that focusing on treatment in one situation does not alter the behavior in another. For example, while treatment is focused on situation A in figure 10.3, it is not directed to situation B, which shows no changes. Third, when treatment is then focused on situation B, desirable changes are observed. Finally, after treatment, both situations should have maintained their desirable changes at follow-up. These requirements make this design impractical in many treatment contexts in which client problems are likely to be highly interrelated.

The time-lagged control feature of the multiple baseline design can be employed sequentially with more than one client. It requires 1. at least two clients with similar treatment objectives, 2. at least two clients who are to receive similar treatment interventions, and 3. at least one of the clients on a waiting list. In this design, treatment takes place sequentially, with treatment beginning with the second client only after a statistically significant improvement has

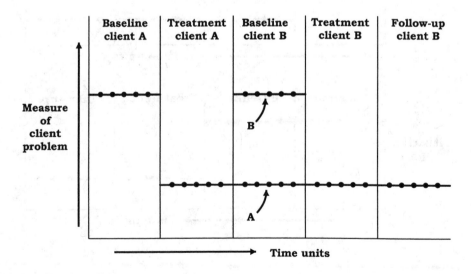

Figure 10.4

been demonstrated with the first client. The ideal data pattern for this design is demonstrated in figure 10.4.

Time-lagged control group designs are most practical in short-term intervention situations with highly specific treatment goals. Thus, they lend themselves to educational settings as well as many managed care practice settings. They are also employed in program evaluations in agencies in which there are large numbers of similar clients and insufficient resources to serve them all at once.

REPLICATIONS OF SINGLE-CASE DESIGNS

Perhaps the simplest strategy for increasing the certainty of knowledge produced by single-case studies is replication. Repeated studies and comparison of results of single clients with similar treatment goals and interventions provide an accumulation of information regarding intervention effectiveness with a variety of clients. Before moving to this broad type of inquiry, however, Hersen and Barlow (1984) suggest that replications be made with clients that are as similar as possible to each other on characteristics such as family compositions, type of problem, sex, age, and ethnicity. As a rule of thumb, three successful replications out of four cases would indicate that the treatment procedures used are generalizeable to a comparable group of clients.

SELECTED BIBLIOGRAPHY

Barnett, D. W., Daly, E. J., Jones, K. M., and Lentz, F. E. 2004. Empirically based special service decisions from single-case designs of increasing and decreasing intensity. *Journal of Special Education, 38,* 66–79.

Besa, D. 1994. Evaluating narrative family therapy using single-system research designs. *Research on Social Work Practice, 4,* 309–325.

Bloom, M., Fisher, J., and Orme, J. G. 1999. *Evaluating practice: Guidelines for the accountable professional.* 3d ed. Boston: Allyn and Bacon.

Ferguson, K. L., and Rodway, M. R. 1994. Cognitive behavioral treatment of perfectionism: Initial evaluation studies. *Research on Social Work Practice, 4,* 283–308.

Hall, J. A., Dineen, J. P., Schlesinger, D. J., and Stanton, R. 2000. Advanced group treatment for developmentally disabled adults with social skill deficits. *Research on Social Work Practice, 10,* 301–326.

Hersen, M., and Barlow, D. H. 1984. *Single case experimental designs.* New York: Pergamon.

Jensen, C. 1994. Psychosocial treatment of depression in women: Nine single-subject evaluations. *Research on Social Work Practice, 4,* 267–282.

Neuman, K. 2002. From practice evaluation to agency evaluation: Demonstrating outcomes to the United Way. *Social Work in Mental Health, 1,* 1–14.

Soliman, H. H. 1999. Post-traumatic stress disorder: Treatment outcomes for a Kuwaiti child. *International Social Work, 42,* 163–175.

Tripodi, T. 1994. *A primer on single-subject design for clinical social workers.* Washington DC: National Association of Social Workers

Vonk, M. E., and Thyer, B. A. 1995. Exposure therapy in the treatment of vaginal penetration phobia. *Journal of Behavior Therapy and Experimental Psychiatry, 26,* 359–363.

Table 10.1 Published Examples of Single-Case Design Variations

Authors	Date	Design Variation
Barnett, et al.	2004	Graduated intervention
Vonk and Thyer	1995	Graduated outcome criterion
Soliman	1999	Withdrawal and reintroduction
Besa	1994	Multiple baseline across subjects
Hall, et al.	2000	Multiple baseline across outcomes
Jensen	1994	Replication of AB design
Ferguson and Rodway	1994	Replication of ABA design

The Use of Sample Surveys in
Follow-up Evaluations

ELEVEN

Follow-up evaluations are studies that take place after treatment has been completed and the client's relationship with the social worker has been terminated. Data collection may involve face-to-face interviews, self-administered client questionnaires, or telephone interviews. Frequently, these data gathering efforts take place weeks or months after treatment has been terminated so that judgments can be made about whether treatment gains have persisted over time or whether the clients' condition has deteriorated without continued treatment. These evaluations may also seek to determine whether clients were satisfied with the services they received.

Often, however, there are not sufficient resources to survey every client who has received treatment from an individual social worker or from a staff of social workers. When this is the case the survey may be administered to a *sample*, a smaller group of clients selected from the *target population,* the total number of clients in question. The results of the sample survey are then used to make inferences about the target population. The greater the similarity between the sample and the target population, the more certain are the inferences that can be made. When sample and target populations are demonstrated to be highly comparable, we refer to the sample as *representative*.

Sample surveys are probably the most often used data-gathering strategy employed by social science researchers. Their uses range from public opinion polls and market research to mental health surveys. In the context of clinical social work they can serve to gather information from a client sample about satisfaction with services received, self-concepts, attitudes, and behaviors, among others. They may be used by clinicians themselves to evaluate samples of their own cases, by supervisors to evaluate sample client outcomes within a treatment unit, or by administrators to evaluate an entire program by sampling service recipients.

Whatever the target population, sampling techniques are designed either to increase the chances of drawing a representative sample or to decrease the cost of data gathering. Unfortunately, however, these two objectives are generally in conflict because, as it increases, the sample size is more likely to be representative of the population, but, at the same time, data collection becomes more costly. This contradiction is a continuing dilemma for the researcher who does not have the resources to study an entire target population. Here a sampling strategy must be devised that both maximizes the chances of representativeness and remains within the resource limitations of the study. Even after the sample has been drawn, however, statistical techniques must be used to determine whether the sampling strategy has in fact produced a representative sample.

An additional problem in follow-up surveys is that they do not provide direct evidence of the causal link between treatment interventions and client outcomes. This is because they generally involve measures that are only taken after treatment has been completed. By precluding before/after comparisons they do not provide direct evidence of client change. Moreover, follow-up surveys generally focus only on individuals who have received treatment. Without a *control group* of comparable individuals who did not receive treatment, they cannot establish with absolute certainty that it was in fact the treatment that produced positive client outcomes.

Nevertheless, follow-up surveys of client samples represent an efficient formative approach for assessing client conditions after treatment has been terminated and for assessing client satisfaction with the treatment they have received. And, while this approach sacrifices certainty of knowledge about the causal connections between treatment and client outcome, it is relatively inexpensive to implement, it does not involve data collection devices and procedures within the treatment process, and it does not involve denial of treatment that is necessary for creating a control group.

SAMPLE SURVEYS AND CLINICAL SOCIAL WORK PRACTICE

Sampling principles and techniques are potentially useful in all phases of clinical social work practice. In diagnosis and treatment planning, for example, the social worker may need to make diagnostic inferences about a child's behavior based on a number of observations of the child at home, at school, and in play situations with other children. Only by properly sampling these behaviors and giving attention to how representative they are can appropriate diagnostic inferences be made.

Likewise, in treatment monitoring, representative samples of groups of clients may be drawn to determine the kinds of services they are receiving, the frequency of service, and the quality of service. Such a monitoring study involves principles and techniques of sampling as well as aggregation and analysis of data.

Finally, sampling techniques and principles are useful in many evaluation designs. Thus they are just as likely to be used in summative evaluations as in formative evaluations. In summative evaluation designs, for example, they may be used to assign experimental subjects to treatment and to control groups. In formative evaluations the same sampling principles and techniques may be used to select samples of service recipients for follow-up evaluation. As a consequence, sampling principles and techniques constitute some of the most useful tools in the clinical researcher's repertoire.

In this chapter we will focus on principles and techniques of sample survey methodology as they apply to follow-up evaluations. We will pay most attention to the discussion of time-saving procedures such as systematic sampling and telephone interviewing. Since sample surveys frequently involve the use of self-administered questionnaires, interviews, standardized instruments, or forms, we recommend that the reader review our previous chapters on these topics (chapters 1, 2, and 7).

PRINCIPLES FOR CONDUCTING FOLLOW-UP SAMPLE SURVEYS

Defining the Purpose of the Survey

Broadly speaking, the purpose of a follow-up evaluation is to acquire information about client outcomes that is not already available through existing monitoring devices. More specifically, such a study can reflect on the quality and effectiveness of treatment, termination, and/or referral decisions. Finally, it is an important source of information about clients' satisfaction with agency services.

Before constructing any data collecting instruments, however, it is necessary to specify the desired information regarding client progress and satisfaction. Since client progress may mean different things in different cases, questions directed to more than one client will have to be sufficiently general and abstract so that aggregation and comparison of client data is possible. Questions about whether the client has maintained the benefits gained during treatment are also useful. Client progress may be indicated as well by questions that concern the presence or absence of negative side effects associated with treatment. Thus, for example, a client who has completed a smoking reduction program may have successfully stopped smoking but at the same time gained twenty unneeded pounds in the process.

Measures of client satisfaction are another important source of information. Although they may or may not be associated with treatment success, they can be good predictors of whether clients would seek the agency's help with other problems that might arise in their lives. High client satisfaction is also likely to lead to clients' recommendation that relatives or friends with similar problems contact the agency. In addition, client satisfaction measures may provide information useful for modification of service delivery. These measures need not be confined to questions about whether the client liked the social worker, but rather should be directed to satisfaction with the type of treatment received, perceptions of the social worker's competence and concern for the client, whether appointment times were convenient, questions about the cost of service, whether the number of visits seemed adequate, and so on. Several psychometrically sound standardized client satisfaction instruments are available and referenced in this chapter's selected bibliography. Overall, the information collected should inform the social workers and agencies regarding future treatment as well as policy decisions and actions.

Designating the Target Population and the Sampling Unit

After specifying the purpose of the follow-up study, the social worker should specify the characteristics of the client population to be surveyed. The basis for determining the target population can vary. Thus, one may want to survey all those clients who have been terminated during a given time period, for example, over the last six months. Another basis for determining the target population is by problem. So, for example, a social worker may wish to survey all clients who were treated for a given type of problem, such as depression or anorexia. The target population also may be defined in terms of the types of treatment received. For instance, a follow-up study may compare the satisfaction of clients who received short-term versus long-term treatment or cognitive-behavioral therapy versus narrative therapy. Target populations can be defined as well by focusing on characteristics of the clients themselves. Here factors such as age, race, income, education, or other demographic characteristics may be the determining features of the target population.

Whatever the basis of the target population, one must consider whether sufficient resources are available to study the whole group of interest. If scarcity of time and money prevent study of the entire target population, then some type of sampling strategy is required. This involves specifying the basic *sampling units* from which to choose. The type of target population determines the sampling unit. Thus, if the target population is all families that received family therapy over the past twelve months, the sampling unit is each individual family that falls in this treatment category and time frame. The *sampling frame* is the list of all sampling units that meet the criteria of the target population. For example, the social worker interested in surveying all families that received family therapy could use records to identify and list all the relevant families.

Choosing a Sampling Strategy

To increase the likelihood that the sample drawn will be unbiased and representative of the population, each sampling unit in the target population should have an equal probability of being selected. Not all sampling strategies make this possible, however.

There are basically two kinds of sampling strategies—*nonprobability* and *probability* sampling. In nonprobability sampling there is no way of determining the probability that any particular sampling unit will actually be included in the sample population. While more convenient than other types of samples, they often fail to adequately represent the population. For example, an agency may request that social workers ask their clients to complete a survey of client satisfaction at the end of their last contact with the agency. This is convenient since it does not involve extra time and resources for follow-up phone calls or mailings. However, since many clients do not have planned terminations from service, the survey will not be completed by clients who do not return for treatment or do not complete their treatment plans. In addition, some social workers may knowingly or unknowingly further bias the sample by "forgetting" to ask clients perceived to be unhappy with the agency to complete the survey. In this case, the nonprobability sample, while convenient, will not be closely representative of the entire population since it leaves out a large percentage of clients, many of whom were potentially dissatisfied with service.

In sum, nonprobability samples are less time-consuming and costly than probability samples. They can be used for generating hypotheses, pretesting research instruments, and getting rough ideas about a given population. They are likely, however, to produce biased and nonrepresentative samples.

Three types of nonprobability sampling strategies are *convenience sampling, quota sampling, and purposive sampling.* Convenience sampling involves choosing the most readily accessible set of sampling units available, without regard to whether the sampling units are representative of the target population. Thus, a follow-up study of the last fifty clients served in a program that has been in operation for years may give a very biased picture of the hundreds of clients served by this program. On the one hand, it may give a falsely positive evaluation if the program has improved over the years—or a falsely negative evaluation if the program has declined in quality. In addition, it would be inadequate for assessing whether treatment gains persist after treatment because the clients surveyed will have only recently terminated agency contact. For these and other reasons, the findings of a study based on such a sample could not be safely generalized to the target population served by the agency since the program's inception.

The second type of nonprobability sampling is quota sampling. It is a more refined form of convenience sampling and is frequently used in less scientific public opinion polls. In quota sampling the target population is classified by certain relevant characteristics such as race, ethnicity, or age. Quotas are set, frequently based on the proportion of each group in the target population. Thus, if clients who are characterized as having "personality disorders" constitute 10 percent of the target population served by the agency, a quota sample of fifty clients should contain five clients who have received this diagnosis. These five are selected on the basis of convenient access. Once this quota is achieved, no additional clients with this diagnostic label are included in the sample. This sampling strategy produces a sample population that resembles the target population in the properties specified, in this case, by diagnostic category. However, since the selection of respondents to fill the quotas is by convenience, the result is still likely to be biased and unrepresentative. Thus all clients within each diagnostic category do not have an equal chance of being selected. Moreover, in quota sampling those who refuse to participate in the study are simply ignored. This is why public opinion polls are frequently wrong.

Purposive sampling is a third type of nonprobability sampling. It involves hand selecting cases for inclusion in a study on the basis of some notion of what is typical or what is unique about the cases. Like convenience and quota sampling, it is inexpensive and quick. It is also highly unreliable, since it is frequently based on erroneous stereotypes. Such a strategy in a follow-up study is likely to lead to the hand selection of those cases that are most successful. While it might provide some hypotheses about the conditions that are likely to lead to treatment success, the study would provide a biased and unrepresentative picture of the target population of clients who have received treatment.

In contrast to nonprobability sampling, probability sampling makes it possible to calculate the probability that any one sampling unit in the total target population will be selected for the sample. Moreover, probability sampling makes it possible to calculate the margin of error that is likely to occur under different sampling conditions and the sample size that is necessary to reduce error to a tolerable minimum. In other words, probability sampling enables the researcher to estimate the degree to which generalizations to the target population can be trusted from findings within the sample. Though they cannot guarantee representativeness, probability sampling techniques greatly increase the likelihood of this outcome.

The most common type of probability sampling strategy is the *simple random sample*. With this strategy, every sampling unit within the target population has an equal probability of being included in the sample population. To draw a simple random sample, each unit within the target population is assigned a number. Then, using a table of random numbers available in any statistics book or generated by a statistics software program—or even by using numbers in a hat—the researcher selects individual units randomly until a sample of the appropriate size is selected. This technique requires no previous knowledge or categorization of the target population. Nevertheless it is more likely to produce a representative sample on every characteristic of the target population than any of the nonprobability sampling strategies. Even simple random sampling, however, does not insure representativeness.

Another form of probability sampling is *systematic sampling*. This technique is particularly useful in sampling case records that are filed either alphabetically or by identification numbers. To do systematic sampling, one must first establish the sampling ratio, that is, the proportion of the total target population that will be included in the sample population. If the sampling ratio were one-fourth, that would mean that one out of every four client units in the target population would be selected for study. Taking a random starting point, the researcher would then select every fourth case until one full cycle of all case records was completed. With populations organized alphabetically, systematic sampling can produce samples as representative as simple random samples with far less difficulty in the mechanism of selection. Here again, however, the technique does not guarantee representativeness.

A more refined kind of probability sampling is *stratified random sampling*. In this strategy the target population is first described according to certain significant properties, for example, agency-based versus community-based cases. Then a random sample is selected from within each treatment grouping. The numbers chosen for each may correspond to the proportion of this treatment group in the total target population. We call this *proportionate stratified random sampling*. This strategy would yield a highly precise picture of the total target population. When emphasis is placed on making comparisons between different types of cases within the total target population, *disproportionate stratified random sampling* may be employed. Thus, if only 10 percent of the clients in the target population are community-based cases, but the study is designed to make comparisons between agency- and community-based cases, a disproportionate sampling strategy could be used to generate *subsamples* of equal size for these two treatment groups. In such a sampling strategy the members of the different treatment categories have different probabilities of being included in the sample, but the probabilities within each treatment group are known. This is not the case with quota sampling.

Depending on the nature of the study, any of the foregoing sampling strategies may be used on a one-time, multiple, or sequential basis. Overall, it is clear that the advantages of probability sampling far outweigh the disadvantages. Consequently, in follow-up surveys probability sampling is recommended. When in doubt, however, about what form of probability sampling should be used, either a simple random sample or systematic sample should be the choice.

Selecting a Sample Size

The decision about the size of the sample population is based on several factors, the most complex of which is statistical probability. That is, the size of the sample is related to the probability that the findings from the sample are accurately representing the population. The degree to which the sample does not accurately represent the population is called *sampling error*. In general, the larger the sample is, the smaller the probability that the findings are due to sampling error. However, sampling error is also related to the overall size and diversity of the population itself. When it is important to have a highly representative sample with low sampling error, the size of the sample that is needed should be calculated. Such calculation is beyond the scope of this book, but a thorough discussion of sample-size analysis, including tables that can serve as quick guides, can be found in Bausell and Li (2002).

Other aspects of deciding on a sample size are more practical. These involve questions of resources. How much time and money are available and how many interviews do they make possible in a day? If a questionnaire is mailed to respondents, initial mailing and return mailing costs must be calculated. More often than not, these practical considerations will determine the sample size in clinical settings.

Recognizing the inevitability of the above, we suggest two rough rules of thumb. First, do not choose samples smaller than fifty for a follow-up survey. Second, if there are categories of sampling units that are particularly relevant to the study, employ strategies that will generate at least twenty-five units of each of these categories in the sample population. So, in a study of treatment outcomes with a target population of one hundred cases, sample at least fifty cases. If the study focuses on the impact of community- versus agency-based treatment, be sure that the sampling strategy provides at least twenty-five cases from each setting. This requires taking into account the probability that a given proportion of clients selected for inclusion in the study will refuse to participate.

Listing Target Population and Selecting the Sample

Once a sampling strategy has been chosen, a complete list of the target population should be compiled. For systematic sampling, sampling units should be listed in alphabetical order or any other order that does not involve an implicit pattern that might bias the sample. In simple random sampling, the ordering of units is of no significance since each individual unit will still have an equal probability of being selected. For stratified random sampling, a separate but complete list should be compiled for each group that is being differentiated in the target population. Thus, if the sample population is going to be stratified by diagnostic category, separate lists should be compiled for each. The ordering within each of these lists will be of no significance since random selection will take place within each diagnostic category.

After compiling the list of the target population, the sample can be selected. In systematic sampling this involves choosing a sampling ratio, starting at a random point, and selecting cases consistent with the sampling ratio.

In simple random sampling, each unit in the listing of the target population is given a separate identification number. Then, using a table of random numbers or numbers in a hat, a sample of desired magnitude is randomly selected. For stratified random sampling, a comparable set of procedures would be employed for each stratum of the target population until the desired subsamples were drawn.

Checking the Representativeness of the Sample

Since probability sampling promotes but does not ensure representativeness, it is important that a sample population is checked to see whether it is representative of the target population on dimensions that are relevant to the study. This process requires some knowledge of the characteristics of both the sample and the target populations.

To check for representativeness, one begins with percentage comparisons between the sample and target populations on those dimensions that are relevant to the study and about which there is complete information for both populations. For example, a target population of one thousand clients may contain 40 percent males and 60 percent females. A perfect, representative sample of one hundred clients would contain forty males and sixty females. If the sample population contained twenty-five males and seventy-five females, one would question the representativeness of the sample. In this case males would be underrepresented and females overrepresented. Consequently, if it were found that gender was differentially associated with treatment outcome, adjustments would have to be made in the inferences drawn from such a sample population. Moreover, if a self-administered mailed questionnaire were used, percentage differences between respondents and nonrespondents should be compared. Here, again, such comparisons tell us whether inferences based on respondent questionnaires are likely to be biased.

A second, more refined technique for assessing representativeness of a sample involves the use of the chi-square statistic discussed further in chapter 13. This simple yet versatile statistic has, among its many uses, the capacity to determine whether data distributions in the sample population are sufficiently like those in the target population to warrant the assumption of representativeness. Similarly, with self-administered questionnaires, it can be used to determine whether respondents are significantly different from nonrespondent populations. In the context of sampling, a chi-square that indicates a statistically significant difference between target and sample populations, or between respondent and nonrespondent populations, means that the assumption of complete representativeness must be rejected.

To assess representativness, chi-square is based on a formula that contrasts the actual observed frequencies in the sample population with those one would expect to find in a perfect representative sample. Likewise, it can be used to statistically compare actual and expected frequencies in respondent and nonrespondent populations. If the computed value of the chi-square is sufficiently low, a high degree of similarity between sample and target populations or between respondent and nonrespondent populations is indicated. This means that the sample population is representative on the dimensions tested and that relatively safe generalizations can be made from the findings in the study.

As an example, suppose we were comparing the gender distribution of the target population of agency clients referred to earlier with a 10 percent simple random sample population of forty-five males and fifty-five females. Given the distribution in the target population, the expected frequencies for a perfect representative sample would be forty males and sixty females. In tabular form the actual and expected (in parentheses) frequencies would look like this:

	Males	Females
Observed and expected frequencies	45 (40)	55 (60)

Using the formula explained in chapter 13:

$$\chi^2 = \Sigma \frac{(O - E)^2}{E}$$

and substituting the numerical values from our expected and observed populations for the letters in the formula, we get:

$$\chi^2 = \frac{(45-40)^2}{40} + \frac{(55-60)^2}{60}$$

$$\chi^2 = \frac{(45-40)^2}{40} + \frac{(55-60)^2}{60}$$

$$\chi^2 = \frac{25}{40} + \frac{25}{60}$$

$$\chi^2 = 1.04$$

With a table of these proportions, a chi-square with any value less than 3.84 indicates that the sample population is not significantly different from the target population. Since the value of the chi-square in our example is only 1.04, we can assume that, at least insofar as gender is concerned, our sample is representative of the population.

If, on the other hand, the chi-square value had been 3.84 or greater, the difference in expected versus observed proportion of men and women would likely occur by chance only five times in one hundred. According to research conventions, this probability level is considered to be statistically significant, and we would have had to conclude that our sample was not representative of the population. For sample distributions with more than two categories, chi-square is computed in exactly the same manner. However, for the samples to be representative, a distribution with three categories should yield a chi-square value below 5.99; with four categories, below 7.82; with five categories, below 9.49; with six categories, below 12.59; and with seven categories, below 14.07 (Cohen and Lea, 2004). These critical values for interpreting chi-square test results can be found in most basic statistics textbooks as well as in statistical computer programs that will both compute the chi-square statistic and provide the probability of the resulting value.

Choosing a Method of Data Collection

Three primary methods of data collection can be employed in follow-up surveys: face-to-face interviews, telephone interviews, and self-administered questionnaires. The least expensive and least time-consuming is the self-administered questionnaire. While self-administered questionnaires are most often sent through the postal service, there is growing use of electronic delivery through email or Internet Web site. The problem with self-administered questionnaires, however, is that they tend to produce low response rates. And, those who do respond may have views that are more extreme, either positive or negative, than those who are not motivated to respond. As a result, unless response rates are quite high (over 65 percent) they are likely to be biased in the picture they present.

The face-to-face interview, on the other hand, is likely to yield the most complete and accurate information. Additionally, it allows the interviewer to make observations while completing the interview. It is, however, a very costly and time-consuming method of data collection. In addition, it may not be the best way to gather highly sensitive information due to respondents' reluctance to self-disclose.

As a compromise between the two, when clients can be reached by phone, telephone interviews are suggested for follow-up evaluation surveys. They yield a higher response rate than mailed questionnaires, but are not nearly as costly or as time-consuming as face-to-face interviews. Moreover, respondents are not required to be literate for telephone interviews, and the anonymity may allow respondents to be more forthcoming.

Typically, telephone surveys are limited in that they cannot use questions that involve visual displays or complex sets of instructions, including questions that involve rank ordering of alternatives. Despite these limitations, telephone interviewing can be an efficient and effective device for collecting information about client progress and satisfaction with agency services. Additionally, telephone contacts may be used in conjunction with other primary sources of data collection. For example, telephone interviewing may be used as a substitute for face-to-face interviewing when a former client is inaccessible. Likewise, when self-administered questionnaires are the primary data-collection instruments, telephone contacts may be used as reminders to those who have not completed their questionnaires or as sources of information about nonrespondents. Finally, it is worth noting that some of the limitations of telephone interviewing can be ameliorated through the use of computer-assisted telephone interviewing (CATI). CATI allows for more complexity in the interview and helps to control errors in recording responses.

Constructing Telephone Interview Schedules

In constructing telephone interview schedules, one should employ the basic principles used in constructing standardized interviews and questionnaires discussed in chapter 1. The interview schedule should begin with an introduction that indicates how much time will be required, why the information is desired, and what will be done with it. Those contacted should be advised that they have a right to participate or not, that the results are confidential, and that the information will not be used to negatively effect the respondents' or their social workers' status in the agency in any way. The interviewer should solicit interviewees' cooperation on the basis of the agency's interest in their progress and opinions regarding the services received and with the understanding that this information might be used to make changes in the existing structure and procedures of the agency. In this way potential respondents view participation as being in their self-interest or in the interest of future clients similar to themselves.

Interview questions themselves should be relatively short and direct. For questions that are somewhat complicated, some redundancy should be built in through summarizing statements. Overall, telephone interviews should not last longer than fifteen minutes. Time and opportunity should be left at the end of the interview for respondents to indicate whether they need or desire renewed contact with the agency.

Pretesting the Interview

Principles for pretesting interviews have been discussed in chapter 1. These can be directly applied to telephone interviews as well. In addition, evaluation planners should get some idea as to how the interviewer's voice transmits over the telephone, whether words are distinguishable and clear, and whether interviewer instructions are nonambiguous. Ideally, the schedule should be pretested with several former clients who are similar to those who are to be included in the follow-up survey.

Preparing for Data Collection

Prior to conducting the telephone interview, potential respondents should be apprised that they may be called. This can be done routinely during the final treatment session or it can be done by letter. Alternatively, a short telephone call might be used either to inform the former client that a telephone interview will be forthcoming or to make an actual appointment for the telephone interview. Under certain circumstances it is helpful to send the interviewee a copy of the interview questionnaire in advance of the interview. This is particularly helpful if the interview is complex in any way. All these techniques help to increase the rate of response and decrease the ultimate cost of the study.

Implementing Data-Collection Procedures

In implementing the actual interviews it is important for the interviewer to distinguish the information-gathering process from therapeutic interviewing. This is especially important if the interviewer is the person who provided treatment in the past. If the former client is again in need of treatment, appointments can be made after the follow-up interview has been completed. It should be made clear to the respondent that the primary purpose of the interview is information gathering for evaluation purposes. Finally, it is important to check for completion of questions by all respondents. If there are questions that tend to go unanswered, the interview schedule has not been adequately pretested and refined.

Tabulating and Analyzing Data

Using the principles described in chapter 13, data should then be aggregated and analyzed in relation to the primary purpose of the follow-up study. Frequency of response and percentages of former clients who respond to various alternatives should be tabulated for closed-ended questions. If there are relatively large numbers of respondents (say more than fifty), it might be possible to cross-tabulate interviewee responses with other important variables such as age, gender, diagnosis, or other relevant variables.

FOLLOW-UP SURVEYS IN ACTION

A social worker employed by a private nonprofit counseling center decided to conduct a follow-up survey of clients treated during the past year. Of the two hundred clients seen, most were treated for problems defined as anxiety, depressive, or adjustment disorders.

Defining the Purpose of the Survey

The purpose of the study is to determine whether former clients have maintained their progress after counseling service has been terminated and whether they were satisfied with the counseling service they did receive. Moreover, the social worker is interested in whether these people have recently received treatment elsewhere and whether or not they would return to the agency if the original problem recurred or if new problems arose.

Identifying the Target Population and the Sampling Unit

The social worker determines that it is possible to interview by phone about 80 former clients in the two-week period set aside for the study. Of the 200 clients seen, 160 completed their treatment plans and terminated service. These represent the target population of the study. Each such former client then will represent a sampling unit for the study.

Determining Sampling Procedures

Since the social worker does not have time to interview all 160 former clients, a 50 percent sample is desired. A systematic sampling strategy with a sampling ratio of 1:2 is chosen. The target population is then listed alphabetically and, after a random starting point, every other case is chosen for a follow-up interview.

Checking the Representativeness of the Sample

After the sample has been selected, comparisons are made between the target population and the sample on characteristics such as gender, race, age, and problem definition. Percentage comparisons and chi-square analyses indicate that on these dimensions there are no statistically significant differences between sample and target populations. The sample is then considered to be representative of the population.

Constructing the Interview Schedule

The social worker then constructs the following interview schedule.

Introduction

Hello_____. This is _____ calling from the Connections Counseling Center. As I told you when we last saw each other, I might be phoning to obtain some information from you and from other former clients that I've seen. This interview should take no longer than fifteen minutes. Is this a convenient time to talk to me? (If "no") When would be a more convenient time? (set up time) (If "yes") Good, thanks for your time. The reason I'm interested in talking to you is so I can get some idea about how you are doing and how satisfied you were with the services you received from our agency. Your responses will of course be confidential and will not affect any future service requests you might make. By the way, if you do wish to resume counseling, time will be available at the end of the interview to discuss that. May we begin?

Interview Schedule

First, I'd like to ask some questions about the counseling service you received.

1. Would you say that your counseling service ended too soon, ended at just the right time, or should have ended sooner? Too soon___ right time___ should have ended sooner___
2. How satisfied were you with the counseling service you did receive? Would you say that you were: very satisfied ____ somewhat satisfied ____ somewhat dissatisfied ____ very dissatisfied____
3. (If "somewhat" or "very dissatisfied" in above) Would you have preferred to have some other form of service? Yes____ no____

4. (If "yes") Can you tell me what that would be? _____

5. Overall, how successful do you think we were in solving the problems for which you entered counseling: would you say we were: very successful____ somewhat successful____ somewhat unsuccessful____ very unsuccessful____

Thank you. Now I'd like to ask some questions about how you've been doing since counseling service ended.

6. In thinking about the problems that brought you into counseling, would you say that since counseling ended you've continued to make progress____ remained about the same____ gotten worse____

7. Compared to how you felt when counseling ended, would you say you are more depressed____ about the same____ less depressed____

8. Again, comparing yourself now with when you ended counseling, would you say you are more anxious____ about the same____ less anxious____

9. Since you ended counseling with this agency, have you received any help with mental health problems form any other providers? Yes____ no____

10. a. (If "yes") Would you describe the kind of help you received? _____
_____

   b. from what agency/provider did you receive this help?_____
_____

   c. How helpful was it? Very helpful___ somewhat helpful___ not helpful___

11. Are you currently employed? Yes____ no____ (If "yes") Where are you working and what do you do there? _____
_____

12. Do you attend school or take any training courses currently? Yes____ no____ (If "yes") Where and what course are you taking?_____
_____

13. Are there any problems that you have now for which you believe you need counseling service? Yes____ no____

14. (If "yes") Would you describe these problems?_____
_____

   Would you like to set an appointment to come into the agency? Yes____ no____ Appointment time_____

15. Finally, are there any comments that you'd like to make about your progress or the services you've received from this agency? _____
_____
_____
_____

Closing

Again, thank you very much for your time. This has been very helpful.

Pretesting the Interview

The interview is then pretested on three former clients not included in the sample but drawn from the target population. Questions that seem to be difficult for the respondent to understand are reworded. It is found that the questionnaire is completed well within the fifteen-minute upper limit. On two out of three pretests, however, it was clear that the respondents were surprised to receive the phone call, indicating that they did not remember being told that they might receive a follow-up telephone interview when their treatment terminated. As a result, a decision is made to send those in the sample a letter telling them that they would be receiving a phone call, describing the purpose of the study, and soliciting their cooperation.

Preparing for Data Collection

The social worker then reviews the case summary for each client in the sample, extracting information about the clients' age, race, gender, employment status, marital status, and problem definition. These data are attached to the interview schedule that will be used in interviewing each former client. In addition, a letter is sent to all those in the sample population informing them that they will be called.

Implementing Data-Collection Procedures

Letters are sent out, followed by telephone interviews. In those few cases in which former clients refuse to participate, they are asked why. This information might give some indication of their general attitude toward the agency and the social worker. In addition, clients who are not reached during the day are called in the evening. Finally, those former clients who refuse to participate or who cannot be reached are replaced by others who are randomly selected for the remaining members of the target population. If, however, a sizable proportion (say more than 25 percent) refuses to participate, some analysis of the differences between respondents and nonrespondents should be attempted.

Analysis

After the interviews have been completed, the responses of former clients to closed-ended questions are then aggregated and placed in percentage form in the appropriate categories of a blank copy of the interview schedule. Open-ended responses are then analyzed by developing mutually exclusive and exhaustive code categories for those responses and filling in the percentages of response that fall into each of these categories.

If the findings of the follow-up study show an increase in depression or anxiety after treatment, the social worker would wish to consider whether criteria used in terminating treatment should be revised. Cross-tabulations with background characteristics might be employed to determine whether some groups (such as anxiety versus depressive disorders) seem to be doing better. In addition, it might become apparent that some groups tend to indicate that they should have been terminated sooner, whereas others may feel just the opposite. Finally, the extent to which former clients take their problems elsewhere may be seen as a serious negative indicator of satisfaction and effectiveness and would suggest some major changes in service method or delivery.

EXERCISES

1. What improvements would you suggest for the interview schedule above? Why?
2. What would be the benefits of using a standardized versus a self-developed instrument to assess client satisfaction? Which do you think is preferable in the example above?
3. Develop a follow-up survey for clients with whom you have worked in the past year. Determine whether sampling procedures will be necessary. If so, draw a sample and determine how representative it is. Implement the survey. Describe the findings of the study. What are the implications of the study for your practice?

SELECTED BIBLIOGRAPHY

Babbie, E. 1990. *Survey research methods*. Belmont, CA: Wadsworth.

Bausell, R. B., and Li, Y. F. 2002. *Power analysis for experimental research: a practical guide for the biological, medical, and social sciences*. New York: Cambridge University Press.

Cohen, B. H., and Lea, R. B. 2004. *Essentials of statistics for the social and behavioral sciences.* Hoboken, NJ: Wiley.

Fisher, R. L., and Valley, C. 2000. Monitoring the benefits of family counseling: Using satisfaction surveys to assess the clients' perspective. *Smith College Studies in Social Work, 70,* 272–286.

Fowler, F. J. 2002. *Survey research methods.* Thousand Oaks, CA: Sage.

Harkness, J. A., van de Vijver, F. J. R., and Mohler, P. P. (eds.) 2003. *Cross-cultural survey methods.* Hoboken, NJ: Wiley-Interscience.

Hawes, C., Phillips, C. D., Rose, M., Holan, S., and Sherman, M. 2003. A national survey of assisted living facilities. *Gerontologist, 43,* 875–882.

Larsen, D. L., Attkisson, C. C., Hargreaves, W. A., and Nguyen, T. D. 1979. Assessment of client/patient satisfaction: Development of a general scale. *Evaluation and Program Planning, 2,* 197–207.

Martin, J. S., Petr, C. G., and Kapp, S. A. 2003. Consumer satisfaction with children's mental health services. *Child and Adolescent Social Work Journal, 20,* 211–226.

Nardi, P. M. 2003. *Doing survey research: a guide to quantitative methods.* Boston: Allyn and Bacon.

Nugent, W. R. 2001. Probability and sampling. In B. A. Thyer (ed.), *Handbook of social work research methods,* pp. 39–51. Thousand Oaks, CA: Sage.

Rubin, A., and Babbie, E. 2001. *Research methods for social work.* 4th ed. Belmont, CA: Wadsworth.

Smith, M. 2002. Program Evaluation. In A. R. Roberts and G. Greene (eds.), *Social worker's desk reference,* pp. 757–763. New York: Oxford University Press.

Simple Group Designs for Use in Evaluation | **TWELVE**

Follow-up evaluations, discussed in chapter 11, are often referred to as after-only or post-test only evaluations because they rely completely on data collected after treatment has been terminated. And, as we indicated earlier, while these types of formative evaluations are relatively easy to implement, they shed little light on the extent to which the client has changed during the treatment process. Instead, they provide a description of a group of clients at a specified time.

As in our discussion of various single-subject designs, the design and the method by which data are collected to evaluate a group of clients' outcomes determine the level of knowledge produced. In order to produce causal knowledge about the effect of social work intervention on client outcomes, more rigorous *experimental designs* must be used. In social science research experimental designs are used to test *hypotheses* about the effect of one variable or condition on another. By controlling how, when, where, and to whom the variables are introduced, researchers can reduce the possibility that *extraneous* variables, or factors other than those under consideration, are responsible for the observed effects.

Experimental designs of intervention effectiveness involve controlling the delivery of a specified intervention, also called the *independent variable,* to at least two groups of clients. In the *experimental* group the clients receive the specified intervention. In the *control group* the clients do not receive the specified intervention; instead, they may receive no treatment or unspecified supportive intervention. Crucial to experimental design is the use of *randomized assignment* of clients to groups. The outcomes of interest, also called the *dependent variables,* are measured in both groups at specified pre- and post-test intervals. The comparison of outcome measures between the groups allows the evaluator to test hypotheses about the effect of an intervention on particular outcomes.

Each of these components of experimental design helps to control for threats to internal validity or alternate explanations for change in outcomes other than the effect of intervention. These threats, as identified by Campbell and Stanley, were reviewed in chapter 9. Random assignment, for example, decreases the potential threat of selection bias, that is, the possibility that change among those in the group that received intervention is due to their characteristics rather than to the intervention. Comparison of outcome measures between experimental and control groups helps to rule out the possibility that the change is due to maturation or contemporary history.

While experimental designs are the most certain way to gain information about the effects of intervention on outcome, they are generally not utilized in practice settings because of practical and ethical concerns. First, random assignment to treatment and control groups is problematic. In a practice setting, social workers are not willing to withhold, nor should they, intervention known to be effective for a group of clients. Next, it is difficult to control treatment integrity, that is, provide evidence that a particular intervention has been implemented and delivered as intended. In practice, social workers rarely apply a standardized intervention to a group of clients, but frequently adjust or change interventions as deemed necessary with a particular client. In addition, it may be difficult in a clinical setting to gather sufficient numbers of clients with similar diagnoses and/or other relevant characteristics.

Rather than use experimental designs in practice settings, other simple *preexperimental* and *quasi-experimental* designs are sometimes used instead. Two of these designs, the *pretest post-test one-group design* and the *pretest post-test wait-list comparison group* design are progressively more complicated than the after-only design discussed in chapter 11. They allow for more certainty of the relationship between intervention and outcome.

SIMPLE GROUP DESIGNS AND CLINICAL SOCIAL WORK

Preexperimental and quasi-experimental designs are most useful in clinical social work practice to build support for associational and causal knowledge about intervention and outcomes for groups of clients. While less rigorous than experimental designs, even preexperimental evaluations of outcomes for groups of clients must be carefully planned. The process of planning and implementing a group evaluation is useful in all three phases of clinical social work.

In the assessment phase the social worker must make decisions about how to measure the client's problem or desired outcomes. This is best accomplished through the use of reliable, valid measurement instruments. However, regardless of how the problems or outcomes are to be measured, the process of deciding on a measure for evaluation purposes works hand in hand with the process of conceptualization and specification of goals. Similarly, in the implementation phase, a process for assessing treatment integrity is needed both for group evaluation purposes and for the purpose of monitoring client or clinician adherence to intervention standards or plans.

In the evaluation phase simple group designs may be used for a number of purposes. While they do not provide information specific to a particular client, they may allow for formative evaluation by using the results to inform future service provision. They may also allow for exploratory outcome evaluation by helping to answer questions related to whether clients are better off after service than before. The information may provide important information to stakeholders. In addition, simple group designs may be used to explore potential differences in outcomes among different groups of clients, such as groups based on severity of impairment, ethnicity, or diagnostic categories.

Several steps are involved for planning and implementing both the pretest post-test one-group design and the pretest post-test wait-list comparison group design. Each of the steps relies on principles discussed in greater detail in other parts of this book. First, goals, objectives, and outcomes must be specified and operationalized in order to be measured. An evaluation will not yield useful information if the outcomes are not logically related to the clients' problems and the planned intervention. Next, an outcome measure must be chosen, using the most reliable and valid method available. As stated previously, this is often best accomplished through the use of a psychometrically sound available instrument. When this is not possible, however, social workers may choose to utilize other methods reviewed in part 1.

The next steps involve deciding on the study design and sample. The evaluation design should be chosen according to the question being asked, the level of knowledge desired, and the practical limitations of available resources. For example, a school social worker may desire causal level knowledge about the effect of cognitive group therapy on the level of depression among children referred by teachers for therapy. While an experimental controlled evaluation would provide the most certain answer to the social worker's question, it is not possible to randomly assign children to groups that receive either cognitive therapy or no therapy. The school social worker, however, remembers that there is always a list of referred children who must wait for service. Since a pretest post-test wait-list design is stronger than a post-test only or pretest post-test one-group design, the social worker chooses the former. It requires only slightly more time to complete measurements than the two other, less rigorous designs.

The sample also is chosen by considering the demands of rigor and practicality. In the school social work example given previously, the number of children receiving therapy in a given semester is only about forty, so it is reasonable to evaluate the outcomes for all the children. In situations where the numbers are higher, it may be reasonable to utilize one of the sampling techniques reviewed in chapter 11.

Next, the intervention should be monitored using the principles discussed in part 2 of this book. The two final steps involve appropriately analyzing the data collected as specified by the evaluation design and then utilizing the results to inform practice.

In the remainder of this chapter, two simple designs will be presented. In addition, for each design, the strengths, limitations, and utility for use in practice settings will be described.

THE ONE-GROUP PRETEST POST-TEST DESIGN

The pretest post-test one-group design is preexperimental and slightly more refined than the post-test-only design in that it relies on measurements taken before treatment has begun as well as after it has been terminated. Although this somewhat more complex formative design does not control for most threats to internal validity, it is a methodological improvement over follow-up evaluations, indicating the extent to which treatment and client change are associated. In other words, it shows whether or not the client has changed along specified dimensions over the time in which treatment took place, but it cannot establish with any degree of certainty that the change was due to the intervention.

Despite its limitations, this preexperimental design is used frequently in social work settings. It is relatively easy to implement and requires few resources, either of time or of expense. It can answer the question whether clients' levels of knowledge, behaviors, or attitudes have changed over the course of an intervention. It may provide assurance that social workers are, at the very least, following the ethical guideline of "doing no harm" to their clients. For example, social workers in a community-based agency, desiring to better serve at-risk adolescents, designed a comprehensive intervention program for those students, ages sixteen years or older, who had stopped attending high school. The program involved the services of the school system, as well as the departments of mental health, drug treatment, and labor, all of whom provided intervention for the youths at an alternative school setting. Evaluation of the program was necessary for several reasons. First, the administrators at the community-based agency needed information about the effectiveness of the program to guide future funding of the program. Next, the social workers and other practitioners needed to know if the program was having the desired effect, that is, to help at-risk adolescents complete their high school education, limit drug usage, and gain skills that would enable future employment.

The evaluators considered several designs, including experimental and quasi-experimental, but both were ruled out. Experimental designs were not possible because of the inability to randomly assign adolescents to treatment or control groups. The quasi-experimental design was ruled out when the evaluators discovered that a relevant comparison group composed of similar adolescents could not be identified. In addition, because it was a new program, there was no wait list. Instead, the evaluators measured indicators of the desired program outcomes when adolescents were assessed and again at the end of each semester while enrolled in the program. The design can be shown in symbols as follows:

$$O_1 \quad X \quad O_2$$

The results indicated that during the time in which students were actively enrolled in the new program, from observation 1 to observation 2, progress was made on the desired outcomes. While it was impossible to be certain that the changes were due to the intervention, the results were strong enough for administrators to base their decision to refund and expand a slightly modified program. Of course, evaluation was continued in the program as well.

THE PRETEST POST-TEST WITH WAIT-LIST COMPARISON GROUP DESIGN

The pretest post-test wait-list comparison group design, a quasi-experimental design, adds even more methodological rigor. In this design the treatment outcomes for two groups of clients are measured before and after treatment. In one group the clients receive intervention. In the other group the clients receive no intervention while they wait for service to begin. In this second group the outcomes are measured three times, that is, at assessment, immediately before the intervention begins when the waiting period is over, and after the intervention ends. A comparison of the outcome measurements for the two groups provides support for causal knowledge of the effects of intervention on outcomes. By adding a comparison group, several threats to validity are diminished. For example, it is unlikely that contemporary history or maturation would affect the two groups in significantly different ways. Likewise, since the process of measurement and instrumentation is the same for both groups, these threats are diminished as well. While somewhat more complicated than the previous design, it is often possible to find a convenient comparison group in social service agencies. Thus, with a bit more effort, the evaluation generates more useful information by strengthening the level of knowledge produced. An example follows.

Clinicians at a university counseling center wanted to find out if the services being provided were effectively decreasing mental health problems for their clients. As in the example given earlier, it was determined that experimental designs were not feasible because of the requirement of random assignment to treatment and control groups. However, unlike the new intervention program described, the counseling center was well established and always had a list of clients who waited for treatment following an initial intake session. Therefore, a quasi-experimental design, the pretest post-test wait-list comparison group design, was chosen. After the outcome measure was selected, clients were asked to complete it at the beginning of the intake session. Those who began their counseling right away completed the instrument again at their last session. Those who waited for counseling completed the instrument at their first and last sessions. The design can be shown in symbols as

$$O_1 \quad X \quad O_2$$
$$O_1 \quad O_2 \quad X \quad O_3$$

For both groups observation one took place at intake. Observation 2 occurred during the last session; while in the wait-list comparison group observation 2 occurred at the end of waiting (at the first therapy session). Observation 3 took place at the last session.

The results of this study indicated that the treatment group improved much more on the outcome measure than the wait-list group from observation 1 to observation 2. In addition, the comparison group improved much more from observation 2 to observation 3 than from 1 to 2. While the counseling center clinicians cannot be absolutely sure that the positive outcomes were due to the intervention, they can cautiously infer that the services provided are producing reductions in their clients' mental health problems.

EXERCISES

1. Referring to Campbell and Stanley's eight threats to internal validity in research design (reviewed in chapter 9 of this book), critique both of the evaluation examples above. What are some of the extraneous variables that might account for the changes in outcomes noted for each?

2. Think about and describe an evaluation question that is relevant to your own practice. Using one of the designs above, describe how you would carry out an evaluation study. On what basis did you make your choice of designs? What are the potential threats to internal validity for your evaluation study?

SELECTED BIBLIOGRAPHY

Campbell, D. T., and Stanley, J. C. 1963. *Experimental and quasi-experimental designs for research.* Chicago:Rand McNally.

Logan, T. K., and Royse, D. 2001. Program evaluation. In B.Thyer (ed.), *Handbook of social work research methods*, pp. 193–206. New York: Oxford University Press.

MacDonald, G., Sheldon, B., and Gillespie, J. 1992. Contemporary studies of the effectiveness of social work. *British Journal of Social Work, 22*, 615–643.

Mecca, W. F., Rivera, A., and Esposito, A. J. 2000. Instituting an outcomes assessment effort: Lessons from the field. *Families in Society, 81*, 45–49.

Neuman, W. L., and Kreuger, L. W. 2003. *Social work research methods.* Boston: Allyn and Bacon.

Pomeroy, E. C., Kiam, R., Green, D. L. 2000. Reducing depression, anxiety, and trauma of maile inmates: An HIV/AIDS psychoeducational group intervention. *Social Work Research, 24*, 165–167.

Proctor, E. K. 1990. Evaluating clinical practice: Issues of purpose and design. *Social Work Research and Abstracts, 26*, 32–41.

Rubin, A., and Babbie, E. 2001. *Research methods for social work.* 4th ed. Belmont, CA: Wadsworth.

Vonk, M. E., and Thyer, B. A. 1999. Evaluating the effectiveness of short-term treatment at a university counseling center. *Journal of Clinical Psychology, 55*, 1095—1106.

Zosky, D. L., and Crawford, L. A. 2003. No child left behind: An assessment of an after-school program on academic performance among low-income at risk students. *School Social Work Journal, 27*, 18–31.

If treatment data are to be useful in clinical practice, they must be analyzed properly. Procedures for doing so involve techniques for aggregating, summarizing, manipulating, analyzing, and interpreting data economically and in such a way that appropriate inferences can be drawn from findings. These inferences may be based on an aggregated data set describing the ongoing treatment of a single client. Alternatively, inferences may be based on aggregated data describing the treatment of a number of comparable clients receiving comparable treatment. In the first instance, generalizations are made about a single client. In the second, generalizations are made about a "class" or set of comparable clients. In either case, data-analytic procedures rely on relatively simple concepts from statistics, measurement theory, and information processing.

In this chapter some research concepts and techniques derived from the foregoing areas are applied to the processing of data concerning treatment compliance and effectiveness. More specifically, the chapter attempts to demonstrate how techniques of aggregation and data analysis can be applied to information about either an individual client's or a class of clients' compliance with treatment contracts or progress toward specified goals.

Three sets of procedures are presented in this chapter. First, data management principles are described. Next, descriptive techniques are described, including the use of whole numbers, averages, and dispersion, the use of proportions, and the use of cross-tabulations. Third, the determination of statistically significant differences is described, including an in-depth explanation of the chi-square test and a brief description of the *t*-test. Principles and examples are presented for each set of procedures.

DATA AGGREGATION, ANALYSIS, AND CLINICAL PRACTICE

Data aggregation and analysis are essential to all types of research and useful in all phases of clinical social work practice. In diagnosis and treatment planning, for example, the social worker may need to make diagnostic inferences about a client based on a number of clinical observations. Only by properly aggregating and summarizing these observations can appropriate diagnostic inferences be made. In treatment monitoring, more than likely, compliance data about client or worker involve sets of client or worker behaviors rather than single instances of compliance or noncompliance. These sets of behaviors must be properly accumulated and analyzed to make appropriate generalizations about compliance or noncompliance.

Finally, data-analytic techniques are useful in evaluating treatment outcomes. Thus, in assessing the success of treatment with a single client, the social worker may need to draw inferences from a series of clinical observation. Likewise, in assessing the effectiveness of a type of treatment with a number of clients, outcome information about these clients must be systematically and accurately aggregated and analyzed.

PRINCIPLES FOR WORKING WITH DATA

In order to analyze and interpret data, it first must be organized in a useful way. Data are currently managed almost exclusively through the use of computer software packages. The three steps involved in data management are described briefly here. Rubin and Babbie (2001) provide a more thorough description of these steps.

Coding

Coding, the first step of data management, involves converting the information about clients into numerical form. This process, discussed in chapter 1 of this book, involves assigning a code and/or number to each variable and a number to each response category for the variable. For example, the variable "highest level of education completed" may be coded as "VAR1" or "EDLEV." The responses could be coded as follows:

> 01—Completed 8th grade
> 02—High School Graduate
> 03—Associate or Technical Degree
> 04—Undergraduate College Degree
> 05—Graduate School Degree

The code can be recorded in a code-book or on the response sheet itself. It is an important part of data management as it both guides the coding process and the identification of variables and data later, during the analysis and its interpretation.

Data Entry

Data may be entered either into a spreadsheet program or a statistical analysis program. In either case, each variable is assigned to a column and each case is assigned to a row. The responses are then entered accordingly. For example, using the EDLEV variable, data entry for three separate clients might look like this:

Client#	EDLEV	Var2	Var3
101	01		
102	03		
103	02		
104…; etc.			

In this example client number 101 completed eighth grade; number 102 completed high school; and number 103 completed an associate or technical degree. The data entry must be done carefully to avoid errors in the transfer from response sheets to computer.

Checking Data for Errors

The last step in data management is to perform a check for errors in the data that have been entered for analysis. Often referred to as *data cleaning*, this step is important to help ensure that the results of the analysis are valid. The simplest method is to check to see that the numbers entered are valid responses for the variable in question. For example, the *possible* responses for EDLEV above are the numbers 01 through 05. Looking down the EDLEV column, a response of 06 would clearly be an error since it is not a valid response category for that variable. In that case the original response sheet could clarify the correct response. Some software packages can perform this task, but, with a small sample and relatively small numbers of variables, it can easily be done manually as well.

Another type of data cleaning involves checking to see that responses conform to the requirements of the questions asked. Turning again to the EDLEV variable, clients under the age of eleven would not normally qualify for any of the responses provided. In other words, any of the responses from 01 to 05 could be an error *contingent* on the age of the respondent. Again, some analysis software programs will perform this type of data cleaning, but it is more complicated and therefore more difficult to perform manually.

PRINCIPLES FOR USING WHOLE NUMBERS, AVERAGES, DISPERSIONS, AND PERCENTAGE TABLES

Computing a Frequency Distribution

The simplest kind of data available to a clinician or a researcher is the frequency of acts, observations, or individuals falling within each category of a single variable or dimension. If, for example, a client who is seeking employment was asked to keep a daily record of the number of telephone inquiries made about potential jobs, the social worker could aggregate and record this information in the form of a simple frequency distribution that might look something like this:

Date	# of inquiries
May 1	0
May 2	2
May 3	1
May 4	0
May 5	1
May 6	0
May 7	0
May 8	2

[continued]

Date	# of inquiries
May 9	3
May 10	1
May 11	3
.	.
.	.
.	.

Total number of inquiries = N

If the number of inquires each day varied considerably, and if treatment lasted for several weeks, a simple frequency distribution might be too unmanageable to compile. In addition, trends in the data might be difficult to perceive. In such instances the data can be aggregated and analyzed in the form of a *grouped frequency distribution* based on the number of job inquires made each week. The weekly frequency distribution might look something like this:

Week	# of inquiries
1	4
2	10
3	12
4	5
5	1
.	.
.	.
.	.

Total number of inquiries = N

These findings could be presented more dramatically by converting them into simple graphs, bar graphs, or frequency polygons. This manner of presentation often helps the person viewing the data visualize trends that may be less apparent in the form of whole numbers. In a simple graph, bar graph, or frequency polygon, daily or weekly intervals are plotted along a horizontal axis, with the frequency of inquiry plotted along a vertical axis. In the simple graph shown in figure 13.1, each day in treatment is represented by a single unit on the horizontal axis. The number of job inquires each day are represented along the vertical axis and the coordinates of these points are connected with a straight line.

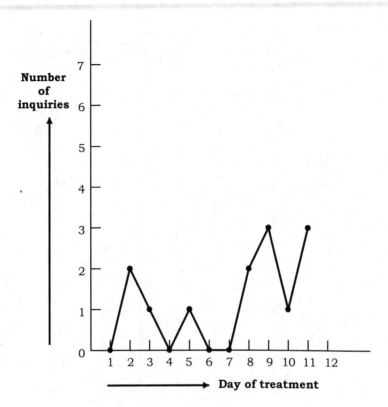

Figure 13.1

For purposes of presentation, grouped frequency distributions can be converted easily into bar graphs or frequency polygons. In both, weekly intervals are plotted along a horizontal axis, with frequency of job inquiries plotted along a vertical axis. In the bar graph shown in figure 13.2, the width of each bar corresponds to a weekly interval, and the height of each bar indicates the number of job inquiries made within that interval.

In the frequency polygon shown in figure 13.3, the number of job inquiries is plotted along the vertical axis at the midpoint of each weekly interval. The points are then connected with straight lines to give a graphic representation of the grouped frequency distribution.

Grouped frequency data that are graphically presented can reveal patterns that are not apparent when the data are not aggregated. For example, figure 13.1 suggests no clear pattern in daily inquiries, whereas figure 13.3 reveals an increasing number of inquires until the end of the third week of treatment, after

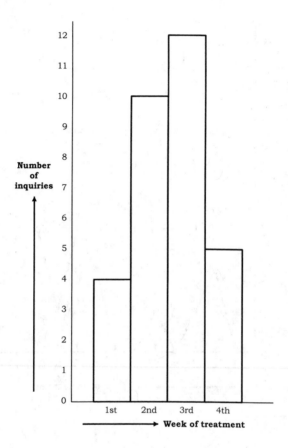

Figure 13.2

which there is a sharp decline in inquiries. Whether this pattern is unique to this particular client or is common to many clients receiving this form of intervention can only be discerned by aggregating other data based on a number of comparable cases.

Choosing a Measure of Central Tendency

Once a frequency distribution has been specified, the data contained within can be conveniently summarized in the form of a measure of central tendency, or, in more common language, an average. These summary measures are useful when there are a great many measurements taken on single variables for individual

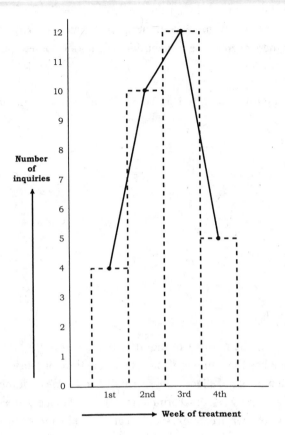

Figure 13.3

clients or when data drawn from individual cases are aggregated in order to determine the pattern for all clients receiving comparable treatment.

Social researchers make use of three different measures of central tendency: the arithmetic mean, the median, and the mode. Each has its own advantages and disadvantages. Each offers a way to make an efficient summary statement about the data contained within the frequency distribution.

The *arithmetic mean* $(\bar{M})$ or the arithmetic average is the most widely used measure of central tendency. It is computed from the frequency distribution by taking the frequency within a chosen interval, multiplying it by the value assigned to that interval, and dividing by the total number of units, observations, or individuals. Thus, for example, if we wanted to know the mean number of job inquires made during the first week by all those clients receiving a comparable form of intervention, we would begin by computing the frequency distribution during the first week for these clients. The distribution might look something like this:

Number of inquiries	Number of clients	Inquiries x Clients
0	3	0
1	2	2
2	1	2
3	5	15
4	6	24
5	2	10
20	1	20
	Total = 20	Total = 73

$$\bar{M} = 73/20$$
$$\bar{M} = 3.65$$

Taking the sum of the number of inquiries made within the first week of treatment, multiplied by the number of clients making those inquiries (73) and divided by the total number of clients (20), we arrive at the mean number of inquiries made within the first week of treatment (3.65). An average pattern for all clients over the course of their treatment can be calculated by following this procedure for each week of treatment. This could be then plotted on a simple or bar graph for purposes of presentation.

Although the arithmetic mean is widely used and does give the most common interpretation of the "average," it is likely to be distorted or skewed by extreme individual cases in the frequency distribution. Thus, if the last client listed made three instead of twenty inquiries, the mean number of inquiries for the first week would be only 2.8. Clearly, then, extreme scores can create a false impression of what the "average" client is likely to do in the first week of treatment.

A second measure of central tendency is the *median*. The median is the point in the distribution that has the same number of scores above and below it, as close as possible to half of the scores on either side of the midpoint. In the preceding example a total of twenty clients produced scores of the number of inquiries made during the first week. Dividing the number of scores in half, the midpoint, at which approximately half the scores are above and half are below, is ten. The tenth client's score falls within the group of clients who made three inquiries during the week. Thus the median number of job inquiries for the first week is three. Note that this category leaves six clients above the median and nine below. Clearly, it is less precise than the mean. The advantage of the median, however, is that it is not affected by extreme values the way the mean is. Thus, the median would still be three whether the last client listed made three, twenty, or sixty job inquiries. As a result, the median gives a truer picture of the central tendency in frequency distributions that contain extreme scores. One consequence of this quality is that the median is frequently used in table construction for dividing populations into low and high categories along a given dimension.

A third measure of central tendency is the mode. It is the category in the frequency distribution that has the greatest number of scores. It is easiest to compute and least precise. Like the median, however, it is unaffected by extreme scores. In the foregoing example the mode is four inquiries, since that is the category in which the greatest number of clients falls. In that sense the most "typical" client makes four job inquiries during the first week of treatment. Note, however, that each measure of central tendency has given us a different score based on the same frequency distribution.

Dispersions

In studies in which measures of central tendency are used, information about the measures is frequently supplemented with information about the *dispersion* of the frequency distributions. This gives the reader a sense of the shape of the distribution and the degree to which they are skewed or distorted by extreme cases. Two common measures of dispersion are the range and the standard deviation. The *range* is simply the difference between the highest and lowest scores in the distribution. In the foregoing example the number of inquiries made ranged from zero to twenty.

The *standard deviation*, on the other hand, indicates the extent to which scores in the distribution cluster around the mean or are highly dispersed. Higher standard deviations indicate greater dispersion from the mean. Information about the computation of the standard deviation can be found in chapter 9 of this volume or in any basic statistics text. Most often, however, it is calculated using analysis software programs. The calculation of the standard deviation is based on a formula that considers the distance of each score from the arithmetic mean and is therefore larger when there is wider variation among the scores. Consider the following as an example. Client Group A and Client Group B both have mean scores of 25 on "The Pretend Depression Scale," indicating very mild symptoms that interfere very little with functioning. It might be tempting to think that the groups are very similar in their levels of depression. The standard deviation, however, yields more information. In Group A the standard deviation is two, which indicates that most of the clients' scores fall between 21 and 29. The high score is calculated by adding two standard deviations to the mean ($25 + 2 + 2 = 29$), the low score by subtracting two standard deviations from the mean ($25 - 2 - 2 = 21$). For Group A most clients' scores fall within the mild range of depression on the "Pretend" scale. The standard deviation for Group B, however, is twelve, indicating that most of the clients' scores fall between 1 and 49. Some of the clients in Group B, then, are in the most severe range of depression, while others are virtually symptom free. The two groups are not as similar as the mean alone might indicate.

Whole numbers, averages, and dispersion are also useful for describing relationships between two or more variables. For example, returning to the job-seeking example above, one could describe the relationship between the level of education of the clients and the number of job inquiries they make by indicating the mean number of inquiries made by clients with or without a college education. To do this, one would plot the frequency distribution for each education grouping. From the two frequency distributions, two means would be computed. To determine whether the two distributions are skewed, measures of dispersion would be computed for each group as well. This would make comparisons possible between clients with lower or higher levels of education. The statistical significance of the difference between the two means can also be determined using tests discussed later in this chapter.

Proportions, Tables, Cross-tabulations, and the Elaboration Model

The most common forms of data presentation are whole numbers and proportions. Each of these, seen alone, can be extremely misleading. For example, two agencies may represent themselves as providing treatment to clients of all socioeconomic groups. One agency, a relatively small one, indicates that roughly 50 percent of its clients are from low-income families. The other agency, a very large one, reports that it served nearly one hundred low-income families in the past year. Only by converting both agencies' service statistics into percentages and determining the comparability of the bases on which they were percentaged can a true comparison of the two agencies be made. The point of this discussion is that in presenting agency or client data, the proportions as well as the numbers upon which they were based should be clearly indicated.

Analyzing Cross-tabulation Tables

Cross-tabulations are simple devices for analyzing and presenting relationships between two or more variables. They make use of whole numbers as well as proportions. However, for any single set of numerical cross-tabulations, percentages can be taken in three different ways: vertically, horizontally, or against the total number in the tables as a base. Each reveals a different aspect of the relationship between the two variables. Take, for example the following numerical cross-tabulation shown in table 13.1, between the types of therapy prescribed in a family agency and the client's continuation in therapy. For the sake of simplicity, type of therapy is divided into two categories—family therapy and individual therapy. Client continuation is measured by whether clients returned after their intake interviews.

Table 13.1

	Family therapy	Individual therapy	Total
Return	30	100	130
Non-return	60	80	140
Total	90	180	270

If the table were converted to vertical percentages, it would indicate the percentage of cases receiving each therapeutic prescription that returned or did not return for treatment. Such a table, shown in table 13.2, would treat the therapeutic recommendation as the independent or causal variable and the rate of client return as the dependent variable or the consequence.

Table 13.2

	Family therapy	Individual therapy
Return	33% (30)	56% (100)
Non-return	67% (60)	44% (80)
Total	100% (90)	100% (180)

Moving from the presumed causal variable to the presumed consequence, this table shows that 33 percent of the cases that are to receive family therapy return for treatment compared with 56 percent of those that are to receive individual treatment. The latter, then, are 23 percent more likely to return that the former.

A table that used horizontally determined percentages would tell us the percentage in the return or nonreturn categories who received a therapeutic recommendation of family versus individual therapy. Rather than tell us about the impact of the recommendation on the rate of client return, that table would tell us the percentage of those who returned that are receiving family versus individual therapy. Such a table would more adequately describe the character of current treatment cases than would the previous, vertically percentaged table. Horizontally presented, the table would look like table 13.3.

Table 13.3

	Family therapy	Individual therapy	Total
Return	23% (30)	77% (100)	100% (130)
Non-return	43% (60)	57% (80)	100% (140)

Table 13.3 tells us that, of the clients who returned for treatment, 23 percent were recommended for family therapy and 77 percent for individual therapy. Rather than shed light on the impact of the recommendation on the client's return as in the previous table, this table tells us something about the impact of clients who return on the type of therapy received.

A third way of percentaging is against the total number of cases as the numerical base. As shown in table 13.4, such a table would describe the percentage of all cases that were processed at intake within each recommendation and return category.

Table 13.4

	Family therapy	Individual therapy
Return	11% (30)	37% (100)
Nonreturn	22% (60)	30% (80)

Total 100% (270)

This table indicates that out of all the cases processed at intake, 11 percent received family therapy recommendations and returned, 37 percent received individual therapy recommendations and returned, 22 percent received family therapy recommendations and did not return, and 30 percent received individual therapy recommendations and did not return. This table describes a typology or multidimensional classification of different types of cases based on these two variables. From it we see that the most typical case receives a recommendation of individual therapy and returns. Alternatively, the least typical case receives a family therapy recommendation and returns.

Although each of the percentage tables reveals a different aspect of the relationship between treatment recommendation and client return, all were derived from the same set of whole numbers. Consequently, it is important to be careful to choose the type of percentaging that is most appropriate for the question the table is intended to answer.

Later in this chapter we will discuss statistically significant difference and provide step-by-step instructions for the chi-square test. In this case the chi-square can tell us whether the higher rate of nonreturn for those who received a family therapy recommendation is likely to be a chance phenomenon or is reflective of a statistically significant relationship between these two variables.

Controlling for Intervening Variables Using the Elaboration Model

The cross-tabulations presented above seem to reveal a relationship between the type of therapy recommendation that a client receives and whether the client is likely to return to the agency for this treatment. However, it would be premature to assert on the basis of this table alone that there is a cause-effect relationship between the treatment recommendation and the client's return. Thus, the relationship between recommendation and return may be the consequence of a third variable that is either accidentally or logically associated with both the type of therapy recommendation and the client's return.

To better understand the relationship between two variables, researchers *control* for the possibility of intervening effects of alternative explanatory variables. Only through such *multivariate analysis* can the relationships among several variables be analyzed at the same time. In multivariate analysis additional independent variables, based on subgroupings of the original independent variable, are examined in relationship to the original dependent variable. Most often multivariate analysis is carried out through statistical software programs because of the sophistication of the statistical tests. It can also be done more simply, however, by constructing and examining new tables that describe each of the independent variable subgroups by the dependent variable categories.

The new tables produced through multivariate analysis are interpreted using the *elaboration model*. The elaboration model provides a guide for interpreting the pattern of change seen in the new tables, indicating how the original relationship changes with the introduction of the new independent variable. Described in greater detail by Neuman and Kreuger, five patterns or interpretations are possible. Each will be explained as it relates to the example above.

REPLICATION

It may be possible that the reason clients who received a family therapy recommendation were less likely to return was that men were more likely to oppose this recommendation than an individual therapy recommendation. To see if this explanation is correct, however, the relationship between the three variables should be empirically tested.

Controlling for, or "holding constant," the clients' gender would require the construction of two additional tables, one looking at the relationship between recommendation and return when the client is male and one looking at the relationship between recommendation and return when clients are female. If the relationship between recommendation and return is replicated in each of these tables, shown in table 13.5, it would indicate that the original relationship between recommendation and return could not be explained by the clients' gender.

Table 13.5

| | Male Clients | | Female Clients | |
	Family therapy	Individual therapy	Family therapy	Individual therapy
Return	30%	52%	35%	58%
Non-return	70%	48%	65%	42%

The tables indicate that, irrespective of the client's gender, clients who receive a family therapy recommendation are still less likely to return. Thus, we see that, for male clients, there is a 22 percent difference between the return rates for those who received one recommendation versus the other. Likewise, for female clients a 23 percent difference exists. Under these circumstances the new variable does not explain why family therapy clients are less likely to return.

SPECIFICATION

Another potential intervening variable may be age, that is, perhaps clients' age has an effect on whether or not they return for family versus individual therapy. Again, tables such as that shown in table 13.6 can be constructed to test this hypothesis.

Table 13.6

	Under 25 years old		25 Years and Older	
	Family therapy	Individual therapy	Family therapy	Individual therapy
Return	10%	54%	56%	58%
Non-return	90%	46%	44%	42%

In this case it appears that clients under the age of twenty-five are much less likely to return for family therapy than for individual therapy. Those who are twenty-five or older, however, are approximately equally as likely to return for both types of therapy. The age variable appears to *distort* the relationship between the two original variables of therapy type and return rate.

INTERPRETATION

In this pattern of the elaboration model the introduction of a third variable provides information about the effect of an *intervening* variable on the two original variables. For example, perhaps the return rate for family or individual therapy is affected by whether or not the client's partner supports or opposes the recommendation. To test this idea, the partner's opposition or support must be controlled. The new cross-tabulations may look like those shown in 13.7.

Table 13.7

	Spouse opposes		Spouse supports	
	Family therapy	Individual therapy	Family therapy	Individual therapy
Return	31%	32%	70%	68%
Non-return	69%	68%	30%	32%

These tables indicate that when the partner's attitude is held constant the differences in return rates by type of recommendation disappear. Thus, when the partner opposes, there is a 1 percent difference between family and individual recommendation in the return rate. When the partner is supportive, a 2 percent difference exists, slightly favoring those in family therapy. By comparing the findings between tables, and within a recommendation type, it is clear that for either recommendation the partner's support contributes a good deal to whether the client will return. Since the partner's support or lack thereof temporally follows the recommendation, these findings would lead us to conclude that partner support intervenes between the therapy recommendations and return rate. In other words, these findings would lead us to conclude that the original negative relationship between a family therapy recommendation and return was explained by the fact that partners were more likely to oppose a family therapy recommendation and that, in turn, led to a lower return rate.

EXPLANATION

A variable that is introduced may also act to *control* the two original variables. In this case the new variable temporally precedes the original independent variable, showing the original relationship to be spurious or false. The social worker's skill level will be used as a variable to illustrate this pattern. Thus it may be that clients who received a recommendation of family therapy were seen by less skillful workers than were clients referred to individual therapy. Since the skill level of a worker temporally precedes providing clients with recommendations, skill level may act to control the return rate regardless of the type of therapy recommended. As a consequence, the client's return rate would most likely be a response to the lack of skill of the social worker rather than a response to the type of therapy. The original relationship between recommendation and return would then be spurious in that it gives a false impression of causality. This pattern might look like table 13.8.

Table 13.8

	Low skill level		High skill level	
	Family therapy	Individual therapy	Family therapy	Individual therapy
Return	31%	32%	70%	68%
Non-return	69%	68%	30%	32%

Note that the pattern looks the same as table 13.7. Just as in table 13.7, by holding the new variable constant the original relationship between return rate and type of therapy disappears. The difference is that the control variable precedes the original independent variable, showing the original relationship to be spurious.

Thus, the new variable, workers' skill level, explains the differences in return rate better than partners' support level.

SUPPRESSION

A variable may also act to *suppress* the relationship between the two original variables. In our ongoing example, this would mean that an extraneous variable acts to diminish the relationship between the type of therapy and the return rate. For example, perhaps client's level of functioning is related to the return rate by type of therapy. This is illustrated in table 13.9.

Table 13.9

| | High functioning clients | | Low functioning clients | |
	Family therapy	Individual therapy	Family therapy	Individual therapy
Return	16%	81%	74%	19%
Non-return	84%	19%	26%	81%

In this example the table shows that the relationship between type of therapy and return rate is even stronger than originally shown in table 13.2. However, by controlling for client functioning level we see that clients with low levels have a higher return rate for family therapy while clients with high levels have a greater return rate for individual therapy. Thus the clients' level of functioning variable suppresses the relationship between the two original variables.

In general, it is important to control for as many possible intervening variables as possible in order to determine the true explanation for a finding or to discover whether the finding is spurious. Without such controls, assertions about causality are premature.

PRINCIPLES FOR DETERMINATION OF STATISTICALLY SIGNIFICANT DIFFERENCES

Determining Desired Level of Significance

Earlier in this chapter we mentioned the use of tests of statistical significance. These tests are calculations of the probability that the observed differences between groups are due to chance rather than an actual difference between the two groups. For example, if a social worker discovers that Client Group A drops ten points on a measure of depression, while Client Group B drops only six points, how likely is it that the difference between the two groups of clients is statistically significant? The social worker would not want to make a big deal about the difference in the two group's scores if there is a high probability that the results could have occurred simply by chance. The erroneous decision that there would be a real difference when the difference is just due to chance is called a *Type I error.*

A full explanation of the logic of probability as it relates to statistical significance can be found in basic statistics texts. For our purposes it is important to know the level of risk that the difference is due merely to chance is called the level of significance. A 5 percent or lower risk of making a Type I error is generally acceptable in social service research; it is usually expressed in an equation such as this:

$$a < .05$$

The actual probability of obtaining particular differences between two groups is determined by using a statistical test of significance; this probability is expressed using equations such as these:

$$p < .05 \quad \text{or} \quad p = .025$$

In addition to Type I errors, there are also Type II errors. A Type II error is the probability that the researcher will erroneously decide that the differences found between two groups are due to chance when, in fact, the differences are real. Again, the social worker with Client Groups A and B would not want to diminish the importance of a four-point difference between the groups by deciding it was merely due to chance if the results were indicative of a true difference. The probability that a true difference will be correctly identified is called *power.*

One other type of significance is important when considering results from a study involving social work practice. *Clinical significance* refers to the practical importance of the difference between the two groups. Clinical significance is not computed mathematically. To the contrary, it is considered regardless of the statistical significance of the results or the power of the study to detect real differences. Suppose that the four-point difference between Client Groups A and B referred to earlier does not result in a statistically significant difference, that is, the probability of finding this difference in this sample is greater than 5 percent. However, although both groups started at about the same level of depression, the ten-point drop puts Group A clearly below the clinical cutting score for depression, while Group B remains in the clinical range of depression. These findings would then have clinical significance. Alternatively, a statistically significant difference would have little practical importance if the depression measure was scored on a two-hundred-point scale and neither Group A nor Group B dropped into lower levels of depression through the course of intervention. In this case the statistically significant difference would have little to no clinical significance.

Choosing and Applying Tests of Statistical Difference

There are many statistical tests of significance, each of which is used for particular situations. One test, the chi-square, will be explained here in detail. Other tests are listed along with an explanation of their uses in table 13.10. Although they are not covered here in depth, they can be found in basic statistics texts, along with the specific requirements for their use.

Table 13.10

Test Name	Use	Scaling
Chi-square	Tests significance of association between variables	Nominal
Wilcoxon matched pairs, signed ranks test	Tests significance of differences between scores taken at two points in time. Does not require normal distribution of scores.	Ordinal
Wilcoxon/Mann-Whitney test	Tests significance of the comparison of differences between scores for two groups. Does not require normal distribution of scores.	Ordinal
Dependent samples t-test	Tests significance of differences between means in two groups that are related, i.e., one group in which scores are compared at two points in time.	Interval
Independent samples t-test	Tests significance of differences between means in two groups that are related, i.e., two groups of clients who receive different interventions.	Interval

Chi-square

Earlier in this chapter the chi-square was mentioned as a test of statistical significant difference for use with cross-tabs. In fact, the chi-square is a simple yet highly versatile statistic that can be used both to measure an association between two variables as well as to determine the probability that the association is due to chance or to an actual relationship between the two variables.

Briefly, the chi-square is based on a formula that contrasts the actual, observed frequencies in the various cells in the table with those one would expect if there were no relationship between the two variables that are cross-tabulated. If the computed value of the chi-square is sufficiently low, the actual findings are considered nonsignificant and as chance occurrences. If there are great differences between the expected and observed frequencies in each cell, this would be reflected in a high chi-square, which in turn would indicate a statically significant relationship between the two variables in the table.

In our example of returning clients assigned to family or individual therapy, we can use the original cross-tabulation of whole numbers to compute the *chi-square* (X^2). The chi-square will determine whether the relationship between the treatment recommendations received and the rate of client return is statistically significant. To calculate the chi-square for our table of whole numbers in table 13.1, we must first calculate the expected numbers of cases receiving each treatment recommendation in each return category. To compute the expected number of clients who received a family therapy recommendation and returned, for example, one would use the following formula:

$$\frac{\text{Total Family Therapy}}{\text{Total Cases}} \times \text{Total Returns} =$$

The numbers taken from the original cross-tabulation are substituted, and the expected number of cases receiving a family therapy recommendation and returning is found to be:

$$\left(\frac{90}{270}\right) \times 130 = 43.3$$

Following similar procedures, the expected numbers for each cell of the original table can be calculated. The following table indicates the observed and expected frequencies for each recommendation and return category. The expected frequencies appear in parentheses.

	Family therapy	*Individual therapy*
Return	30 (43.3)	100 (86.7)
Non-return	60 (46.7)	80 (93.3)

The final computation of the chi-square involves adding the sum of the squared differences between all pairs of observed (O) and expected (E) frequencies, divided by the expected frequencies for each pair. This is expressed as a formula, using the summation sign (Σ):

$$\chi^2 = \sum \frac{(O-E)^2}{E}$$

Substituting the numerical values from our expected and observed findings for the letters in the formula, we get:

$$\chi^2 = \frac{(30 - 43.3)^2}{43.3} + \frac{(100 - 86.7)^2}{86.7} + \frac{(60 - 46.7)^2}{46.7} + \frac{(80 - 93.3)^2}{93.3}$$

$$\chi^2 = 11.81$$

With a table such as this, that is, a 2 × 2 table, a chi-square with any value of 3.84 or better indicates that the relationship between the variables in the table is statistically significant.[1] Since the value of the chi-square in our table exceeds 3.84, we would conclude that the relationship observed between the type of treatment recommendation received and the rate of client return is not a product of chance variation.

Significance Tests for Grouped Data

T-tests are frequently used both in simple group and single-case designs to determine the significance of findings from grouped data. Computation of a t-test is based on a formula that utilizes the means and variances of the two groups. If the computed value of the t-test is sufficiently low, the actual findings are considered nonsignificant and as chance occurrences. If the difference between the means of the groups is large, this would be reflected in a high t-test statistic, which in turn would indicate a statistically significant difference between the two groups. In other words, the probability would be low that the differences between the two groups were the result of chance. Specific t-tests are selected based on the characteristics of the groups. For example, the two groups of data are considered to be *dependent* on one another when comparing pre- and post-test scores from one group of clients. The data are *independent* when comparing scores of one group with the scores of another group.

---

1. For tables with expected frequencies below 5 in any cell, additional adjustments have to be made in the computation. However, for a 2 × 2 table with expected frequencies greater than 5, and a chi-square value over 3.34, the findings could occur by chance alone less than 5 times in 100. According to research convention, this probability level is considered statically significant. Discussion of adjustments for small numbers of cases and various levels of statistical significance are contained within standard textbooks on statistical methods.

Other significance tests with which social work clinicians should be familiar are listed in table 13.10. Scaling, explained in chapter 5, refers to the type of scale utilized for data collection. It should be kept in mind that statistical tests of significant differences are almost always calculated by statistics software programs on computers. While these are available in some agencies, some clinicians may need to seek assistance from a professional who conducts evaluation research.

DATA ANALYSIS IN ACTION

A clinical administrator in a women's crisis center has introduced a cognitive-behavioral therapy counseling program in her agency. The program offers women individual counseling as well as mutual support groups. In the course of the first year, the program has served 120 women from all segments of the community. Recently, however, program critics have suggested that the services it offers are primarily geared toward middle-class women. The clinical administrator decided to collect and analyze data relevant to this issue and to interpret the findings to her staff and board members. If the data were to reveal any class bias, she would want to take measures to correct it.

Collecting the Data and Computing a Frequency Distribution

To collect relevant data, the administrator reviews client termination statistics available in the agency's records. Her intention is to see whether women of lower socioeconomic status have significantly fewer agency contacts than do middle-class women.

From the agency's records the administrator is able to calculate a grouped frequency distribution based on the clients' reports of their family income. Using the median income as her dividing point, she divides the client population into those who are above and those who are below the median.

Next, she computes a frequency distribution based on the number of times individual clients have come to the agency within the past year. Again, using the median as a dividing point, she identifies clients who are above and those who are below the median in attendance.

Computing Cross-tabulation and the Chi-square

Next, she cross-tabulates client income and client attendance. Indeed, her findings reveal that clients from lower-income families are served at the center much less frequently than clients from more middle-income families. A computation of the chi-square for this table reveals that the inverse relationship between class and attendance is statistically significant.

Controlling for Intervening Variables

To determine whether this relationship between socioeconomic level and agency participation can be further understood by other variables available to her, she extracts other quantifiable information from the case records that might serve to explain the finding. One control variable that she is able to cull from the case records refers to the client's level of education. Again, on this variable she plots a frequency distribution and divides the population at the median into those with relatively high and those with relatively low educational attainments. By controlling for educational level, in a multivariate analysis she discovers a pattern that specifies the original relationship. Among highly educated women there is no longer a relationship between income and attendance. For women with low levels of education, however, income is still significantly related to attendance.

These findings are then brought to staff and board members for discussion. Various possible explanations are offered, ranging from the need for programming designed particularly to serve low-income, low-education clientele to providing babysitting or transportation for the women so that they can more regularly attend counseling and support group sessions.

EXERCISES

1. Concerning the example above, what are the potential advantages and disadvantages of utilizing the mean, mode, and median as a guide for dividing the women into groups based on income? What other intervening variables might affect the relationship between women's income and agency usage? How could you gather data related to those variables?

2. Select a program that can provide you with descriptive data on clients' income, types of presenting problems, and whether or not clients were accepted for service. (If data for one of these variables are not available, you may substitute another. Just make sure that there is some logic involved in your choice.)
   - Compute the frequency distributions for the clients' income; and the mean, median, and modal income of the total client population.
   - Compute the percentage of each client income group accepted or rejected.

- Compute a chi-square to determine whether there is a statistically significant relationship between the two.
- Finally, construct a table controlling for problem type.
- Interpret the findings.

SELECTED BIBLIOGRAPHY

Bausell, R. B., and Li, Y. F. 2002. *Power analysis for experimental research: a practical guide for the biological, medical and social sciences.* New York: Cambridge University Press.

Cohen, B. H., and Lea, R. B. 2004. *Essentials of statistics for the social and behavioral sciences.* Hoboken, NJ: Wiley.

Grant, D. 1996. Generalizability of findings of exploratory practice-based research on polydrug-addicted mothers. *Research on Social Work Practice, 6,* 292–307.

Neuman, W. L., and Kreuger, L. W. 2003. *Social work research methods.* Boston: Allyn and Bacon.

Orme, J. G., and Buehler, C. 2001. Introduction to multiple regression for categorical and limited dependent variables. *Social Work Research, 25,* 49–61.

Rosenthal, J. A. 1997. Pragmatic concepts and tools for data interpretation: A balanced model. *Journal of Teaching in Social Work, 15,* 113–130.

Rubin, A., and Babbie, E. 2001. *Research methods for social work.* 4th ed. Belmont, CA: Wadsworth.

Stocks, J. T. 2001. Statistics for social workers. In B. Thyer (ed.), *Handbook of Social Work Research Methods,* pp. 81–129. New York: Oxford University Press.

The majority of this book has focused on the use of research to inform and evaluate practice. Within that focus we have shown how to apply research concepts, techniques, and knowledge to clinical social work practice. More specifically, we have tried to show that research procedures can be employed as practice tools, particularly for obtaining information relevant to diagnostic assessment, implementation of social work interventions, and evaluation.

In addition to focusing on research-based practice, however, we have mentioned that practice can and should inform research. By this we mean that the evidence base that informs ethical clinical practice is stronger when knowledge gleaned from practice in real social work settings is included in its foundation.

The influence of practice can be introduced into research that leads to further knowledge in several ways. First, practitioners are frequently aware of important practice-related questions long before scholars and academicians. Such questions may arise out of difficult clinical situations, policy changes that affect delivery of service, or demographic changes that affect the characteristics of those who seek service from clinical social workers. In addition, new practice techniques are sometimes distilled, promoted, and delivered widely prior to finding answers to questions about their effectiveness and efficacy. Practitioners are in the perfect position to bring these questions to light. Once questions have been identified, practitioners may decide to bring their questions to social work professionals who specialize in research, such as academics. Time and interest permitting, clinicians may also decide to engage in research themselves or to collaborate with researchers.

The use of research skills and techniques in the practice setting to answer emerging questions in ways that further inform practice may be referred to as *practice-based research*. Practice-based research is often less rigorous than research designed by and implemented in research institutions because of several characteristics of the practice setting. First, the research questions are derived from practice wisdom or experience. Next, the research designs are almost always nonexperimental or quasi-experimental. The level of knowledge produced is descriptive or associational. The instruments used are tailored to the practice setting and are not always known, standardized measures. Finally, the research is generally carried out through collaboration between researcher and clinician, but the practice needs are considered primary. While the constraints on research within the practice setting do not allow for true experimental research, practice-based research produces valuable information applicable to social work practice and its contingencies.

In this chapter we will briefly describe principles related to one technique for gathering data that is useful to clinicians who want to engage in practice-based research. Clinical *data mining* is a procedure that allows practitioners to make use of information already available in records to answer questions that emerge from practice. In addition, we will discuss and provide further resources for learning how to report on practice-based research. Reporting is crucial; without it the new information produced through research cannot be disseminated and utilized.

CLINICAL DATA MINING

Clinical data mining is a term coined by Irwin Epstein (2001) as a metaphor for the process of gathering data from information available in client records to answer practice-related questions. Data mining begins with "prospecting," or searching, available information resources for data relevant to the practice question. Although labor intensive and sometimes frustrating due to false leads, the search continues until reaching "pay dirt," that is, useful data are found. Once located, the information must be "extracted" and "refined" in order to determine the value of the "findings." The principles for gathering data in this manner are listed here. Many of the principles are similar to those described in chapter 6 on content analysis.

Locate and Identify Available Information Sources

In order to begin, the clinician must identify what types of information are available in records. This may include demographics, client problems, type and frequency of interventions, clinical notes, and much more. A simple list of the types of information available may be developed as the clinician reviews records.

Assess Accessibility and Credibility of the Information

In addition to noting the type of information available, the clinician must make a judgment about how accessible and credible the information is. In terms of accessibility, how difficult will it be to retrieve the information? If records were handwritten, are they legible? In terms of credibility, were the records written during or immediately after the relevant event? Was the information provided by a reliable source? The findings of the research project will be only as credible as the data on which they are based.

Determine Unit of Analysis

The unit of analysis refers to the informational units that will be categorized or coded. For example, if records in an agency indicate whether termination with the client was planned or unplanned, the unit of analysis would be "type of termination" with two possible categories, either planned or unplanned. In addition, a decision must be made to determine the time frame from which records should be utilized.

Literature Review

After determining what information is available, a scholarly literature review should be conducted to help conceptualize and contextualize the research question. The literature provides information about how related research questions have been studied and answered in the past. It also may spark new ideas about variables relevant to the research question.

Inventory of Variables

Next, an inventory of potential variables should be made. This will involve not only listing the available variables but also indicating exactly where those data may be found in the records. In addition, the variables should be categorized as predictors, such as demographics or psychosocial factors, intervening variables, such as social work interventions, or dependent variables, such as quality of life factors or accomplishment of client goals.

Preliminary Development of Data Forms

Once the variables have been identified, a coding form should be created. This form will contain space to organize data related to every variable and related category. The form should be tested with a sample of records in order to check for reliability and completeness of data retrieval.

Revise Data Forms and Extract Data

Based on the test of data extraction with the preliminary form, the next step is to refine the data retrieval form, potentially eliminating variables if reliability or completeness is inadequate. The refined form can then be used to extract the desired data from the records.

Create Database

Data should be transferred to a data base in preparation for analysis. This is the final step, after which the study may be conceptualized and implemented. The detailed step-by-step process and excellent examples of data mining are available in Epstein's articles listed in the bibliography below.

REPORTING ON PRACTICE-BASED RESEARCH

In order for results of practice-based research to add to the social work knowledge base, they must be reported. Reporting is important to inform future practice, policy, and research. While reports on evaluative research findings may be required by funding organizations, quality control departments, or other local stakeholders, they may also be of interest on a broader level. For instance, an agency that finds a particular intervention to be highly associated with positive outcomes for an emerging and expanding ethnic group may be able to assist other similar agencies by sharing the results of their study. In fact, it may be just as important to report results that indicate a strong relationship between a particular intervention and negative outcomes. In either case, in order to spread information beyond the local level, the usual method is to publish the report in a scholarly journal.

Whether informing locally or broadly, research reports follow a specific format. The principles are briefly described below and are more fully detailed in references listed in the bibliography. Before we describe the steps, however, we want to acknowledge that report writing may intimidate, excite, or burden clinicians. Or the process may feel too much like being in school. Whatever your reaction, one of the best ways to learn how to write good reports is to read and critique reports published in social work journals. Guides, such as those written by Thyer and Pyrczak, for evaluating research reports are useful tools. Finally, keep in mind that report writing is again a process that can be shared through collaboration with research professionals who are accustomed to report writing.

Abstract

The abstract is a brief summary of the entire report, including a statement of the problem and purpose of the study; highlights of the methodology; important findings; and how the results are contextualized in the discussion section. Although this is the first part of the report, it is often written last after the rest of the report has been completed.

Review of Literature

The literature review provides a context in which the problem under study can be nested. Utilizing scholarly literature, it generally begins with an overview of the problem that was studied. It continues by describing what is known about the problem from previous relevant research. In some cases the literature review is also used to show how the research problem is related to relevant psychosocial theories. Writing a good literature review is part scholarship and part art. Rather than being a string of sentences describing "who said what" about the research question, it should be a synthesis and analysis of related literature that logically leads the reader to understand the purpose and importance of the study at hand.

Methodology

This section describes how the study was carried out. The information needs to be thorough and succinct.

DESIGN

The design refers to the type of study, e.g. single-case design, one-group pre-post-test design, etc.

SAMPLE

The sample describes the clients who participated in the study. This generally includes the number of participants, the selection process, and inclusion criteria. In addition, it may describe client-participant demographics.

PROCEDURE

The procedure describes the steps implemented for data collection. This usually includes answers to how, when, and where data were collected.

MEASUREMENT OF VARIABLES

In this section the variables are defined in terms of how they were measured. In addition, instruments used for measurement are described, along with any available information about their psychometric characteristics.

Results

This section presents the results of the study. Results may be presented in narrative form, but graphs and tables are also used to make the results more accessible to the reader. Again, it is important to be thorough but succinct in this section. Thus, information is not repeated, that is, it is presented either in table or narrative form. In addition, any interpretation of the results is saved for the discussion section.

Discussion and Implications

This is the last section and, once again, is used, at least in part, to contextualize the current study. The researchers' interpretations and conclusions about the results are provided here. These interpretations are based not only on the current study but also on how the current results fit with results of previous studies or with theory. This section generally also includes the researchers' ideas about what the results imply about social work practice and policy. Implications for future research as well as the limitations of the current study are also discussed.

CLINICAL DATA MINING IN ACTION

The administrator of a nonprofit social work agency that serves teenager mothers with children under the age of four is curious about the ways in which various aspects of their programming is related to outcomes for the teens and children they serve. Consulting with a professor who provides field liaison for social work students at the agency, the administrator realizes that contacting an adequate sample of former participants in the program would be very difficult. Instead, the administrator, in collaboration with the professor, decides to try to use already available information in client records.

Locate and Identify Available Information Sources

The administrator's first step is to look through records kept by the agency. This includes extensive intake information that provides demographics, the mother's current living situation, medical problems, children's age and condition, and more. There is also a record of each visit to the center that includes whether the young mothers were there for concrete services, support group, child care instruction, tutoring, or any of a number of other services. Finally, each case file has a termination report that indicates whether the termination was planned or unplanned, the status of the mother, and the status of the child.

Assess Accessibility and Credibility of the Information

The administrator notes that the records have all been entered electronically by the social workers themselves, with the exception of a few case notes that are handwritten. There appears to be a time lag between actual termination and production of some of the termination reports, which raises some concern about reliability of the information.

Determine Unit of Analysis

The administrator considers all the available information and decides to focus on several informational units from the intake report as well as the number and types of contacts during the service period. In addition, several factors from the termination report will be considered, including the status of mother and child, living situation of mother and child, medical condition of mother and child, and so forth. The potential response categories are then listed for each unit of analysis. For example, responses for "status of mother" include attending school, working part-time, working full-time, and other. In addition, the administrator decides to utilize records of all case files closed during the previous calendar year.

Literature Review

The social work professor completes a literature review and provides a few of the most important articles to the administrator to read. After discussion, the two decide on a research question. It is very similar to the administrator's original question: What factors at intake and types of agency services are associated with positive outcomes for mother and child?

Inventory of Variables

Next, an inventory of potential variables is made. The administrator lists the available relevant variables, indicating exactly where those data may be found in the records. In addition, variables are categorized as predictors, such as the mother's and child's condition at intake, intervening variables, such as the types and number of agency contacts, and dependent variables, such as the status of mother and child at termination.

Preliminary Development of Data Forms

The administrator then creates a coding form to organize data related to the chosen variables and related response categories. The form is then tested with a sample of records to check for reliability and completeness of data retrieval. As suspected, a few of the termination reports have not been fully completed. In spite of this, the administrator decides to move forward with the project. While not ideal, the termination reports are the best available evidence of client outcomes.

Revise Data Forms and Extract Data

Based on the test of data extraction with the preliminary form, the administrator refines the data retrieval form, eliminating the information related to mother's medical condition at termination. The decision to eliminate a variable was made because this particular item was often left blank on the termination reports, which resulted in a high rate of missing data for the variable. The refined form was then used to extract the desired data from the records.

Create Database

The administrative assistant transferred the information from the data form to a database in preparation for analysis to be conducted by the social work professor. The study was implemented, a report was prepared, and results were discussed among staff members.

EXERCISES

1. Think of one other potential research question related to the example above. What predictor, intervening, and dependent variables would be needed to answer your question?
2. Is there a research question about your practice that might be investigated using information gathered systematically in records kept at your social work setting? State the research question. List the relevant predictor, intervening, and dependent variables. Explain where that information might be available in records. Choose two variables and describe the unit of analysis and response categories for each.
3. If you were to carry out your investigation from question 2, would the results be of interest to a broad audience of social workers, i.e., more than just those with whom you work? Why or why not?

SELECTED BIBLIOGRAPHY

Berger, R. 1997. The common logic of research and practice in social work. *Social Work and Social Sciences Review, 7,* 112–121.

Blumenfield, S., and Epstein, I. 2001. Promoting and maintaining a reflective professional staff in a hospital-based social work department. *Social Work in Health Care, 33,* 1–13.

Epstein, I. 2001. Using available clinical information in practice-based research: Mining for silver while dreaming of gold. *Social Work in Health Care, 33,* 15–32.

Harrison, D. F., and McNeece, C. A. 2001. Disseminating research findings. In B. Thyer (ed.), *Handbook of social work research methods,* pp. 501–512. Thousand Oaks, CA: Sage.

Neuman, W. L., and Kreuger, L. W. 2003. *Social work research methods.* Boston: Allyn and Bacon.

Pyrczak, F. 2005. *Evaluating research in academic journals.* 3d ed. Glendale, CA: Pyrczak.

Rubin, A., and Babbie, E. 2001. *Research methods for social work.* 4th ed. Belmont, CA: Wadsworth.

Thyer, B. A. 1991. Guidelines for evaluating outcome studies on social work practice. *Research on Social Work Practice, 1,* 76–91.

Sainz, A., and Epstein, I. 2001. Creating experimental analogs with available clinical information: Credible alternatives to "Gold Standard" experiments? *Social Work in Health Care, 33,* 163–183.

Zilberfein, F., Hutson, C., Snyder, S., and Epstein, E. 2001. Social work practice with pre- and post-liver transplant patients: A retrospective study. *Social Work in Health Care, 33,* 91–104.

Postscript

This book is geared to social work students and to practitioners who do not have a high level of research sophistication. Accordingly, we have presented relatively simple research concepts and techniques that be can easily be mastered. In trying to present this material in an understandable and approachable form, it is inevitable that we will be accused of oversimplifying research by some of our researcher colleagues. Clinicians also may accuse us of oversimplifying clinical issues.

Our intent has not been to oversimplify. Rather, it has been to link some basic research concepts with the fundamentals of clinical practice. Similarly, the bibliographies at the end of each chapter are selective. They provide the reader with some basic sources. Rather than being exhaustive and redundant, they are representative. Finally, they were selected with a mind to what consumers without extensive research training could read and understand.

Although for the purposes of this book we divided treatment into three phases, we recognize that assessment, intervention, and evaluation are interrelated in practice. Moreover, the research techniques introduced in the context of any one of these phases might just as easily have been applied to one of the others. So, for example, rating scales can be used in diagnostic assessment, treatment monitoring, and in evaluation of effectiveness. Consequently, a complete understanding of the book requires flexible application of the research concepts and techniques discussed to different areas of clinical decision making.

Perhaps the most difficult idea that we have tried to convey is that the logic of research can be applied to clinical practice. In other words, research thinking can be used for purposes other than pure research. In this vein we hope the book contributes to bringing research and clinical social work practice closer together.

Index